A HARD PLACE TO FIND

BY RONNIE TEE SMITH

Dedication

I dedicate this book to a loving wife, who gave all she could to me, and to my two extraordinary children. Elaine, Jemal, and Gavin—my family was a pinnacle of joy.

Acknowledgments

I give heartfelt thanks to Bruce Brownell and Cynthia Stead for carefully reading my manuscript. The keen eyes of both Lin Meredith and my memoir-writing teacher, Christine Cutler, suggested that I separate my original memoir into two different books. I am most appreciative of their recommendations. I also wish to thank the fellow writers in my memoir group, who have generously provided constructive criticism and encouragement: Joy Bellis, Deborah Bonds, Nancy Craddock, Nabila Khanam, Temple Kinyon, Beth Parker, Linda Sanborn, and Penny Yazzie. I am grateful for the many hours that Angel Luna spent examining my family photos and selecting those in which he incorporated into the book cover design.

Introduction

A *Hard Place to Find* is a continuation of my first two published books. In this third book everybody's looking for something although true peace with one's self is a hard place to find. This story explores my journey from being stuck in a compromising lifestyle to acquiring a better understanding of life and what it takes of me to live a joyous, authentic life.

My second book in this series is entitled *Stuck*. It begins with my release from the United States Marine Corps at age twenty after serving my country, fighting in Vietnam.

My first book, *An Unnoticed Casualty of War*, explores my life from infancy to age twenty. Readers, who are interested in obtaining a copy of Book One, *An Unnoticed Casualty of War*, may contact me directly at Teelonious@yahoo.com.

Prologue

"I believe most children are damaged to different degrees and struggle with perceived guilt. Innocence is a gift of life for a very short time at best." Geraldine Pantle

I refuse to wear the cowardly color yellow. It's a sunshine color that haunts me. Wearing yellow, I feel exposed—like I'm on stage, moving against a moonless backdrop, and I'm acting beneath a 200-watt light bulb shining directly above me. I don't have any yellow shirts, sport coats, ties, pants, socks, or underwear. Yellow, on me, triggers childhood memories, making me want to moan.

I was five and happy before Miss Overweight got to me. She was not my complexion, a sweet dark chocolate, but as black as soy sauce. She made me do things I felt uncomfortable doing. At fifteen, older than I by a long shot, she pulled me to her lips and made me kiss her. I was only an innocent five. The thought of making-out with a girl was repulsive. It seriously grossed me out. Then, worse yet, she opened up her yellow blouse and pressed my head onto her ebony nipple. "Suck, suck it," she demanded. "Circle it with your tongue."

I obeyed her orders. Being so young, I felt I had no choice. I reluctantly sucked and sucked. So young, barely past being a baby, what was I to do? Suddenly, I changed. This hellish transformation came. Encasing me within its mangled, mysteriously hypnotic fingers, I transcended to a place where murky, moody misery seemed to incarcerate me. My unsuspecting parents were at work. They left me in her care. Sexual abuse-so young. So young! I cried. Crippled. I changed. And not just for the moment. My innocence lost, forever. I was only five. From then on I struggled, wanting to escape the pain. Eventually, I pushed it deeply down inside to the point where I no longer thought about it—confused, convinced my agony had gone away.

Bullied by boys in elementary and junior high school, I never physically fought back. I didn't know how. I tried using my intellect, taking a less combative, softer way of complying with their demands. These pre-hoodlums didn't ask for my lunch or money. (I was too cheap to tolerate or give in to any of that.) Although I can't remember exactly what they did, they repeatedly inflicted their hateful fear and painful shame, scaring me forever. I suspect they used carefully chosen words. Perhaps they poked and nagged at my skin color, as I was the darkest of my friends and family—

maybe a shade darker than my twin, at least that's the way I imagined it. I recall one of them saying, "Ronnie, you so black, you're invisible at night."

Another said, "Boy, your sweaty skin's so black, it sparkles like a newly paved asphalt road."

I became bitter when all the bystanders laughed. I laughed along with them and replied, "Okay, you got jokes," pretending it didn't hurt. Looking back, I now wonder: Perhaps that's one of the reasons I always saw myself as the black sheep of the family.

Those slaves of old whose first acknowledged how sticks and stones could possible break bones got it all wrong. Derogatory words hurt far more. They can crush, exposing bone marrow.

Feeling wounded, utterly damaged, dethroned, I contrived the notion, *It must have been my childhood, which caused all of my dysfunctional relationships.* Trying desperately hard to hide all my shame and to control everything around me, I decided to take a hard, defiant stance. *I'd show them all, that I'd become somebody, that I'd go places? I'll do whatever it takes; I'm not going to sell myself short.* From then on, I spent my adult life protecting and passionately nurturing children—especially the damaged ones.

CHAPTER 1

In the State of Nevada, first-year teachers receive a minimum of three performance evaluations during the year. It seemed my principal, Mr. Twithcell was always in my classroom, putting me in front of his spectacles, examining my lesson plans, and observing everything I did. I kept telling myself, Teacher Corps had taught me well, preparing me how to be a successful first-year teacher. How could I fail? I emulated my master teacher, Mrs. Resse, in everything I did. Perhaps it started in the Marine Corps, with all of the inspections I endured— back then, I couldn't and wouldn't dare show any uneasiness or any signs of my eager, hopeful anticipation to pass them. No one wanted to fail because it usually resulted in cruel and grave consequences, especially in boot camp and more so in Vietnam. Yet, through severe conditioning, my nerves, like bad allergies, blossomed whenever Mr. Twitchell, entered my room. I often told myself, *He can be as hard on me as he wants. He genuinely loves children and only wants to bring out the best teaching in me for them.* But it didn't help. I still got extremely nervous each time he entered my fifth grade room.

His school was impeccably clean, and all of his teachers were passionately dedicated to their students. It didn't take me long to discover the school was a stellar school, one of the highest rated in the District. Mr. Twitchell was demanding, and I respected him for it. He even collected his faculty's lesson plans at the end of the day each Friday.

He'd read them over the weekend, make notes on them, and return them in our mailboxes each Monday morning before the school day started. One of the teacher's commented in the teachers' lounge when Mr. Twitchell was not around, "There are so many comments, but he stopped short of giving us grades."

He made a big production on the playground celebrating each child's birthday. Mr. Twitchell would wrap his loving arms around a child's waist on his or her birthday, twirl them high in the air, while lightly spanking them on their bottoms and calling out the number of years they were old. He knew the name of every child in his school. I don't respect too many men, but Mr. Twitchell was genuine to the core—he earned mine.

CHAPTER 2

K nowing that my dealings with the principal and with my students wouldn't consume my entire life, Jim Perkins, a special education teacher on our faculty, was the first to invite me into his family's life. He knew I didn't have any family or friends in this town. From the start I knew I would always have a special relationship with Jim for as long as I lived in Las Vegas. His compassion for me touched my heart. I had never experienced a White man, with a southern accent as pronounced as Jim's, take so much interest in me.

The evening I went to Jim's home for dinner, I met his wife, Janie, and their newborn daughter, Stacey. That night, I learned Jim had earned his college degree and state certification while stationed at Nellis Air Force Base, and that he joined the Gene Ward teaching staff after retiring from the Air Force. Janie told me they were from Kentucky, and that I was the first Black person ever invited into their home—the first Afro-American that she would truly get to know. I didn't know how to take what she had shared, so I replied, "Well, I'm a good first start."

CHAPTER 3

There were only two separate occasions ever, where Mr. Twitchell initially pissed me off. One day after lunch, my students and I entered the classroom. The light monitor switched on the lights, and there sat Mr. Twitchell in the dark. It was math time. Though a little nervous, I did my teaching pretending that he wasn't there. He wrote his notes for about thirty minutes and was gone. This did not upset me. I was glad that he was there observing my teaching—unlike the pastor of the parochial school where I had taught just out of the military, without a college degree or State teaching credentials.

Then a day or two later, during my one-on-one mentoring session, Mr. Twitchell asked me to share some of my weaknesses as a teacher with him. Trusting him, I did. A few weeks later, I read those weaknesses in my performance appraisal. I felt betrayed, like he should have helped me to improve in those areas without putting them in writing.

CHAPTER 4

Months later, during another mentoring session, Mr. Twitchell asked me to reveal more weaknesses. It took all I had to not put my index finger in his face and shake it. I wanted to move my head from side to side saying, "Oh, no. I'm not doing that again." Instead, I said, "I'm happy with what I'm doing. I think I'm doing a good job. I see great growth in those areas of weakness I shared with you some time ago."

I talked every night with my previous girlfriend, Elaine. We had mutually agreed to separate after college so that we could start our lives anew. Missing each other, I drove to Los Angeles to be with her almost every weekend. She was my best friend, ever. I longed for her, my sidekick, throughout the weekdays. I chose only to remember the good times when we lived together. I wanted more. Mentally, I wasn't whole. I looked to Elaine to complete me. I guess Elaine felt equally the same way, too.

By October we decided to get married. Elaine would drop her substituting in the Compton Unified School District and move to Las Vegas with me.

I let Mr. Twitchell know about the upcoming marriage, which would be on a Saturday. I filed a written request to take that Friday off, so I could have the day preparing for the wedding. Mr. Twitchell approved my day-off request, but he docked me a full day's pay. *Why did he have to be such a "by-the-book" person? Why couldn't he just mark me absent due to illness?* Then I caught myself. *Why did I have to be so honest? Why didn't I simply lie and call in sick?*

CHAPTER 5

With passengers sneezing and coughing while once riding a Greyhound bus back and forth, from Las Vegas to LA, I vowed to never do it again. Their sniffling and hacking was far too much. I kept my promise. I splurged and took a plane. By purchasing a one-way ticket, I could help Elaine drive her Datsun to Vegas.

I spent Friday morning moving all of Elaine's stuff to my mother's garage. (We figured we'd take something back to Vegas each time we visited L.A.) I spent Friday night dicing boiled potatoes so her mother, Helen, could make potato salad for the wedding. The ceremony would be held at my former master teacher's home. My minister, Reverend Tryon, whom I highly respected, would conduct the ceremony. Elaine's master teacher, Tishumi, would bring sushi, enough to feed everybody.

We ordered, picked-up, and distributed normal white ruffled shirts, black tuxedos, shirt studs, bow ties, and cummerbunds for all of the guys participating in the wedding. Naturally, my twin, Donnie would stand at my side as best man. Elaine would be wearing a cream-colored gown. We had the license and her gold wedding band. I thought we were prepared for everything.

****

I convinced myself long ago not to wear jewelry of any kind. I didn't need to make a fashion statement. I didn't need to be that pretentious. *No blood diamonds or precious metals for me.* If I had wanted to wear a ring, it would have been made out of copper or aluminum, with a polished granite stone. That would have been my fashion statement. Besides, the thought of wearing a ring gave me the jitters. This feeling came about long ago--back in high school, while trying on a class ring. It felt too confining and gave me the heebie-jeebies.

****

"Will you take your bride for better or worse, in sickness and in health, until death do you part?" Growing up in the church, this part of the ceremony meant so much to me. I committed this vow to myself, Elaine, and to God. This part of the wedding, I got. It meant Elaine and I would stay together no matter what. Human beings aren't perfect, and each of us, at various times, will test each other's nerves, but no matter what, we were vowing to stay committed to each other, to ride together in the same vehicle, even if the wheels fall off.

Back to the ring—during one part of the ceremony, I felt a slight bit dishonest. While sliding the ring onto Elaine's finger, I knew in my heart wearing a ring for me would be life changing. I'd be committed to explore those jittery, uncomfortable, heebie-jeebie feelings. Fearfully, not wanting to risk what I'd find out, I quickly buried the thought. The rest of the ceremony went without flaw.

I spent time trying to talk to each and every wedding guest. By the time I sat down to eat sushi, it was all gone.

CHAPTER 6

Elaine started substituting in the Clark County School District while waiting to get a full-time teaching job. Many times, she taught at my school. As my faculty got to know her, they would request her by name. When Elaine met Janie Perkins, they took to each other like white paste and paper. Elaine's parents had been raised in the hills of Kentucky—Janie, too. Even Janie's husband, Jim, hailed from Kentucky. Maybe Janie's accent is what drew Elaine to her. Perhaps the accent reminded Elaine of her mother.

Elaine quickly got me out of my studio. We moved into the same apartment complex as Jim and Janie. It was several blocks from my school and a few blocks from the University of Nevada, Las Vegas. How nice it was to have two bedrooms and lots of living space. We even had a community swimming pool. I built a stained oak frame for a new king sized waterbed for our bedroom. I also made a small couch and loveseat out of oak. Elaine cut the foam and covered it to make pillows and decorative cushions. To celebrate and showoff our creative furniture-making skills, we invited Jim and Janie and one male teacher, Grady, who was the lead-teacher of my fifth grade team, to join us often for dinner.

Elaine got me to drag a huge mulberry tree stump from a nearby wash back to our apartment. We placed it near the front door as a decoration. One evening I took an elongated striped watermelon and sliced out a piece from end-to-end. I sat on the stump and lost myself in biting into the melon. I was lost in that melon, but after coming to my senses, I looked up into the neighbor's window directly in front of where I was sitting. A White couple were pointing and laughing at me. I could only imagine what they were thinking and that stereotypes truly do come from somewhere. Could they be saying, "Look at that Nigger, sitting on that stump, smiling, not a care in the world, as happy as can be, tearing that watermelon up?" I was so embarrassed. I couldn't eat anymore. With head bowed, I took my watermelon and went inside.

CHAPTER 7

❝ If you put a penny into a jar for a year every time a newlywed couple has sex, and then extract a penny for the next two years, there would still be pennies remaining in the jar," my father-in-law said. A few months after Elaine and I got married, Elaine could sense it, but I knew it: I didn't want to be married anymore. I felt this heap of adult responsibility rush upon me. One part of me longed to be free and irresponsible, like those imagined days after returning from the war. Fear of marital failure made me feel like I wore handcuffs, with my arms locked down tightly behind my back. Perhaps I was continuing to hold onto the notorious notion of one day turning into my alcoholic father. I don't know, but I felt trapped. I just wanted to be free—on my own. We didn't have any real intimacy, so I never talked with her about it. I simply found myself creating all kinds of ridiculous reasons why she disappointed me. It aggravated me to no end how she continually left the glasses turned up in the kitchen cabinet, knowing they could gather dust. She would sometimes forget and wash my lights with darks or, worse yet, my colored clothes with my whites. It was her consistently doing minor things like these I blamed for causing me to start drawing further and further away from her, retreating more—both emotionally and physically.

Outwardly, I was a man, but deep down inside I knew that emotionally, I was nothing more than a child. Unprepared for marriage, I didn't want it anymore. I thought it was my not wanting the responsibility that goes alone with marriage, but the truth was that I was not ready to acknowledge and share all of my fears and pain. Even that late in our relationship, I still didn't have the courage to be totally honest with my wife about something as simple as having sex. I didn't even have the courage to admit to Elaine that I had never been totally up front with her. Some parts of our marriage were a lie. Now would have been an excellent time to start discussing them. But I didn't. I couldn't. I should have told the truth about my lack of experiences with sex. Yet, for me to have done that, I would have needed to be totally honest with myself. Being well-endowed and by having a magnificent, slender-framed, muscular, well sculptured body—created by the Marine Corps—I found it easy to hide behind the stereotypical, conspicuous sex appeal of a worldly, young Black buck. Pretending to be well-experienced, standing upon myth and falsehood, I faked everything I did. I knew little about sex, except for what I had heard in sinfully whispered, adolescent boy-talk during my pubescent years. Prior to sleeping with Elaine, excluding the one time I had paid for sex while in the military and the one time I did it with a girlfriend, I knew so little about actual fornication. Those two separate experiences certainly didn't elevate me to the status of a Don Juan or a professional pimp-daddy, one who knew how to turn a woman on or out. Instead, my mother's lectures and the church's teachings produced a "good man," one who feared the Lord and was afraid of having sex outside of marriage. All the time with Elaine, I had discovered that I still felt equally uneasy, uncomfortable having sex inside of marriage, too. Perhaps I felt bad because I sensed that having sex was for adults—something restricted solely for grown-ups. Inside my heart and head, I certainly wasn't one. Not knowing what to do and not having an authentic self, I was stuck—way back somewhere in my past. Yet, wanting to be normal, wanting to be like everybody else, I continued living the lie.

All the while I kept telling myself, *I'm not going to let go all the way and completely lose myself. I'm not going to give up that much guarded control.*

Eventually, she left. Elaine went to Tucson, Arizona, to live with her brother, Edley, as he had recently divorced his wife. Patsy couldn't continue living with him working as a cop. Refusing to acknowledge the trauma buried inside, my life made no sense. Like Satan, who couldn't see his major problem—his refusal to submit—I, too, continued to heap sorrow onto my life. I wasn't ready to deal with the underlying issues I needed to face. I continued my existence, justifying my irrational behavior. I missed Elaine, but had my job as a teacher and my drinking to comfort me and occupy my time.

CHAPTER 8

As my friend and next-door fifth grade teacher, Grady, was single, we spent a lot of time together. Besides going out to dinner and to movies together, we'd spend a lot of time at Jim and Janie's. Perhaps by being a happy family of three, they wanted to bring some joy and comfort to their friends— two lonely bastards.

One Friday night, after consuming a lot of beer at a bar, Grady and I decided to take in a movie. I don't know who fell asleep first, but near the end of the movie, I awoke first. He was still snoring. I don't know if it was the beer that caused the nodding off or the amount of work we both put in as dedicated teachers.

To conserve money, I moved out of the two-bedroom apartment, into another studio. My salary was $9,000.00 for the entire year, and I got it through monthly paychecks.

I ate lots of dinners at Jim and Janie's, but not wanting to wear out my welcome, Grady and I began spending more time together. On the surface, he was a jovial, single, excellent fifth grade teacher, who easily socialized with everyone on our staff. And after school, Grady drank as much beer as I did. Throughout the weekdays and especially on early Friday evenings, about 4:30 P.M., Grady would invite all the staff's drinkers and me to join him at a nearby restaurant for cocktails and dinner.

Afterwards, rather than go home to our separate, lonely, partnerless abodes, we'd often go to the movies or frequent additional bars. We were together so much, I wondered if people thought we were closet lovers.

I eventually learned that Grady had lost his high-school sweetheart in a fatal car accident many years ago. His way of grieving included drinking and isolation—not getting involved in a new relationship with another female. Perhaps he thought he owed it to her to romanticize her death by remaining celibate and clinging to the cherished memory of her love.

Maybe I felt the same way about Elaine and wanted to worship her into martyrdom. I didn't want anybody, but her.

One thing I had learned about drinking beer came early in my reclaimed civilian life, immediately after Brenda dumped me. Beer, with its two-percent by volume alcohol content, never got me completely drunk. I could drink it endlessly, and I never got obliterated, totally out of control, or became a falling-down-drunk. Grady probably had discovered the calming effect beer had on him as he self-medicated to quiet the pain of losing his girlfriend many years ago.

While believing I was the one responsible for making my life incredible, I was hyperactive, fearful, and forever thinking—relentlessly trying to keep it all together. Beer calmed my nerves and helped me sleep at night. I think it was the same for Grady. We understood each other, and that is why we got along so well. Thinking we managed our lives with satisfactory control, the fact was, we were extremely immature and completely out of control. Thinking and wanting our lives to improve, we never entertained the possibility that things could get much worse.

Strange as it might seem, Grady was one of the best teachers on our staff. He was by far the informal leader of our school. Everybody respected him, and many envied his teaching.

He was entirely in a teaching league of his own. No classroom environment ever came close to matching his. His bulletin boards were crafty and most unique.

Annually, his students would put on an one-hour end-of-the-year school performance in the multipurpose room. Dressed in full costume they would dance, bump, or grind while lip-syncing the most popular tunes on the current musical charts.

One weekend Grady drove me to my mother's house. We left Las Vegas bound for L.A. immediately after school that Friday afternoon. Our first stop before leaving town was to fill our two ice chests with beer and ice. We bought two twenty-four-can cases. (I say our first stop because we made frequent stops, reliving ourselves, as we traveled down the highway in his brand new, red, 1976 Cobra II Mustang.)

When we reached the bottom of the grade at Baseline in San Bernardino, Grady called out, "Reach in the backseat and give me a beer."

I swished my hand around in one chest, found nothing. I raked through the ice and cold water in the second chest. "Grady, you aren't going to believe this," I said. "All the beers are gone. We've drunk them all."

CHAPTER 9

O ften, Elaine and I talked over the phone. I even wrote her love notes. "Laney, Laney, I miss and love you so," was included in every note.

"Ronnie, I love you, but you will have to change," was her constant refrain, every time we communicated.

"Laney, Laney, you know I love you so. I promise I will change. It's you and me 'till the wheels fall off, so, Honey, come on home." I honestly meant what I had said. I wanted to change, but, unfortunately, I didn't know how.

For escape and entertainment, whenever I wasn't at school or with Grady, I spent many lonely hours singing and playing my piano or jumbo, acoustic guitar. Singing ballads, work songs, spirituals, field songs and the blues sometimes caused my actions and intent to work in reverse. Instead of cheering me up, I'd sink into depression. I'd think about the many hours I had spent singing and playing in the past, trying to relieve the anxiety from being dumped by an old girlfriend, Brenda. Then God. Then Elaine. (I had met Brenda in church after getting out of the Marine Corps. Prior to dating her, I had asked God for a sign to let me know if it was the right thing to do. Since He kept putting us in situations that brought us closer and closer together, I trusted Him and gave her what I could of my heart. Not too long into the relationship, Brenda dumped me, setting my world and plans into a tailspin. How could I ever trust God again?) Sometimes I'd stop singing and playing, get completely silent—so silent, I'd hear troubling thoughts from my past. *You isolated yourself after your breakup with Brenda. You wallowed in self-pity. All you had was your music, and you used it every day. But them you were about ready to go, to mentally slip off the edge, and you probably would have if Elaine had not come along.* Each time these thoughts arose I'd listen for a second and then send them back into the dark pit of suppression. *Been there. Done that. I'm not going to return to that living hell because of this new break-up with Elaine. I've got my friends, my work—loads of it—to keep me strong.*

Near the end of the school year, Elaine reunited with me. I knew I could never divorce her, and I guess she had learned to feel the same way about me.

CHAPTER 10

My teaching mainly consisted of utilizing management systems, which were taught to me during evening and weekend in-service training programs. Using them, how could anyone fail? I would pre-test my students on certain concepts, teach the concepts, and then post-test the students to see how much they learned. When the majority of my students passed, at a satisfactory eighty-percent rate, I would move on to teaching other concepts. If they did not pass, I would re-teach—utilizing different methodologies—post-test, and do this until enough students passed. By complying with the use of these teaching strategies, I felt my life, as a teacher was rubber-stamped. *Where was the need for my creativity? What about my individualism? The hell with their systems,* I thought. I resented using them, but I continued using them, dutifully.

I was miserable teaching most of my fifth grade students how to add and subtract. After all, these were fifth graders. They should have been ready and prepared to learn the order of operations for rational numbers. Most of them should have been ready to learn about fractions and reviewing how to divide. The sad fact was most of them couldn't read or write. What exacerbated the situation was my inability to teach fifth grade students who were heterogeneously grouped. I tried to group them into Red Birds, Blue Birds, Yellow Birds, and Green Birds. I wanted to devote teacher-instruction to a specific group while others worked independently, but I never had time for the extremely bright students. I'd always end-up giving most of my time to the students having the most learning deficiencies. And I never got it right.

I loved the children and never blamed them for my own inadequacies. No one would ever hear me say, "These kids can't do this or that!" I always believed the onus was on me, not on their previous teachers, not on their parents, and certainly not on them. Besides, blaming others or making excuses for my students' deficiencies did nothing to improve their skills. I always believed I'm the Pied Piper, and I should posses the necessary skills to "Pipe" my kids away.

By the end of the school year, I had had it. I told my principal (and my close friend, a veteran teacher, Bruce) that in spite of their on-going mentoring me, I was going to quit and return to Los Angeles, with the hopes of perusing a career in cabinetmaking.

Close to the end of the school year, I signed a document in the principal's office acknowledging I would not be signing a contract for the next school year.

I rushed home to tell Elaine I finally had mustered up enough courage to sign the document. She first hugged me and said she was proud of me. After all, I had discussed my dissatisfaction with teaching with her off and on all year. Then, she said, "Ronnie, I'm pregnant."

With my jaw still dropped low and my eyeballs about to pop from their sockets, I immediately called Mr. Twitchell on the phone. Thank God, I got through. I asked him if he had turned the signed contract documents in to the District office. When he said, "No." I didn't hesitate to ask if I could sign my contract for the up-coming year.

"Will you, Mr. Twitchell, allow me to sign my contract declaring my intent to return?" I begged. "Will you destroy the document I foolishly signed this afternoon?" I pleaded. "Elaine just told me she is pregnant."

After hearing my reason for suddenly changing my mind, Mr. Twitchell replied, "It's a good thing you are a good teacher, Ronnie Smith. You know, you've already signed the document? I don't have to take you back. But I will. Come in tomorrow, and sign your intent to return.

"Thank you, Mr. Twitchell," was all I could say.

After hanging up the phone, I thought more about Mr. Twitchell. I knew for certain that he, like a patriarchal father of his flock, genuinely loved and cared about the members of his staff. Most times, right after special evening school events, certain members of our faculty would go out to drink. Immediately after the phone call, I sat and thought, *How painful life must be for Mr. Twitchell—a bishop and the devoted leader not only in the District but also in the Church of the Latter Day community. How difficult it must be for him to know half of his teachers were sinners--drinking and partying all the time.*

This time I welcomed a child. I wanted to be a Daddy. With a secure job, I knew I'd be able to financially provide for my child. I wanted to nurture him or her emotionally, as well—giving my child the security, outward expressions of love, and my time, attributes I felt I never received as a child.

Knowing how thoughtless Elaine could be, especially about satisfying her immediate sexual needs, I thought back to her being in Syracuse, New York, when she went to visit her old boyfriend, while we were in college. I hadn't entirely let that go. Since people rarely change, I wondered if she'd lain with a loving friend when she left me and ran off to Arizona. I pushed all negative thoughts out of my mind and hoped that the baby was mine. Because I loved her, I didn't want to bring up the past and hurt Elaine. I was happy, content at having her back with me. *If the baby's not mine, I don't know what I'll do. Will I abandon her and the child? Will I lovingly keep them both? No need to make a decision now. I will deal with that issue, if needed, once the child arrives.* I didn't confide in sharing my thoughts or concerns with Bruce or Donnie. Something deep inside kept telling me there was no need. Some people you know so well, you already know exactly what they are going to say. There's no need asking.

CHAPTER 11

Bruce sent Elaine and me a letter inviting us to his wedding, which would be held on a Saturday, at his new house located across the road of the Botanical Gardens, above the Santa Barbara Canyon. His bride was not "Miss Cute Girl." As attractive as she was, being the first girl on the rebound of his marriage, they had mutually broken up, as I had expected, a long time ago. As the wedding would be held in June, school would be out. Teachers and their students would be on summer break. In addition, Bruce wanted Elaine and me to housesit his ranch for a week, when he and his new wife, D'Anne, would be enjoying their honeymoon.

****

I spent a lot of weekends with Bruce while Elaine and I were separated. He had sold his old house, divided the equity with Rosie, moved onto 55 acres of land. His caretaker owned the property when Bruce was a troubled adolescent who had run away from home. The place was a burned-out mansion, constructed with adobe brick, one-foot thick. When Bruce first moved in, the adobe was the only thing standing after the historical Santa Barbara wildfires of 1969. He first began rebuilding by putting a corrugated tin roof over the kitchen, a toilet room, and a small guest bedroom. Although the burnt-out place was palatial, these were the three areas he lived in. Bruce took his showers outside, using a water hose. When I first got there, I used the toilet. Unsteady, unleveled, it rocked and hissed when I sat down. I thought it was a snake. It 'bout scared me out my mind. Water sprayed at the bottom and leaked all over the floor.

****

The wedding took place on the patio. The bride and groom faced the preacher. They could see the burned adobe. The guests marveled at D'Anne and Bruce as they took their vows. What a backdrop—the clear sky, working its way down the mountain, onto the beaches, and out to the Pacific Ocean.

Once the guests left, I had to feed the chickens, goats, and horses. All of it was easy. I watched Bruce do it many times. But my fighting with Bruce's big red rooster, whom I nicknamed Chant éclair, caught me by surprise. He kept on trying to strike me with his spikes located just above the claws on his scaly legs. I wanted to take a hoe, rake, or shovel and take him out for good. But I knew Bruce wouldn't like that. Not having an inkling of any kind about being a farmhand, I was more afraid of the rooster than he was of me. I'd kick at it each time he tried to spike me. If psyching out an opponent were the sole criterion for winning a fight, Chant éclair would have claimed the victory. I only won each battle because I was much bigger than he.

At sunrise, I could not get up to feed the livestock. That rooster could crow and crow for all I cared. I was not getting up. I reminded myself of the poet, Robert Frost. He, too, I have been schooled, was not a good farmhand. Like Mr. Frost, I never got up before eleven o'clock to start my non-city chores. How glad I was when Bruce and D'Anne finally returned.

CHAPTER 12

Elaine and I spent most of our summer away from hot Las Vegas. We took frequent trips to L.A. to visit my family and friends, or go to Santa Barbara to visit her family, Bruce and D'Anne, and her other friends. We spent a lot of the summer helping Bruce fix up his home. One day, he and I got the largest, cheapest aboveground pool pump and jerry-rigged plastic pipe and fittings to old galvanized steel in order to attached the new pump to the original pool filtering system. To our surprise, the pump worked fine. We now had a swimming pool to cool us off during the heat of the day. We ate breakfast, lunch, and grilled-meat dinners on the patio beside the pool. Andy, Rosie's father and Bruce's ex-father-in-law, would often fly over in his piper-cub broadcasting on his megaphone, "Hey, you guys, I see you skinny-dipping," even though we weren't. Bruce explained that Andy was a spotter for fishing boats, working the Channel Islands. One day, Andy got extremely upset when a fishing boat could not use his longitudinal and latitudinal coordinates to net the fish. He was so angry, the next day he mounted a megaphone onto his piper-cub to use it whenever necessary.

One day, Bruce saddled Andrea's tamed quarter horse, Ranger. I packed a sack lunch, and was going to spend the afternoon taking a trip around the fifty-five acres. I saddled-up and rode a quarter of a mile. Bruce's steed, a beautiful brown and white Appaloosa, called from the corral. Ranger heard the call, started bucking and trying to throw me. Holy cow! I held on for dear life. The saddle slipped to the horse's side. The horse galloped back to the house, with me hollering, still seated, riding side-saddled. All Bruce could do was laugh.

One morning, I saw what Bruce had told me was a turkey buzzard soaring above the canyon. I ran into the house, grabbed Bruce's field glasses, and dashed back outside. Locating the buzzard in the glasses, it looked big enough to grab me up with one claw. Up close, its face looked blistery and loaded with purulent, green algae and fungus. I dived under the patio table and waited for the buzzard to pass before I dared to stand up. Huffing and completely out of breath, but glad to be still remaining on the ground, I said to myself, *This city boy still has a lot to learn about outdoor life.*

During the summer of 1976, Elaine and I took advantage of every opportunity we had to spend time with Bruce. Unlike the fresh, cool air above Santa Barbara Canyon, the awful heat in Vegas did nothing but tire us out. Santa Barbara's weather and natural landscape invigorated our bodies. minds, and spirits. That's where we wanted to be, and that's were we went, again and again. We would either have breakfast on the patio or drive down the mountain into town. Our lifestyle was so relaxed, so slow, many times we road our bicycles. Breakfast at Rose's Café was always a delight. Skillet-fries, warm tortillas, and Spanish omelets with chorizo were the special on the menu. Every time I ordered it, I'd complain yelling out, "Spicy, Rose! Too many chilies, and the seeds inside the jalapeños are too hot."

She'd yell back from behind her kitchen, "If you don't want it hot, don't order a Spanish omelet. That's the way I make them. That's the way they're always going to come."

Typically, we wouldn't eat lunch. We'd drink beer and wine throughout the day. For dinner, we'd eat out occasionally, but no dinners were better than those grilled above Bruce's sand-stoned terrace. Be it chicken, steak, lamb, or seafood, he always made excellent kabobs. Like The Great Gatsby, Bruce surrounded himself with friends. The parties never ended.

For two weeks, we sat out on the terrace in the evenings watching the Olympics on an old 24-inch black and white portable T.V. Bruce had mounted crinkled tin-fold arms to the base of an antenna. It took me awhile to not be distracted by the spinning, twisting, tin-fold spindles being propelled by the breeze.

While watching the athletes perform, I often asked myself, *Will I ever become famous? Will I ever rise beyond the ordinary?*

Then, I would remember what Mother had always instilled into her children's minds since childhood. "Don't ever ask anyone to do for you what you can do yourself. You can become whatever you want, but don't count on others to do your work for you."

Recalling my mother's words, I could no longer simply enjoy watching the Olympics at face value. Watching the athletes achieve their aspirations, the accomplishments of their dreams, I, too, didn't want to be ordinary. I wanted to be exceptional at something.

CHAPTER 13

At the end of the school year I talked our principal, Mr. Twitchell, into letting me teach second grade. I wanted him to know how I felt about my inadequacies in teaching fifth grade. "Come on, please give me a chance," I told him. "I promise, no child will leave my class next year not knowing how to add and subtract. No child will be passed on to third grade not knowing how to read. In college, I minored in early childhood education. Trust me, I know exactly what to do." I believe after hearing all of this, he was convinced to let me give it a try.

Believing good teaching is all about establishing great relationships, I wanted to work hard to create positive relationships with my second grade students, their parents, and my team of second grade teachers on our staff. I had learned the importance of the teacher/parent relationship part last year from the best—my principal, Mr Twitchell. He told me, "If a child's parents believe you are doing your best for him or her, they will be more forgiving when you make a mistake."

Unlike the previous year, this new 1976-77 school year was starting out with promise—except for Mr. Twitchell's frequent visits to my classroom prior to the day of the students' arrival. It seemed he was always there, watching all I was doing to prepare the room for the kids. He chatted with me and watched me construct a bulletin board. He watched me add teacher-made and commercial displays to the room. Though he would never say it, I guess he was there to make sure I'd get off to an excellent start— that I'd do nothing wrong.

After obtaining permission from the principal, I used a permanent black marker to draw lines on all my modern, brown chalkboards. I used a yardstick to make the lines straight. Making one solid line across the entire length of the board, then one dotted line I repeatedly drew until the entire board was completed. My purpose for doing this was to draw words on the board. My penmanship, like my life, was shaky, insecure. It held secrets of "less-than-ness," self-doubt, and fear. I wanted my printing to be beautiful—especially for the students to emulate. That is why I drew the lines. I would not simply print; like an artist, I knew I would draw. I would craft every word. I wanted my penmanship to reflect confidence. Knowing my art is in my penmanship, I wanted my letters standing sturdy and tall, showing regality or prominence, super fashion, and great style.

When Mr. Twitchell wasn't there, I took an old, wooden folding ladder and painted it a flat jet black. To create a positive, motivational learning environment, I painted each rung a different vibrant astro-bright, fluorescent color and added a little glitter on the very top rung—just to make it pop! I went to the store and purchased candy, lots of hard candy on a stick. After drilling holes the size of each candy stick, I mounted the confection on each row. The bottom rung contained small blow-pops and small suckers, individually wrapped. The higher the row, the bigger the candy. There were tall, spiral, rainbow candy licking sticks and round, braided suckers, which grew to be as much as nine inches in diameter, as they climbed their individual way to the top. Above the ladder, I hung a self-made poster from the ceiling, which read, "READ YOUR WAY to the TOP." Each time one of my students completed one of the reading books in our required series of reading grade-level texts, and had successfully passed the mandatory management post-test prescribed for the book, he or she could go to the ladder. Starting on the first rung for the first book completed, my students could earn candy for each book read and climb their way up the reading ladder.

Once my students arrived, I wanted to involve them in setting up the learning environment. Over a long period of time, during art, we took newspaper, rolled it and stretched each piece out into a long cylinder. We'd staple each end and then vertically staple each cylinder to the burlap-paneled walls. My students painted the newspaper with brown tempera paint and added black knotholes, for effect. I even went to the extent of stapling their painted paper cylinders to the ceiling. The inside of our classroom looked like a log cabin. I'd like to think this was before fire code standards because my students, their parents, other teachers, Mr. Twitchell, and I loved it.

CHAPTER 14

M r. Twitchell wasn't the only one to make frequent visits to my room. Ann—Mrs. Chapman—a young, slender, dark-complected, attractive, Afro-American teacher showed up just as much. She taught first grade in the primary section of our school for the last three years. But I had not gone out of my way to get to know her, especially while I taught fifth grade on the other side of the school last year. After several chats, she invited my wife and me to dinner, and to meet her husband and daughter. I think we went on a Friday night, so we could spend some time together.

Elaine and I learned that her husband, Billy, was also an elementary teacher, who started teaching fifth grade the previous year just like me. Billy was six-foot, a high-yellow, mulatto-looking man who wore bifocals and his hair in a short, military flattop. Although both Ann and Billy were Afro-American, their three-year-old daughter, Jennifer, looked mulatto, like she belonged to Elaine and me.

Ann was a gourmet cook. It was something she did for pleasure. She set an impressive table—lace tablecloth, crystal stemware, bone china, and silver flatware. What a night of eloquent dining. Her presentation equaled the variety of subtle flavors delicately gracing her cuisine.

After dinner, we played board games, and Billy and I drank lots of beer. It did not take long to know this relationship was going somewhere. Elaine would have a new female friend in addition to her friendship with Janie. Billy was an avid fisherman, which matched one of my favorite hobbies. Elaine and I could frequently take Jennifer out for a Happy Meal or a stop at an ice cream parlor while proudly claiming her as our own. Pretending to have a child, a family felt so good—probably because we didn't. There were no cares, frustrations, nor worries about her being sick, sleepless, or moody. We took her home, to her real parents each night.

CHAPTER 15

Although I worked with my students every day, at times, even I found it almost unbelievable how well they articulated their thoughts. One day, during my second-graders' introduction to rational numbers, I drew a straight, horizontal line on the chalkboard. I drew a vertical line through the middle. "What did I just do?" I asked one student.

"Since it's math time, you are probably introducing fractions, Mr. Smith," one student proposed.

"Yes!" I joyously exclaimed. Then I drew more vertical lines—one through the middle of the first half and one through the middle of the second half of the original line. I asked another student to explain the concept.

"Mr. Smith, you have dissected the horizontal line, indicating one fourth of the plane." After she gave the correct response, I asked the "slowest" student in math class to predict what I was probably going to do next.

"Mr. Smith," he said, "you now have one-fourth and one-half. Next, you are going to go to one-eighth, then one-sixteenth, then, one-thirty-second, and then one-sixty-fourth. Need I go on?"

I was exceedingly proud of this child, Charles, because of his accurate prediction. A few days earlier, his father had stumbled into my classroom—drunk, accusing me of not teaching Charles how to read. Before I could convince the father not to interrupt my teaching and to go to the front office to pre-schedule an appointment with me, my students came to my aide—one in particular bellowed, "Charles is the only one Mr. Smith spends the majority of our reading time with. How dare you accuse him of not teaching Charles."

I was glad of what she said, but I had to end the confrontation right away. "Don't be discourteous in speaking to an adult." I then looked directly at Charles' father and demanded he leave the room immediately.

"Great job," I exclaimed. "Let's go bake a cake." I had brought in enough boxes of cake mix and frosting to do something special with my students. We mixed the ingredients in the classroom but had to take the cake pans to the oven in a special room for baking. I wanted the students to pile layer upon layer to see how many layers they could stack before the cake fell in or over.

Later that day, Carolyn—the student who defended me regarding Charles' father—got me back. She was standing at the blackboard, looking as cute as Shirley Temple, and explaining a social studies concept to the entire class. I was at her student desk socializing with another student. "Mr. Smith," she said, "you are being discourteous, talking while I'm trying to teach. You, too, must pay careful attention if you want to learn."

Fully understanding one another, we shared a smiled as I said, "Touché, My Dear, Touché."

One Friday afternoon, we made pizza during art. I supplied all the ingredients. With tomato sauce smeared all over their mouths, joyous smiles filled the classroom. One student exclaimed, "Cutting, dividing pizza slices to everyone in our class is the best way to learn fractions, Mr. Smith."

CHAPTER 16

Elaine and I invited Ann and Billy over for dinner one evening. I wanted them to experience my culinary skills. Living in an apartment, we didn't have a formal dining room, let alone a dining room table. We knew Ann and Billy would accept us for the quality people we were. We knew eating at our inexpensive kitchen table would not turn them off. Nor did we have a linen tablecloth, crystal glassware, or fine china. Our silverware was stainless steel. But the roasted leg of lamb, seasoned with garlic and rosemary, and served with minted chutney totally satisfied their pallets. Billy and I drank beer while the four of us played Scrabble well into the night.

From then on, it was on. The Chapmans introduced us to other friends of theirs. Our dinner parties grew in size and number.

Billy liked to fish, and he owned a 16-foot Sea Ray. He introduced me to one of his many brothers, Jimmy, and to his best friend, Curtis. The four of us spent many weekends at Lake Mead fishing from his boat. Using different techniques than the ones I utilized for ocean fishing, Billy taught me how to catch catfish, largemouth bass, and strippers. Often we'd meet at each other's house for a fish fry and to drink large quantities of beer.

Not having family in Las Vegas, Elaine and I spent so much time at Ann and Billy's that Elaine once commented, "We should be paying rent." And how wonderful it was to be a part of a social group, which turned our new lives in Las Vegas into the special place we could now call home.

During these gatherings, I learned that Curtis was married to May, and Jimmy was married to Ruby. Elaine and I introduced our new friends to Jim and Janie during a party held at our home. Since Curtis, May, Jimmy, and Jim were all elementary teachers and Janie was working on her teaching credentials, we all hit it off pretty well as a group of special friends. Ruby, Jimmy's wife, drove a school bus, so she in no way felt left out.

CHAPTER 17

W anting to be an exceptional teacher like my role model, Grady, I spent time seriously planning my lessons instead of teaching off the top of my head. I wanted my students to be able to recognize patterns in various concepts and be able to apply newly acquired knowledge, not to merely memorize stuff.

Once, I gave my students a take-home science project. We were learning about wind, force, time, speed, and velocity. Their assignment was to work with their parents to create any type of contraption they wanted that would move as fast as it could and as far as it could—propelled solely by the wind. Being second-graders, smiles came on most of their faces when I said," Each of you has the creativity within you to construct a project that will be able to move like the wind." I further explained, that on a good, windy day we would take their science projects outside and see whose project traveled the farthest and whose traveled the fastest. I let them know I'd videotape the entire race to determine the winners. Of course we discovered the principles behind scientific concepts as we played and applied the concepts to our fun.

Second graders from other classrooms came up to me during recess and at lunchtime begging me to transfer them out of their classrooms, into mine. "Why?" I would ask. "Don't you like your teacher?"

"Yes, she's nice and likes me a lot," many of them would say. "But all we do is work. Your kids get to play, and that's exactly what I would rather do."

"My students work," I would tell them.

"Yeah, but your kids tell us about the cakes and pizza. That's fun work, and I want to be transferred to your room."

One afternoon, after returning to our room from lunch, I decided to have a heart-to-heart talk with my students. "What we do in this classroom stays in this classroom," I instructed. "There's no need telling other students what we do. Not being in our class makes them feel bad. And we don't want to be the cause of other students feeling bad, do we?" I ended my little speech and moved on to a different subject.

One of my female students kept playing with something inside her desk instead of paying attention to the lesson. First, I looked at her askance, showing my disapproval. She continued moving something inside her desk—even to the point of sticking her face close to the desk and peering inside. I went over to her desk and looked in to see what she was doing. I didn't see anything out of the ordinary. In a calm, quiet voice I spoke only for her to hear me. "Laura, I really want you to learn. Please pay attention."

I must have hurt her feelings. She rolled her eyes at me and burst out in silent tears. At dismal, I bent down beside her and quietly asked if I had done something to offend her. She didn't say a word.

The next morning, long before the start of school, her mother showed up at my door. With an unlit cigarette dangling from her lip she said, "Mr. Smith, yesterday you embarrassed my daughter."

"It has never been my intent to embarrass any of my students. It's not my style," I tried to assure her. "But something went wrong yesterday with your daughter. I can't figure it out."

She looked at me with contempt and said, "Laura told me you asked your students to keep what's done in your room a secret. Why would you do that Mr. Smith? Why would you tell kids to keep secret what they are doing with you?"

Then, I caught on to what she was implying. I knew there was no way I could get her to listen to the truth.

"Mr. Smith," she continued, "Don't do that again, or I'll take our little chat to the principal the next time you tell your kids to keep little secrets."

From then on I said as little as possible. I did not want to add fuel to her private flame. I did not want her to twist any more of my words. I was glad when she left my room.

I took the incident to the principal as soon as I had a break. I discussed with him my lesson learned. From then on, I was passionate in telling my students: "Always tell your parents everything that happens in this room."

I enjoyed the freedom my principal gave me to be creative with my students, so much so, work wasn't work. In fact, it was almost like those other second grade students, from other second grade classrooms, had described, "All fun instead of work." Yet, I knew deep down in my spirit that possibly the more unstructured something appears, the more structured it actually is. I took all the credit myself—proud of my college-quality written lesson plans.

The outcome of my students' standardized test scores turned me into a braggart. It didn't take me long to showcase their test results with the other teachers during lunch in our teacher's lounge. Until one day, another teacher, Jody, who also taught second grade, came to my classroom after school. She sat next to me at one of my small tables. With a serious demeanor, she put her arms around me and said, "Ronnie, I hate to be the one to deflate your ego, but you are bragging far too much in the teachers' lounge. Before school started, Mr. Twitchell asked the three of us, your other second grade teachers, if we would give you our top, most intelligent students. He wanted to ensure your teaching at the primary level would be most successful."

Boy, did my bubble instantaneously pop. But I thanked her for her honesty in putting me in my place. Her kind words made me appreciate my team of grade level teachers and our wise principal even more.

Keeping in the back of my mind the athletes who had medaled in the 1976 Olympics the previous year, I wanted to be self-crowned teacher of the year. I didn't have the need for recognition from others. This was an internal craving that desired a motivational accolade. I didn't literally seek the award, but I wanted to feel that I taught my first year of second grade well enough to merit the achieving, reaching one's personal best award. Since I played my guitar and taught my students many traditional children songs all year long, I decided to emulate Grady by having my students dress in parent-made costumes in late spring and perform many of the songs we had learned for all the primary grades. Two of the audiences' favorites were, "Frankie and Johnny," and "Froggie Went A Hunting."

Although I wasn't standing on the winner's podium at the Olympics, the principal, the audience, the parents raved about the program, and no one was more pleased with the outcome than I. The school year ended as quickly as it had come, and I was ready to start my summer.

CHAPTER 18

Elaine and I busied ourselves with preparing for the baby. I stripped, sanded, and stained an old wooden baby crib that had been given to me by Sue Rivers, a third grade teacher on my faculty. I stained it lime green. It looked good once I reinstalled all of the white plastic protectors and polished metal hardware. Elaine and I went out and bought a lot of cotton diapers and large safety pins because she wanted to change diapers the old-fashioned way. I went out and bought two or three baby-sized face clothes and drying towels. We faithfully attended Lamaze Birthing classes. I thought we were all set.

Elaine and I didn't have any problems. We were getting along well, and excited about the baby on the way, the new addition to our family. As delivery time got closer, I could not restrain myself any longer. I wanted to know the truth, if the baby was mine. *Although it would be the Christian thing to do, how could I take responsibility for a baby—a White baby—that wasn't mine, especially when Elaine conceived this child with another man when I wanted her to be with me?* Wanting to, my spirit was right, but my flesh was weak and wrong. And I did not want to add extra stress to Elaine by confronting her with the issue. I kept telling myself to simply wait it out. *Don't upset Elaine. Just wait for the baby's arrival. But will it be White? Will it be Asian? Exactly what ethnicity will it be?* Driving myself crazy with all kinds of ridiculous, probable scenarios, one night, I selfishly popped the question, "Elaine, is the baby mine?"

She should have smacked me, but she didn't. I was lucky. She loved me and knew that I would eventually ask that question.

She smiled and said, "If it's not yours, you'll certainly know it."

I didn't ask any more questions. I stopped to think about what she had said. It filled me with jealousy, disappointment, and hurt, but I also felt I had placed her in this situation. I needed to forgive her for what she had done. I thought about the wedding vow—specifically the, "For better or worse, 'til death do us part."

On the morning of July 7, 1977, Elaine's water broke. We thought we'd have a 7/7/77 baby. I stayed in the hospital with Elaine the entire day. I never once thought about who would be the baby's daddy. All I wanted was for both Elaine and the baby to come out of the delivery extremely well. At one point, the nurse, while examining Elaine blurted out, "Oh my God!"

Elaine and I, in unison inquired, "Is something wrong?"

"Oh, no," the nurse calmly replied. "There was just a glitch in the equipment. I thought I had seen something that wasn't there."

I knew she was lying, that she had slipped and had spoken out unprofessionally. I knew something was wrong. All I could do was pray to my God. *Heavenly Father, if something is wrong, please intercede, and work it out for good. If something is wrong with the baby, I give him to You. Take his life and bless it, Father, I give him to You!*

Elaine did not want an epidural. She wanted no medication. She did not want to further harm the baby. She huffed and puffed, sometimes turning blue. She would often call my name, saying, "Honey, squeeze my hand. Squeeze it harder. Squeeze it harder." She did this until the baby came.

After tying off the umbilical cord, the obstetrician placed our baby, Jemal Tee Smith in my arms at 12:40 A.M., July 8, 1977. As I held him, Jemal looked me dead in the eyes and smiled. I left the hospital about 1:00 in the morning, stopped at a convenience store, got a six-pack, and drove home.

The next morning, I saw Jemal through the glass window in the nursery of the hospital. The entire family of a couple I had met at the hospital the previous night came to me and asked which child was mine. I had to hunt and search for Jemal. While looking at the infants, I made the comment, "Well, you know, they all, at this age, look just alike."

Several members of that family looked at black me like I was crazy. Without thinking about it, it was the middle of summer. I had tanned to a black-black. Seconds later I got it—after it had slipped out of my mouth. *How could this dark-skinned man make a comment as ridiculous as that? 'They all look alike."* He doesn't even know his *child,* they must have thought.

Jemal had had no complications and was born on July 8, 1977, weighing seven pounds, seven ounces. That family's newborn came out weighing thirteen pounds, five ounces. Wow, I thought, no wonder theirs took so long.

Boy, did her feelings change—fast, I thought as I picked up Elaine's mother, Helen, at the airport in the afternoon. While driving her to the hospital to see Elaine and the baby, I could not stop my thinking back to the time Helen first met me. Elaine had driven me to Santa Barbara to meet her parents. At the end of the weekend, as we were driving home, Elaine broke out in tears. "Ronnie, I have to tell you something," she said. "My mother told me if I marry you, and if we have children, she'll never have anything to do with them." Then more tears gushed. Helen had certainly changed. What a relief it was for me to learn my child would not have to suffer from his grandma's ignorant, racist social upbringing.

After visiting with Elaine, Helen and I went shopping for baby stuff. She saw what Elaine and I had collected and knew it wasn't enough. Along with toiletries, baby blankets, and towels, Helen purchased a large, upright, wooden rocking chair. I was so glad to have her with me. She was just what Elaine, Jemal, and I needed. I explained to Helen our reasoning behind naming Jemal and spelling his name the way we did. Elaine and I had met a couple in Santa Barbara who had a son named Jamal. We liked the child and decided to name ours after him. However, being teachers, we knew how some troubled children could poke fun at others. We did not want to take a chance on a child calling ours "Jam." That is why we had decided on spelling his name "Jemal." I decided to give him his middle name, "Tee," after my father, Robert Tee, and after me, Ronnie Tee. I did not want to have a junior.

I brought Elaine and my son home two days later. Being completely new to caring for an infant, I felt thankful having Helen, an experienced mother, in our home. She stayed with us for a week. She held her grandson with such pride, confidence, and love, I'm sure he was comforted, too.

My mother came to rock Jemal, a week or so after Helen departed. I noticed a difference in Helen and my mother, Mattie, as they spent time with their grandson. Because Jemal was Helen's first grandchild, he brought her great excitement. Helen was younger than my mother by thirty years. My mother was an experienced grandmother—a great grandmother by her three sons from her first marriage—before she had married my dad. Mattie also had rocked my sister's boy and girl, babysat my brother, Donnie's, first-born son, and she had kept my youngest sister's son. (My two sisters, Donnie, and I all had sons at approximately the same time.)

When I held Jemal, I felt appreciative and proud. Naturally with the baby, Elaine and I grew closer. We loved each other and our son. And, as Jesus would be the first to say, "A person's actions begin with a thought," I thought only of the present—this new life with my wife and our offspring.

CHAPTER 19

My parents purchased land and property all over Southern California when they were young and also had a little spare money. Perhaps this extra money came from my dad, when he was serving his country overseas during WWII. Besides living in L.A., they owned land in Ventura, Palmdale and Riverside. Each time they bought a home in L.A., they'd keep it as a rental, letting that property work for them to acquire the means to purchase a bigger and better home.

My father taught me well. Like him, by age fifteen, I could build and repair anything related to a home. I considered myself the superintendent of all the properties my parents owned. I repaired the plumbing, replaced broken windows, hung sheetrock and doors, patched and painted, and installed new roofs. There was no house repair job I couldn't do. That is why I never wanted to own a home. I considered it a blessing to call the apartment manager whenever something broke and service was needed.

However, we knew apartment living was out of the question for raising our son,

Jemal. Elaine did most of the home hunting. All the new homes were far too expensive for a teacher's budget. Finally, we had to settle for a home like Jim and Janie. They had purchased a new duplex, with two bedrooms, two bathrooms, and a den, on the far west of town near Rainbow and Flamingo for $35,000.00.

We followed them once more, moving into the same complex, living two blocks from them.

I put a sprinkler system in the backyard and dug out a garden. Wanting my son to have soft, cushiony grass to play upon, I took sprigs of Saint Augustine grass from my mother's home every time we'd visit. I planted the grass in both our front and backyards.

Back then, it was a breeze driving my Bug down Tropicana to my school, which was near Maryland Parkway and Hacienda. It would take less than ten minutes for me to get to work. In fact, very little existed west of Decatur and south of Sahara. It was common knowledge the town virtually ended at that intersection. All the way down the road on both sides of the land were nothing but open desert.

I loved my wife. I loved my child. I loved my job. Every time I looked at Elaine, I thought of the pain she had endured in the hospital while giving birth to Jemal. I often thought of how she gave up drinking alcohol during her pregnancy to ensure better health for our son. All of her selfless sacrifices caused me to love her more. Each late afternoon, when I'd come home from school, I felt the love of a happy marriage, the comfort of a well kept home, and the joy of a good-tempered, well-rested infant.

CHAPTER 20

At the start of the school year, Elaine brought Jemal to school to present him to my staff and students. How proud I felt in showing off my son.

Shortly after their visit, one of my parents confided in me that her daughter, Tara, had Elaine as her substitute teacher in first grade several times. After Elaine brought Jemal to school and introduced him to my class, Tara eventually made the connection. She went home and told her mother, "Mom, old Black Mr. Smith is married to old White Mrs. Smith, and they have a TAN baby."

I wanted my son to grow up having a father—one who was loving, intimate, and believing his son could and would one day conquer the world. With Elaine by my side and my baby in my arms, nothing had ever brought me more joy.

Elaine gave Jemal over to a babysitter at age three. She accepted a full-time elementary teaching position. I returned to my school, teaching second grade. I retained my elation in being a loving husband, father, and second grade teacher—even though I no longer had the brightest second grade class.

One day, while driving to work, I witnessed an automobile collision, which ended in a fatality. A young female was t-boned in an intersection. *Was she a wife, a mother?*

News of her untimely death would certainly change her family's life. This could have been Elaine. This stranger's death caused me to focus on my family and to appreciated them all the more.

Elaine and I kept our two old cars, but for family safety, we purchased a brand new car, which Elaine drove. It was a white Honda Civic—small but reliable. I had peace of mind, knowing the car would never break down, leaving Elaine and Jemal stranded.

CHAPTER 21

The summer heat is lessening by a few degrees. It's the end of August. The three of us are living in our first real home. Both Grandmas frequently come to visit. I'm eager to begin the 1977-'78 school year. Three years in Las Vegas when I was only going to stay one. Vegas is good to me and my family. I couldn't ask for a better life!

I treated my new students as if they were just as smart as my previous class, and we got along just fine. I allowed the parents to come in and throw the afternoon parties each time one of my students had a birthday. This was great for parent/teacher relationships—a family. Word got around that I had earned my teacher degree specializing in teaching mathematics, which I had to tell the parents wasn't true. And I once had a parent frantically enter my room worried to near death because her child was not at school to be picked up at dismissal time. I calmed the parent down by telling her, "Remember, your child, Chance, had a dental appoint today. His father picked him up early."

One of the highlights of the entire year was teaching social studies. At one time, one student, Amy, made the comment, right out of the blue, "Those Indians, killing chickens, just for their feathers."

She shook her little head and added, "It makes no sense."

I got it. One of the reasons I enjoyed teaching young children was because they were natural artists, filled with creative genius. Each framed their individual world with unadulterated perceptions. I saw no need to correct Amy. In her mind she had confused eagles with chickens.

One other time, Amy said, "Mr. Smith, you think you're all that with your big muscles, but my father said, 'Blacks aren't so strong; their muscles are just closer to their skin.'"

Okay, I thought, immediately after hearing her. *Many times students go home and disagree with their parents. In protest they exclaim, "But that's not what my teacher said." Dad's probably tired of her mentioning my physique—maybe even comparing mine to his.* I never made a comment in response to that racial statement, either.

I was proud to have an Afro-American in my class. His name was Ivan. Physically, Ivan was this miniature, buff dude, just like me. But that's not why I was proud. I was happy in knowing he was bussed from the Westside to the school to receive the best education possible. And he was getting it from me. I was glad to be a good role model, not only for him, but also for all stakeholders within the school. Intellectually, I didn't need Jessie Jackson to tell me, "I am somebody." I knew it. I knew everybody is somebody, but I felt I had to prove my self-worth to affluent Whites.

One day, after lunch, Ivan asked the question, "Why are Black men stronger than most Whites?" In my youth, I eagerly wanted to answer his question. But first, I was careful to turn on a tape recorder—just in case I might be miss-quoted and would have to explain to an angry parent, perhaps one like Amy's dad.

After turning on the recorder, I started explaining the concept of "natural selection," and how many weaker Afro-Americans died-off while being brought to America. We discussed how the stronger survived. The students understood. I made sure I wasn't teaching above their level of comprehension. My students gave examples of Black athletes excelling in or seeming to dominate some specific sports. And I eventually segued our discussion into a totally different lesson, with the emphasis on, "Whatever you spend your time doing, that's what you will eventually become good at doing." We all memorized a poem entitled, "Myself," by Edgar Guest. I called on different students to quote it throughout the entire school year. I can still quote it today.

"I have to live with myself and so,
I want to be able for myself to know.
I want to be able as days go by,
To always look myself straight in the eye.
I don't want to sit in the setting sun,
And hate myself for the things I've done."

We continued baking cakes and "designing" pizzas, but since I no longer had the entire top, brightest students, out of all second grade classes, we didn't bake as often. I had to spend more time "teaching."

CHAPTER 22

It seemed like every holiday, Helen and Ed were in Las Vegas. Grandma could not spend enough time with Jemal. She was always buying him clothes or furniture for the kitchen or his room. First, it was an expensive, solid wood child's rocker. Then came the yellow, plastic, combo highchair, car, and rocker. How fancy it was, with its padded, cushioned, blue, vinyl seat. I'll never know why she bought a kid's dining-room table, with four matching chairs, which she placed in a section of our formal dining room.

If she wasn't visiting Jemal, we were headed to Santa Barbara to visit her. I remember Jemal's first Christmas. Being on Christmas break for two full weeks, I over-packed the Honda Civic with everything we would need. Our plan was to stay with Helen and Ed for Christmas, and then eventually spend some time with my mother in L.A. before returning home.

Taking Jemal's car seat, his stroller, warm clothes, light-weight clothes, clothes in the middle, toys to keep him entertained, our own clothes, and presents—lots of presents for both of our families—it didn't take long to fill the car up. In fact, I piled all kinds of extras on top of the car. Using yards of heavy-duty, nylon rope, I tied everything down under a plastic tarp.

After completing the work, I marveled with pride on my job well done. The white, shiny car looked like a Christmas gift itself. The wrapped baggage on top of the car looked like an extra, special gift. All it needed was a red, gigantic bow on top.

My pride caught up with me as soon as we got ready to start our trip. Backing out of the garage, Elaine, who thoughtfully was standing outside the car, yelled, "Stop! The car's not going to clear the garage. You've piled it too high."

After eliminating some of the gear, we headed on our way.

CHAPTER 23

Seeing Helen as much as we did wasn't enough for her. Being a college professor teaching radiological technology, she chose to be on vacation during the summer. She spent all of her time off with her grandson, Jemal.

With my continuing to do the cooking, and with Helen living in our home, Elaine enjoyed the break from parenting, watching her mother gladly do the work.

Mother and daughter enjoyed each other's company so much, they invited Helen's mother to join them by coming to our home.

Over the years, I had come to deeply cherish my relationship with my mother-in-law. I loved her. She had come to treat me as her son. This love of mine had nothing to do with comparing my initial feelings about her to the present. Throughout the years I didn't. Her change came as natural as the changing of seasons. And for me, I never even wondered how or why she changed her thoughts about her grandson—and me. Having no thoughts about her over the years regarding her progress, I certainly couldn't ask her, "Why the change?"

I did look often at Mammaw, Helen's mother, while she visited our home. Looking, without staring, I could see slight traces of what was once dishwater-blonde, thinning hair resting atop her weatherworn wrinkled face. Great-grandma's hands were wrinkled, too—especially around the joints and knuckles of her pallid skin. Her tired, dull, blue eyes were slightly glazed over from glaucoma, making it difficult for me to see her pupils. Her puffed face, with soft, round corners, looked slightly square, especially at the chin. Sunlight rested on the tip of her pointed nose and high cheekbones. Her big-bosomed body was partially shielded by her loose-fitting, floral-printed dress. The sagging skin and muscles hanging below Mammaw's biceps would wobble whenever she lifted her hands above her shoulders. Unlike Helen and Elaine, she had lost her sex appeal a long time ago. She was round, extremely round at the waist, causing me to think, When Elaine gets this old, will she be as hefty as *Great-grandma? Probably so, but I'll continue loving her all the way. For us, our relationship will continually improve—the wheels will never fall off.*

About 4:30 A.M. one day, when I couldn't sleep, I took myself to the living room only to find Mammaw rocking in Elaine's chair.

I made coffee. Wanting to talk and not awaken others, I invited Mammaw to join me for a ride—a ride to my special place. I wanted her to see the sun rising above Red Rock Canyon, a short trip from where we lived.

With large coffee mugs in our hands, we were on our way at slightly before first dawn. No crowds, no wind, only ninety-degree heat.

The loop, at that time, was a two-way narrow road. I did not want to collide with some drunk, racing towards us, so I drove carefully focused. We stopped at the scenic site to marvel at the spectacular mountains of Red Rock. "Yes, Mammaw, this is one of my favorite places in Las Vegas. I couldn't care less about the casinos on the overly lighted Strip."

We sat and talked for about two full hours—with me doing all the talking. I ranted on and on about how I wanted to make a movie with Red Rock being the backdrop. I described how I wanted it to be cowboys and Indians, doing their fictitious do, with lots of external action.

During my verbosity, what I really wanted to ask was for Mammaw to tell me her story. *When and where was she born? Was it during the last days of slavery? What were her thoughts concerning Negroes? How had her parents raised her regarding this issue? How had she raised Helen?* I wanted to know it all—even how she felt staying with her daughter, granddaughter, and Black great-grandson, in a Black man's home. But I didn't dare ask. I merely thought, *When Elaine and I started our relationship we innocently believed my mother's opinion and her mother's opinion on "crossing-the-color-line" didn't and wouldn't matter.* (As Elaine had shared her mother's comment about me, after first meeting me, I, too, shared with Elaine what my mother confided in me. Sitting on her Queen Ann couch, which was wrapped in thick, crunchy plastic, she sat erect—dignified and enunciated, "At least she ain't White trash.") *How we felt about each other and treated each other was the only thing that truly mattered.* Yet, since my time spent with Elaine's family, I gained a little wisdom. Whoever said, "When two people marry, they marry not just each other, they marry the entire family," spoke from experience.

After we left the scenic site, we stopped at a few more places in the canyon. I showed Mammaw the huge scooped-out area at the top of one mountain. I shared my fantasy with her, hoping she could imagine a symphonic orchestra playing Bach on the inside of that gargantuan bowl. "Now, Grandma, how would that sound?" I asked. "Awe-inspiring music at the start of a new day, imagine how that would sound."

When we arrived home, I started cooking breakfast. Mammaw cheerfully talked about our trip and how much she enjoyed it.

While listening to her, I felt good in what I had done, bringing a little joy and probably some racial enlightenment into her life.

CHAPTER 24

Where had the time gone? In July, Jemal would be two years old. By then, I didn't spend time at school working on preparing for the upcoming school year. In fact, I rarely thought about elementary school at all. I found a new distraction to occupy my time. Summer school, at UNLV, working on my masters degree in school administration is how I spent my days.

From my honest point of view, the education classes were a breeze. It took rigor for me to read hundreds of books and write numerous college papers while obtaining my undergrad degree in English. My English professors were like master trainers of language. With reading, writing, logical thinking, and grammar usage they constantly demanded discipline. They used drilling, driving forces and made me pull, push, and pump to exercise and stretch my mind. All of that training made getting my masters degree easy—no one corrects a paper like an English professor.

I spent quality time with my family in the evenings. Yet, there was still time for me to fish on the weekends with my male friends and have cookouts and parties with our group of personal friends. One of our favorite games during a get-together was to play Spoons. We would sit on our butts in a circle and throw one less spoon into the center—one less spoon than the number of participants. Someone would yell, Go," and we'd all grab for a spoon.

One time, while playing the game, someone commented, "I wonder what would happen if we'd use knives instead of spoons."

It didn't take long for summer to come to an end.

After one year of schooling, having a grade point average of 3.7, I earned my post-grad degree.

Now that I was a parent, I learned and deeply understood that graduations aren't for the recipients. These special ceremonies are for the grad's family—especially the graduate's parents. How good it felt to fly my mother to Vegas and have her attend the ceremony with my wife and child.

CHAPTER 25

After spending three years as a mom and housewife, Elaine was ready to return to work. She took a job teaching third grade at one of the schools in the district. She also met and became close friends with a lady named Deborah Crier. I think their friendship geminated as a result of both of them working together and both having three-year-old sons.

I thought it interesting that Deborah's and Elaine's principal was the husband of one of my second grade team members, Kathleen Gaston. Compared to Los Angeles, I now lived in Las Vegas—a small city of about 300,000 residents.

It didn't take long for Deborah and her husband, Michael, to join our gourmet dining parties group.

Since everybody in the group was an educator, I talked Jim and Janie into joining our teaching circle of friends. Billy's brother, Jimmy, and his sister-in-law, Ruby, also joined into our family of friends. And it seemed like overnight, friends of May—Rosemarie and Allan—likewise joined our circle of close friends.

Whenever we went out to dinner or sat at a table in one of our homes, we must have, color-wise, resembled a living chess set. Elaine, Jim and Janie, May, Deborah, and Rosemarie were all Caucasian. Billy and Ann, Jimmy and Ruby, Curtis, Michael, and I were all Afro-American. I often looked at the group and thought it interesting—many of the Black men were married to White women. *What did this say about us? Did our bi-racial babies have anything to do with our forming our teaching klatch?*

As these curious thoughts traveled through my head, one day, I decided to ask Jemal, "What color is Ruby?"

He shrugged his shoulders and said, "White?"

With Ruby being as Black-Black as I, I decided to end it there. *No need in my complicating racial issues for Jemal.*

CHAPTER 26

While in her first year of teaching elementary school after staying home with Jemal, Elaine had had enough. She talked me into taking one methods course with her at UNLV in teaching secondary English. We would need this class in order to obtain secondary licensure from the Nevada State Department of Education. Having the credential, we would be qualified to teach English at the junior high and senior high levels.

Since Elaine had already convinced herself elementary was not her forte, she transferred to high school the next school year. I knew better. I knew I was too immature for high school—that emotionally, I was stunted and nothing more than an adolescent myself. I instinctively knew, *Nothing but trouble could come from a move like that.* Even though I wasn't historically a female chaser, those young girls might start looking enticing. I did not want to put myself in a position where I could eventually find myself embarrassed, fired from teaching, and maybe facing a prison sentence.

However, after having taught one year of fifth grade and several years of second grade, it was time for me to leave. I needed a promotion. I was tired of my students slipping and saying, "Mom," and then recognizing their mistake, correcting it by saying, "Oh, I mean Mr. Smith." I was tired of doing the same activities in the evenings with Jemal that I was doing with my students all day long. I interviewed for a teaching position to open a brand new junior high school.

During the interview, I apologized for not typing the 25-page application. I explained how I wanted to but didn't have the time. The application was complete and written in my best "artist's" penmanship. (Much later it occurred to me the principal and assistant principal probably never read the applications. Taking time to fill out 25-pages for a teacher who already had a job, simply wanting to transfer, was proof enough that I was passionate about education—just the type of educator any principal would want on his staff.)

I got the job, teaching English I (freshman English), Speech I, and Theatre I, all ninth-grade classes at Kenny Guinn Junior High School, in the suburbs of Las Vegas. From the beginning, I was impressed with the other nine teachers in our English department. Given their displayed professionalism, I figured they had all typed their applications. In fact, the entire faculty was as sharp as any teachers I had encountered in my life.

The principal promised us any and everything we needed in order for us to teach our classes, and everyone of us played into that hype, even to the extent of the ladies daily wearing dresses and the men dressing in suits and ties. The smell of new books, new carpet, and new desks evoked commitment, with each of us trying to out-do each other. No wonder the school became one of the best in the district. But I eventually became discouraged.

Initially, I thought I would have students old enough to read and write well. Unlike second grade, where I could read a student's printed story in less than ten seconds, I thought I would have depth and breadth in my ninth graders' written work. But that presumption was far from what I got. I was not given the academically bright students. I taught basic, remedial English. I had students who did not want to be there but were required by state law to attend class. It felt like I left heaven and had been transported to hell. Often, during speech class, I'd think, *I've watered the content down so much, so the students could manage success at something, I don't think anyone in the field would even call it Speech. I don't know what it is I'm teaching!*

To put it bluntly, I was miserable—downright miserable.

Thank God, my theatre class and after-school thespian club brought me some relief.

Although I was essentially a first-year teacher at the secondary level, this time, out of frustration and ignorance, I blamed the students for their shortcomings instead of blaming it on my lack of experience. These kids wrote no better than my second grade students. And in some cases, I experienced total apathy—they didn't even care. I often asked myself, *How in the world could I have been so naïve?* I thought I was moving up when in fact, I merely moved across grade levels—from good to deplorable.

During our inaugural open house activities, my theatre students wooed the audience with their presentation. I got compliments for weeks. This and our end-of-the-year play is what kept me sane. These students were my joy, my delight. Elaine even came to help with make-up and costumes.

My students enjoyed playing with Jemal. During the end of the school year, I made a tragic mistake. I don't know what I was thinking. Perhaps I wasn't thinking at all. I volunteered to play on the faculty team during the end-of-the-year Faculty vs. Male Student Basketball Game. The students were all members of our basketball team. To not be outdone, our team practiced from time to time. At first, I made a fool out of myself. As we are good at what we do, what did scholarly me know about basketball? "Get out of the key, get out of the key," someone would yell at me.

"What's a key?" I'd ask.

I didn't take playing basketball seriously. I naively wanted to be a contributing member of an activity that promoted school spirit. Yet, during each practice, I gave my best. By the end of our practice sessions, I was slamming the ball through the hoop, performing alley-hoops.

"You have got to be our most improved player," one of the team members commented.

His comment gave me false confidence because the actual game didn't go that well, especially for me. As physically strong as I was, for some reason I could not shoot "free-throws" whenever I was fouled and awarded them. The ball would always fall short of the hoop. I discovered it was better for me to stand at the free-shoot line, take the ball, put it between my legs, and release the ball doing a pelvic thrust.

We lost—with little help from me.

I was glad that I had tried something new.

However, I'm certain most thought it would have been better for me not to have attempted this quest. One of my Black special education students voiced it best. On our way out of the gym he said, "Mr. Smith, you cain't play no basketball."

CHAPTER 27

Over summer vacation I was miserable. At times I was so irritable, I didn't even want to be with myself. For years I had driven myself staying busy. I didn't know how to sit down and relax. Not having any work to do placed my mind in overdrive. The last thing I wanted was to think, especially about me. I wanted to be preoccupied—busy. Then I got lucky. Through one of my student's parents, I got a job working for a national moving company. All my jobs were local, and it brought in a lot of extra family income.

I was up each morning and at the company yard by 5 A.M. I'd work with my driver and leadsman, loading our truck with all of the moving materials we would need for the day. I learned about bookcase boxes, 3-cube and 4-cube cartons, dish packs, and wardrobe cardboard boxes—each designed to do a specific job. I learned how to pad dishes and wrap furniture, and how to load and unload all types of items—even pool tables and pianos. I hadn't had years of working knowledge or experience loading and unloading furniture. I was a novice, but I wanted to do my best. Because it was summer, it was too hot for some families to do the work of moving. Accordingly, they hired our company, which accounted for extra work. During these extra jobs, the owner assigned me a small truck and my own crew of two—three of us not knowing what to do. Stressed by being responsible, I fell into a series of nightly dreams. During my worst nightmare, I moved a home filled with cheap chrome and glass. We dropped and shattered everything we lifted.

One day at the yard, a colleague called out to me, "Smitty, why you look so sad? Where's the smile? You look like hell."

It was then that I broke into a polished, deceptive smile and learned to wear it as a disguise many years of my life. I worked that job up until the last week before the start of school. Smiling all the while, I knew I was disenchanted with my life. I didn't feel like a superstar. *There must be more to life, more than running on a treadmill to avoid the painful, fearful memories of childhood.* I felt less than ordinary—confused, dismayed, and overwhelmed. Filled with fear of not being a good husband, father, or teacher, I wanted to run away. And I did—right back to school. I allowed my work to consume me for the school year.

CHAPTER 28

It didn't matter how much extra effort I put into my work, it didn't change my feeling—my emptiness. By not getting out what was festering deep inside, at the close of the school year, I still longed for more of life. I felt I was missing out on something—what, I didn't know. But I wanted whatever it was I was missing. I left Elaine and Jemal.

I stayed in L.A. with my brother, who had recently divorced his wife, Linda. The two of them had owned a four-bedroom newly constructed house in Chino, California. Donnie and I dated all kinds of girls, inviting them over to his grand house for an impressive dinner (cooked by me.) For fun, messing with our dates' heads, Donnie sat at the head of his dining room table equipped to seat twelve people. I sat at the other end. We carried on as if this is what we normally, routinely did each night. The girls sat in the middle. After dinner we went out to various clubs for more entertainment.

One evening, I slept with one of the girls, only to find myself crying throughout the night. Why is it that the best of life's lessons come coupled with a lot of pain? Why did I do it? I didn't even know anything about the girl—only that she was Black and pretty. Although her being Black had nothing to do with it, I didn't stop to question myself as to why I wanted this girl. *Was it male ego, simply juvenile lust? Was it my caveman, primitive instinct to see if I could sexually conquer this female prey?* Immediately after ejaculating, I knew that I was wrong. I didn't want the girl: I wanted my wife. I wanted to be having sex with my wife—the one special person that I truly loved. *Lying with her, not my wife, only served to hurt her and my family. Why was it so easy for me to leave Jemal and Elaine—the two people I cared about? Was it echoes of my father's sin that I had listened to, telling me to run away?* All I knew was that I only wanted an unstressful, loving marriage. If Elaine would only do this, or if only Elaine would do that, I blamed. Coupled with suppression and denial, I hadn't bothered to see that I was the one bringing on the stress.

CHAPTER 29

I stayed away for two weeks, but talking to Elaine and Jemal on the telephone was too much for me to continue doing. I gathered up my belongings and came back home. Elaine gladly took me in. We went to counseling, seeing a Catholic priest. He told me three things I'll never forget. "You are a wonderful teacher. You'll learn to have your students gladly comply with your requests. The reason for my saying this is because you are a child yourself. Your students can easily identify with your emotions and behavior." Next, he said, "If the two of you divorce, you two will end up building your lives and your child's life upon rubble." Lastly he said, "Go and make a second child. There's no way the two of you would ever destroy the lives of the four of you in your family."

Elaine and I followed his advice regarding having a second child. I spent the rest of the summer sweating in the Vegas' heat—smiling, packing and unpacking boxes, and hauling furniture for the moving company.

We joked around about naming our second child Whole-wheat if it was a girl. Elaine and I seriously liked the name Gavin, if we were to have a boy. I wanted to name him after one of my favorite writers, Gavin Lambert.

Elaine chose the name after Gavin MacLeod, the captain of a television show named *The Love Boat*.

However, how can something change when my thinking never did? Unconsciously, naively, unknowingly, without bothering to acknowledge my trauma, I worked out hard at the gym to give me something extra to do—thinking that that would be enough.

CHAPTER 30

Donnie remarried, and his new wife gave birth to a daughter, Antoinette Marie Smith. He now had a son, Matthew, by his first wife, Linda, and a beautiful daughter, who was four years younger than her brother.

About the same time as Toni's entrance into the world, Elaine and I named our new son, Gavin Tee Smith. Like on a racehorse, Gavin charged and arrived into the world on July 18, 1981—a few months early. Little did we know, his entrance into the world predicted his story.

To our surprise, Gavin wasn't anything like Jemal. Jemal was a nearly perfect child—in the womb, not rushing to come out. That was not the case with Gavin. As if he had so much to do, he was eager to get his life started. Elaine had to cut work short, remain at home, and rest in order to carry Gavin full-term. Her obstetrician prescribed medication. I worried. I had heard that women giving birth to a second child spend no time in labor. There's little wait-time. Contractions don't begin and last an entire day. When it's ready, the baby pops out. I did not want my second son born on the side of the road or in the backseat of my car. We experienced several false calls. Each time en route to the hospital, I feared a policeman would be delivering the child. Thank God, Gavin stayed in the oven the full nine months.

Jim and Janie had a second child, also. They moved into a larger home, located on the Westside—about as far west as anyone could go. Elaine and I followed them into the new development being constructed near Tenaya and Washington Boulevard. We purchased the identical model one block away.

Elaine decided to stay at home with the children, and not to return to a teaching position in the district.

One Friday afternoon, I came home from work finding Elaine sitting crossed-leg, on her buttocks, on the kitchen ceramic counter top. Her hands were pressed to her facial cheeks. "Ronnie," she cried, "I can't. I just can't take it anymore."

"Where are the children?" I asked.

"They're both asleep."

"What's wrong, Laney? Have I done something wrong?"

"It's not you," she replied. "It's Gavin. He's nothing like Jemal. If I had known he would have been so different, I would have thought twice about our having him."

"Shuuuu," I said. "One of the kids might be awake and hear you."

Still seated, she continued, "Today, when Gavin was far too quiet, I caught him. He was sitting in the dining room eating an old, crunchy dragonfly. When I looked at him, before I could take it away, he knew he was wrong. With malicious eyes and a victorious smile, he looked me dead in my eyes. Gavin gave me that look of, 'You can't tell me nothing; I'm just as smart as you.'"

I wanted to chuckle, but I gave no expression. Although an immaculately clean and tidy house, I could picture that easily happening. Our dining room had tile flooring and wall-to-wall, ceiling-to-floor glass windows on two walls of the room. All kinds of bugs and insects died in that room, bumping into the spacious glass, trying to get out.

"Then, the toilet in the kids' bathroom wouldn't flush. I don't know what's wrong with it. I don't think it's clogged up because Gavin took off his wet diaper and left it in the room."

"Well," I said, "at least we know he didn't try to flush down the diaper. Calm down, Laney. I'm sure I can fix the toilet."

Elaine ended the conversation saying, "I called the pediatrician, asking if anything was wrong with our hyperactive son.

The doctor asked if Gavin could sit quietly for a few minutes, maybe while watching cartoons or something. When I told him, 'yeah,' the doctor told me Gavin was fine and that maybe I was the one hyperactive."

I held Elaine for a while and told her, "Get some rest. I'll take care of the boys for the rest of the evening."

When I had time, I took a wire snake and dislodged the whole green apple Gavin had attempted to flush down the toilet.

With two healthy sons and a wonderful wife who lived within my world, I had no need to ever enter her's. In my head, I saw Elaine and me as equals, but we always did everything my way. I always pretended to wear the pants in our family. This concept had been indoctrinated into me during all my years of growing up in the church. I felt the need to always be the one in control—or at least pretending to be in control. At times, I would think *Elaine married me, a Blackman, because she had a weak father. She wanted someone strong—a man who would set her world upright.*

It's interesting how life always gifts us more of what we hate and are continuously trying to unconsciously escape. It's true. Elaine unknowingly married a man like her father—driven, with an awful lot of secrets. My deficit dealt with emotion. Ed, socially and with housekeeping issues, needed a lot of help. Although I wore the mask, I knew she was emotionally more mature. It was my private secret; I counted on her to mother me. I think Ed counted on his wife, Helen, to also mother him. Ed gave the appearance of being meek, weak, and gentle although he was selfish and manipulating as all get out. Yet, he still needed a mother—someone to take care of running the day-to-day tasks of living.

I, on the other hand, outwardly portrayed self-assurance and a strong command of presence. I think when it came down to reducing our lives down to the lowest denominator, both Ed and I were, in many ways equally the same.

I trusted Elaine with my life as much as I could. But there was only one major problem. I couldn't trust myself enough. How could I love her to the depth and breath she wanted and required when I was a phony—incapable of loving myself?

I loved Elaine as best I could, and I wanted to love her more. Adoring my two beautiful children, I wanted to have the perfect family, but how could I as I refused to face my fearful, dreadful ghosts? This I did not do deliberately. I simply did not know how to handle my life any better.

God knows I was giving my best.

The doorbell rang one Saturday morning about 6:00. *Who could that possibly be? It's so early in the morning.* I got up to answer the door, wanting Elaine to stay in bed. To my surprise it was Gavin and our neighbor, Chuck, who lived several houses down the street. He was holding a smiling Gavin.

"What are you doing with Gavin?" I asked. "I don't get it. I'm confused and still asleep."

"Gavin decided to have breakfast with me about four-o'clock this morning. I guess he waddled down to our house, pushed the doorbell, and invited himself in."

About this time, Elaine was at the front door. "What did you say? Did I hear you right?"

We both looked at Chuck, then at Gavin, and finally at each other.

We thanked Chuck for taking care of Gavin. After his departure, we talked for hours about Gavin, asking ourselves, *Why can't he be like Jemal?* "That's it. Gavin's gusto, his robust, *joie de vivre*—zest for life—could get him into great trouble. We're putting plastic slip rings onto the front, back and hallway door leading into the garage," I announced.

"It wouldn't be a bad idea to mount safety latches onto all the ground-level cabinet doors, too," Elaine added.

"Are there any other precautions we can take?" I asked out of concern and safety for our children—especially Gavin.

Over the years I learned to keep myself busy, fanatically working during the day. I never drove while drinking with my children in the car. Wanting to give them my best, I played equally as hard with them up until their bedtime and reserved my drinking for later in the night. I accepted the fact that Elaine and I would be married for life and that I would do my best to take care of her financially, and to raise my children well.

CHAPTER 31

O ver the next three years I got better at molding my students instead of having them manipulating me—especially the ones who didn't want to be there.

My teaching and classroom discipline improved as the result of my having a dream—no, an outlandish nightmare. I was teaching an English class and a non-student, about eighteen years old, barged into my classroom. He started lifting up the skirts and dresses of my female students. I immediately pushed the call button and asked for assistance. "We're busy right now. Please call back later," is all I got back from the person monitoring the other end of the intercom system.

I pushed the button again. *This time they will automatically realize I have a major problem, and I am in need of big time assistance.* Instead, I got the same response, "We're busy right now. Please call back later."

I was so enraged; I grabbed the perpetrator by his neck and threw him out of my classroom.

I pushed the intercom button one last time and said, "Someone needs to come to my classroom right away. I don't need assistance. The students do. I'm tired of your bullshit. I quit. I'm going home. The students need your assistance."

I learned a valuable lesson from that dream, not to count on anyone but myself in dealing with my students. *They're mine the fifty or so minutes I have them in my classroom. If I want to see improvement in their work and behavior, I can't blame anyone other than myself if the change doesn't come. Discipline is unspoken; the students know if I have it or not. All the harsh looks, loud yells, and empty threats will not change a thing.* I stopped sending students to the dean of discipline. I stopped expecting anyone to help me. I didn't even count on the students to change their behavior by themselves. I knew I had to learn more about behavior management or behavior manipulation. I knew from my dream, I had to figure out a way to get them to see things differently. They had to first realize I wasn't their enemy. I wasn't just another teacher who'd care little or nothing about who they were or what they felt about themselves. *Ronnie, you big dummy, it's all about relationships,* I had to remind myself. From then on, for the next three years, I enjoyed junior high school, and I learned how to "pied-pipe" my students into becoming the beautiful children we all wanted them to be.

CHAPTER 32

When Jemal turned six, and Gavin was two, Elaine went back to work, teaching English in a junior high school. Since the junior high schools let out an hour before elementary school, Elaine had time to leave her job and pick up Jemal before going to the babysitter's to get Gavin.

By then, I figured I was mature enough to promote myself to high school. At the end of my final days teaching at the junior high level, I applied for and was accepted as a teacher of English at Las Vegas High School for the 1983-1984 school year. My principal at Kenny C. Guinn Junior High told me he'd give me one year at the high school level. "You'll come running back to me, begging to be rehired. Just you wait and see."

Being the new teacher in the department, the department chair assigned me all ninth grade Basic English I classes. I soon discovered that teaching five classes of remedial English to freshmen who didn't appreciate the subject and honestly didn't want to attend the required classes placed my wanting to be there on the same rung as theirs. They would do everything within their power to not let me teach. Some would sleep. A few would try to distract me by talking, doodling, or trying to pull me into an argument. Most had learned the easiest route was to simply, apathetically comply—"Teacher said, 'Do this,' so I'm doing it."

During passing periods, students carried flattened cardboard boxes. Music blasted from portable boom boxes, while students twirled on their backs and sides, atop the spinning, cardboard boxes, effortlessly moving on the highly waxed, linoleum tiles in the hallways. They called it break-dancing. Others carried two-dozen sized doughnut cartons while calling out, "Doughnuts for sale. Doughnuts for sale."

I shook my head in dismay, thinking, *Good schools don't just happen; they are made.* I knew the students were selling the doughnuts for their clubs and activities; yet, I continued to think, *Why does the principal allow this type of behavior?*

Most of the students were kind and respectful, which made it easy for me to respect them. Unlike the elementary and junior high schools, in my two previous assignments—stellar schools in high-middle class communities where parents saw educators as servants—my students at Las Vegas High School were mostly poor, underachievers, with low self-esteem. They thought teachers, in terms of education and social status, were up there with lawyers and doctors. They gave me respect.

Most of my students couldn't write a simple sentence—correctly. *What have they learned over the past eight years?"* I continuously asked myself. One student entitled his paper, "My SA." I was the slow one. It took forever to figure it out. I didn't—until I said the title out loud. I often sat at my desk silently judging them.

Another student innocently asked, "Mr. Smith, where is Hawaii? Can we drive?" With that one, I paused my lesson and abruptly pulled down the world map and had her discover why she could not drive.

Some days I thought, *My previous principal must know me better than I know myself. At the end of this school year, I'm definitely out of here. I'm going to transfer back to my high-middle class, affluent, stellar junior high school. This lower end of the teaching profession certainly isn't for me.*

But the more I thought about it, the more I knew I had to stay. *You call yourself a teacher, I said to myself. But you want to run from the kids who need you most. If I can take these kids from reading at a third grade level and bring them up to reading and writing at a fifth or sixth grade level within a school year, then, I can truly call myself a teacher. I can't, I can't simply run away.*

CHAPTER 33

O n the home front, I learned something new about myself. I liked toys as much as my children. Elaine and I bought as many toys at Easter and on their birthdays as we did for Christmas. She often looked at me and laughed, "You didn't buy those toys for the kids; you got them for yourself."

The toys allowed me to relive my own creative, imaginative childhood. Instead of having Donnie to share magical playing time, I now had Jemal and Gavin. Oh, what fun. I bought old fashioned, aluminum train track. We laid it in every room of our house. Lionel trains ran over switches, bridges, trusses, and platforms of every kind. The metal dump trucks and wind-up airplanes with flashing strobe lights brought absolute joy.

I continued to hone my cooking skills, too. Most nights I took pleasure in preparing dinner. And it was something new and flavorable each night. Both my mother and father were culinary artists. Fortunately, their talent in the kitchen was passed on to me. I could bake and cook anything—even pickled beef tongue.

The highlight of each day was coming home from work, donning an apron, preparing a wholesome meal, and sharing it and conversation at the table with my family. It felt good when Elaine or one of the boys would compliment me when I prepared something special. One night, I made a quick meal—hamburgers and French fries. The fries were prepared with extra love. I took long baking yams, carefully cut them into long, ¾" x ¾" strips. I fried them tempura style, and served them with a ginger/pineapple/currant sauce. Jemal was the first to say, "Great job, Papa. You know how to cook a good French-fry."

Not yet ready to add balance or a complete overhaul to my driven life, I kept doing the best I knew how. I couldn't force it into my behavior. Like the replacement of a mechanical part, if it's difficult to install, won't slip in just right, a lay-technician must be doing something wrong. Since I had no idea of how to replace my faulty parts, I wasn't totally satisfied with how I functioned. I wasn't running like a well-tuned BMW, Mercedes, or Cadillac. Yet, I daily utilized what tools I had just to get by. Knowing in the back of my mind that improperly installed parts will malfunction or wear out sooner, and shamed by some of the things I had done, I continued—like my father—trying to purge the pain or at least intoxicate it enough to substantially quiet it. I won't say my drinking didn't work. It did—for a season. Although booze wasn't the best remedy, I didn't suffer a breakdown. I didn't lose my mind, my job, or completely fall apart. Over the years the quantity I consumed increased—going from two beers to a six-pack, from a six-pack to twelve in one setting, and eventually to hard liquor. In late spring and summer, it was difficult to distinguish gin from sweat as both poured from my pores.

****

Feeling I had certainly gotten my money's worth out of taking that dream interpretation class way back in college, there was more to come. Elaine, one night, rescued me from a nightmare. I dreamed I had reenlisted in the Marine Corps and was on my way to a second tour of duty in Vietnam. Shaking, almost convulsing, Elaine awoke me. We sat up talking about my time in Vietnam. I unexpectedly and uncontrollably burst out in tears. When the sobbing ended, I felt like I had finally released all my secretive, personal horror of the war.

After my catharsis, I was sure Elaine could see a change in me. Although I couldn't create a specific list, I felt a huge burden had been lifted off me. Eventually, I gave up drinking.

I began attending a twelve-step program. During one of my first meetings, an old-timer came up to me and said, "You're not going to make it in this program."

I was crushed because I knew in my heart alcohol no longer worked for me. It only served to create crazy thinking and irrational behavior within me. "Why is that?" I responded.

"Because I can tell by the why you read and talk. You think you're smart. You're the type who will always out-smart yourself. You'll be back to drinking in no-time."

I did not get angry at the "well-wisher." Instead, I became afraid. I tried to figure out what it was he was actually saying. *Could it be that he had seen far too many newcomers fail?*

I believe his comment helped me from ever returning to drink. But long-lived bad habits are difficult to break. My passion for teaching consumed half my life. Jemal and Gavin got the other half, leaving nothing, no part of it for Elaine. Stuck, I could not open myself up to and for her. I had convinced myself that I was happy. I even wore a perpetual, believable smile so no one would question me. I thought Elaine was happy or at least contented, too. We never argued, fussed or fought. Not since my one unfaithful sexual encounter, did we ever "cheat" on each other. Neither of us gambled. We had no financial problems. Outwardly, all of our friends thought we had the best relationship possible.

CHAPTER 34

Sometime during the time when Jemal was six and Gavin was two, my sister, Betty, called me on the phone. She told me Dad was frail, nearing death, and resting in a senior citizen home. Betty also shared he was dying of prolonged prostate cancer and cirrhosis of the liver.

I took both of my sons to L.A. to visit him at his assisted living facility. Gathered next to his bed, I said, "Dad, I don't know if you remember, these are two of your grandsons, my sons, Gavin and Jemal."

He nodded as if he understood.

"Dad, after having sons of my own, I better understand some of the issues regarding your life. I love you, Dad," was all that I could say. There was no need for me to blame or ridicule him. "Thank you for being the best dad that you could be to Donnie and me." I stopped and only thought, *I hope I'll be a better dad to my sons than you were to us.* Without wanting to harbor any further resentment or judgment I said, "I forgive you, Dad, for all of your shortcomings. Thanks for giving me your best."

He didn't say anything. He only nodded as if he understood. Leaving the assisted living home, I decided to drive to Cabrillo Beach, in San Pedro. It had always been a peaceful, joyful place for me—the first place where my mother taught me to fish.

I sat on the pier with my two sons and thought long and hard about my upbringing. That is, until Gavin pooped in his pants. After cleaning him off as best I could, I decided I'd take him into the ocean to thoroughly rinse him off.

Holding Jemal by his hand with one outstretched arm and naked Gavin with my other hand, we walked toward the water. The roar of the surf and the size of the waves must have frightened Gavin. "Go the other way, Daddy. Go the other way, Daddy!" he repeatedly yelled.

I knew he could swim and did not have any reason to be afraid, but I did not want to traumatize him, causing permanent fear of the ocean. We turned around and walked back to the pier. Wading in the water will have to wait for another day, I thought.

Three weeks later, I drove my family back to L.A. to bury my dad.

CHAPTER 35

While talking to Elaine off and on about my father's life and death, she shared with me her feelings regarding her mother's state of health.

"Cancer, Ronnie—my mother's got lymphoma all through her body."

I didn't know what to say. *Do I ask, "And when did you find this out?"* I didn't want to upset Elaine any further, so I kept my thoughts to myself. *What stage is the cancer? Is it terminal or not? Would these be prudent questions to ask?* I wanted answers to my questions, but how dare I ask them right away.

Over a period of time, I found out more about Helen's condition. More came from Grammy than it did from Elaine. Whenever Helen came to visit or whenever we went to spend time with her, I'd learn more about her health.

Reluctant to ask, "So how are you doing, Helen," upon our next encounter, I asked it anyway.

"I'm doing as well, as best my life has to offer me," she replied. "I've got lymphoma, you know. It's stage-four, throughout my body, but I know God doesn't put upon us anymore than we can bear," she said with confident courage.

Over the years, I came to greatly respect this lady and to cherish our relationship. I learned to listen to her wisdom and to feel and treat her as though she was my second mother. I didn't know if she ever came to truly love me, but I knew for certain she loved her grandchildren. She didn't merely tolerate or accept them. She loved them with all of her heart.

I wanted to ask, "So how long have the doctors given you to live?" but using sound judgment, I didn't. Instead, I looked at her with careful observation. Her skin looked soft, but firm, and it had good color, which complimented her beautiful blue eyes. Mass dosages of radiation probably caused her dish-water-blonde hair to thin a lot, but she didn't wear a wig. Helen's weight was perfect—slender but not skinny. Each time we came together, I marveled at Helen's good looks and inner strength. She was still working, focusing on living, and spending as much time as she could with her grandchildren.

Once, while discussing Grammy's life with Elaine, Elaine shared her regret in not allowing Helen to witness the birth of Gavin, which Helen had privately requested. If she had asked me directly, I probably would have conceded, as I had learned from my own mother's voice since childhood, "It's far better to give than to receive." But I didn't know her wish at the time. She only sought Elaine's permission.

After hearing how much Helen wanted to attend the birthing, I did not feel any remorse or regret. I had been right there with Elaine during the delivery of Jemal, and I also wanted to be with her for Gavin's entry into this world. Watching Elaine endure the process of birthing, the heavy breathing, and her almost turning purple from the pain drew me closer to her. Being a part of this process made me feel like I was right there with and for my children, from the very start of their lives. There was no way I could ever regret being a part of that process. I was glad Elaine or Helen hadn't asked me to switch places.

As one thought led to another, I began wondering how Jemal felt about both of his grandmothers, Helen and Mattie. He was far too young, but I wanted to know. I imagined if I had waited for him to turn thirty or forty, his conversation might have gone something like this, "I've always felt disconnected from Mattie, but I didn't want to. Going to her house felt a bit strange. It seemed as if you and Uncle Donnie had achieved so much more outwardly. In a material way, you were going backwards each time you visited your mother's modest home. It was like you wanted to go see her, but not go to the ghetto. This has always been a strange feeling for me. Going to Grandma Mattie's I always sensed a division between Blacks and Whites even though I've always known that I'm just human—not White or Black." Knowing Jemal the way I do, and taking his intellectual aptitude into consideration, I believe he probably would have added, "All of the racial issues that seem to be a huge deal to many Americans, seemed kindergarten to me. Of more importance is the goodness and values Grandma Mattie imparted to you."

On the other hand, I believe Jemal was so secure in his relationship with Elaine's mother, he didn't have to think about it. He was free to enjoy his emotions. I imagine if asked about his feelings about her, in his late thirty's he would have said something like this, "Since familiarity breeds comfort and trust, I've never thought about my relationship with Grammy. I'm used to the experienced way in which she held me. I'm used to her breathing and her tender voice, for as far back as infancy. I'm used to her middle-class existence. In every way, I felt loved and totally secure around her."

My speculating about Jemal's possible thoughts spoiled it for me. From then on, an overwhelming feeling of extreme anxiety robbed me of joy each time I entered into my mother's impoverished neighborhood. Wanting to stop, almost unable to travel, the deeper I drove into the ghetto, the more I felt entombed in a hopeless atmosphere. The heavy, weighted air seemed sickly, decaying, and brought on depression. The more it became difficult to breath, the more unpleasant, fatalistic memories returned. *I had to survive. The rent was cheap. I could have saved a lot, but I didn't want to run the risk of becoming not broke but totally broken. A little bit stuck in my past, leaving without great savings, I had to get out of there.* I refused to become another ghetto-statistic. *Trapped for all their life in this disparaging milieu, its residents became either religious fanatics or "career, professional" pimps, prostitutes, alcoholics, or addicts. Daily, they "used," to anesthetize themselves from the hurt of hopelessness and despair.* I knew my black self too well. I had to do whatever it would take to survive. I refused to end up having my dream deferred—looking like one of James Baldwin's dried-out, shriveled-up raisins in the sun.

CHAPTER 36

Mindset, like the rudder on a ship, greatly influences destination. Perhaps the school's administration had noticed the change in my attitude once I decided to give my all to the students at Las Vegas High. One afternoon, about 3 P.M., I met with my supervisor to discuss a new class she wanted me to teach. For some reason, both Gavin and Jemal were with me. Jemal read a book while Gavin entertained himself at my feet. Crawling on the office floor, he decided to tie both of my shoelaces together, hoping I'd trip when I got up to exit the meeting. I allowed him to complete his task while my boss and I talked. *What fun. When he trips and falls, how embarrassing Dad is going to be*, he probably thought. I wish I could have seen the glimmer in his eyes as he waited for the conclusion of the meeting. Meanwhile, my supervisor explained that I could sell my preparation period to teach one special applied study-skills class to pre-selected freshmen. "These students had incredibly high test scores during junior high but demonstrated complete apathy to academics," she said. "What a tragic waste of talent.

It would be my joy to have you get them academically motivated." All in all, I could teach one Advanced Composition class, two Honors English II classes, two Basic English II classes, and the special, prototype applied study-skills class to pre-selected freshmen during the 1984-1985 school year.

In addition, I could teach an after-school study-skills class to any students needing help. "This extra money, she said, "I'm sure will help you with your children."

At the close of our meeting, I got up and took a long pause to tease Gavin. I bent over, retied my shoelaces, and exited the office with my children.

It is strange how a person can direct others toward the road to paradise, but they can't find it for themselves. One of the first things I did for my freshmen study-skills class was to make copies of my student's second grade photos, which I got from their cumulative school records. I gave each student his or picture and had him or her write a paragraph, telling me about the kid in the picture. The next assignment was for them to explain what happened to that child.

We talked about high school not being the end of their educational journey, the salaries of college grads verses high school grads, and more. The easy part was getting them to see how their grades would greatly improve if they'd do their best on every assignment and make sure they turn it in. The students and I agreed, their grade for my class would be the average of all their other grades in the classes they were currently taking.

My *"raison d'etre"* while teaching Advanced English Composition and Honors English II was to always go beyond the obvious. Eventually, my students started making jokes regarding my teaching, saying comments like, "Mr. Smith doesn't teach English; he teaches Life 101." As applied learning is one of the highest forms of learning, I required my students to enter their written work in various contests and age-appropriate publications. Some of the students entered student public speaking contests, as well.

Educators know that when learning takes place, change in behavior also occurs. I was ecstatic that most of my study-skills students consistently earned B's in my class. Since it was virtually impossible to earn an A by averaging grades, (one of their teachers seemed to have grading standards off the charts) I gave one grade higher on their semester report cards. At the end of the year, all of my Advanced Placement students took the College Board Exam. Of course, I would have to anxiously wait until the next school year to get their test score results.

CHAPTER 37

Although she died at fifty-seven, Helen's death came as no surprise. She was the first person I knew to be cremated. Thinking back, my grandmother on my father's side, Josie Taylor, and Dad, too, both had grand homecoming services. One would have thought professional mourners were paid to make the ambience of each funeral pop. Their half-open coffins were decorated with a huge splay of roses. At their gravesites, I actually saw their polished caskets being lowered into their permanent resting places. I'll never forget the minister sprinkling flower petals into their graves, saying, "Dust to dust and ashes to ashes." But during Helen's memorial service, I looked at a beautiful, enlarged, relatively current photo of her. The picture, mounted on an easel, captured her smiling, being full of life. I thought, *How sad. Many of us allow tradition to dictate our actions. Perhaps it's out of ignorance we accept an embalmed, overly cosmetic face as the last visual of a loved-one.* Seeing Helen's photo placed on that easel and with a small flower arrangement around it, changed my idea of what I wanted for my own big send-off. No funeral. No casket. A memorial service, with happy photos of me. I, however, wasn't ready for cremation. I hadn't progressed quite that far.

During the ceremony, I looked about the room. I saw Edley standing next to his new Japanese wife, Noboko. There was a pocket of Indians from Asia, Hispanics, and a few other Blacks. I felt good in not being the only one.

What a delightful rainbow of racial color. Including all the Whites, the place looked like a United Nations meeting. I could not stop thinking, *A person's funeral service portrays and speaks volumes about the loved-one—how many people attend and their various backgrounds.*

I enjoyed meeting Elaine's extended family, who had traveled from across the United States. Although they spoke with varying dialects and inflections, they were all Caucasian—except Noboko, my two children, and me. I thought this was strange, especially in this day and age. Out of all of that entire family, only Elaine and her brother married people of color. *Must have had something with the way they were raised.*

They were pleasant, cordial around me—especially Aunt Patsy and her husband, Fat-Pat-The-Democrat from Arizona. These two went out of their way, letting me know they genuinely accepted my family.

Wanting to be near his family, Ed moved from Santa Barbara to Las Vegas. I helped pack up and drive the U-Haul. I cursed the "researched" articles contained in entire newspapers, every one of Ed's wooden-board-shelving, his cinderblock stands, and numerous file cabinets as I loaded and unloaded them during the move. In addition, Elaine had me bring all of her mother's furniture. We moved a lot into our house.

We started out having Pampaw over often for dinner. I'd also take the kids to his apartment to visit, which gave Elaine a little time to herself. The boys would spend hours swimming in his apartment's pool.

How embarrassing it was for both Elaine and me to take Ed out to dinner or to take him with us to our friend's homes for dinner, but we did. Ed would take sea salt from his pocket and sprinkle it from a plastic bag onto his food at the table. He then would give his dissertation on the values of sea salt verses the properties of kiln-dried, regular, man-made salt. Wearing the mask, pretending, trying to socially be whole, mentally healthy, and happy, I found his behavior to be most embarrassing.

What concerned me more was the bed that Pampaw slept in. After his move to Las Vegas, he invented a bed that looked more like a coffin—solid pinewood on the sides, head and foot areas, and bottom. He used a foam cushion for a mattress. Worse, yet, were the vertical and horizontal pulleys and chords, with weights and springs that were attached to his comforter. *How morbid, how strange? With the loss of his wife, what sad, depressed state of mind Ed must have been in. Was he secretly wishing death and halfway living it out?*

When I asked him about his contraption, curious to know, he said, "Son, you know I'm both lazy and busy. I wanted a warm bed that would automatically make itself."

Helen had left Ed in a position where he no longer needed to work. Her savings, retirement plan, insurance, social security, and all, would take care of him for the rest of his life. To our surprise, we also discovered Grammy left fifty thousand dollars to both of her grandsons—although it was a chore in getting the money. Elaine and I had to officially prove to the Nevada Court that we were both the legal and biological parents of Jemal and Gavin. Our neighbor, an attorney and friend, did this without usurping any of the funds.

It did not take long for Elaine to have a garage sale to get rid of most of her mother's furniture. She explained to me that the furniture constantly reminded her of growing up in her mother's house. It also continually reminded her of her mother's death.

CHAPTER 38

A pparently, the administration liked what I was doing. They appointed me Department Chair for English, Reading, and Foreign Language for the 1985-86 school year. In this quasi-administrative position, I would be responsible for my allocated financial allotment. I ordered books and supplies and prepared the teachers' room assignments and schedules for the upcoming school year. There were special reports that had to be completed by the chairmen, and in a timely manner. I welcomed the challenge. I remember saying to myself, *Wow. After teaching high school for two short years, I've been promoted to Department Chair. That's pretty impressive.*

Taking the actual position wasn't bad. Prior to leaving, the out-going chairman didn't leave me in a state of having to catch up on any of her deferred work—instead, she included me in the process.

At the first part of summer vacation, I took all of the textbooks from all of the English teachers. I inventoried them all and talked my supervisor into giving me a storeroom to house all of the unissued books. I reissued only the books each teacher needed according to the teaching schedule, with a few additional books for the unexpected students. I was amazed to find books hoarded in some teachers' rooms— boxes of books for subjects they hadn't taught in years.

While cleaning the dust and cobwebs from my new storage room, I found four large, unopened boxes. Inside, I discovered brand new 1930 Underwood, pica typewriters, still wrapped in their original shipping plastic, four to each cardboard carton. Boy, did I want to keep those typewriters. *No one would ever miss them,* I thought. *They didn't even know they were there. Pawnshops in California would give a good price for my finding.* But, I did the right thing. I gave them to my supervisor.

With the textbooks placed in the appropriate classrooms and the rest organized and stored, I was ready to spend the summer with my family. But I had to drive to Idyllwild, California, to see them. Elaine had decided to help her girlfriend. This friend and her husband had quit teaching. They wanted to go into business for themselves, starting a school of the arts, high in the mountains of San Bernardino County. I think Elaine was their "Good-Man-Friday," doing whatever she could to help them out. Our children got to take free art classes, eat free meals, and hang out at the swimming pool when Elaine wasn't working.

When I arrived, I gave Elaine a break by taking the kids fishing at Hemet Lake. We had a blast catching rainbow trout and bluegill. I had taught both boys well. Jemal out-fished me two to my one, and size mattered, too. Gavin caught the largest bluegill I had ever seen.

One day while Elaine was busy working, I took the kids to the pool. Jemal was eight. Gavin was four. Gavin started climbing the ladder to the high-diving platform. People started yelling, "Look at that kid, he's going to drown for sure." My only concern was his possibly falling off the ladder. Gavin was an excellent swimmer. His mother had taken great care to provide water safety classes for both boys long before they could walk. As Gavin climbed the ladder more people began to take notice. He made it to the top and stepped out onto the platform. Tension filled the air, but I was relieved. He hadn't fallen from the ladder. Gavin stood, probably deciding if he wanted to jump or dive. More tension filled the air. One adult screamed, "Where's that kid's parent?" A second or two later, Gavin dove off the platform. He looked like a minnow swimming to the side of the pool. I went to the edge of the pool and lifted him out of the water. I hugged him and told him how proud I was of his fearlessness and his super, great dive.

I stayed at the school of arts for a week and then returned home. All of July and some of August I drove back and forth to be with my family. Although our marriage wasn't full of passionate sex and romance, I thought it was as good as a family spending a day at Disneyland. I had finally committed to our marriage, trying to do the best I could. I brought the kids home with me mid-August. Elaine wanted to stay longer. I sensed that something was wrong, but I didn't ask to find out what.

I didn't know it then, but our biggest problem was a lack of honesty on my part and a lack of communication on both our parts.

Too closed-off to my emotions, I never looked at them. Managing to survive each day is how I had learned to function since high school. Intuitively, I knew that I needed to be ready to open wide the closed-off doors to my demons. Common sense told me I was not, and if I dared, they would whoop my ass. I thought being the dutiful husband and father was enough. I didn't know Elaine needed more.

A couple of days before the start of school, Elaine still hadn't made it home. I started feeling uncomfortable. It brought back the feelings I had had when she went to Syracuse to visit her friend, way back when we were in college. Each day, I'd call the school of arts, trying to find out when Elaine would be coming home. She never returned any of my calls.

Elaine took her leave of absence all the way to the very end. She arrived home Saturday afternoon—a day and a half before the start of public school.

When Elaine entered the house, she was as cold to me as a sheet of steel in a deep-freezer. Walking pass me she said, "Take the credit card and get you a room in one of the casinos. I don't want to live with you anymore."

"Laney, what's wrong? What have I done to deserve this?"

I gathered clothes for the first day of school.

I stared at her.

I looked at my children.

I left.

CHAPTER 39

I think I stayed with a friend at first. About to lose everything, there was no way I would have retreated to a hotel room. I knew Elaine would eventually take me back, like she had always done. That is why I didn't immediately respond, saying, "Since you want out, you take the credit card and go. I'm staying here with my children." I figured she probably needed a longer break.

I rented a room in a house shared with three other strangers—two guys and a young, unkempt, alcoholic gal. I didn't care. So much was going on in my life, I didn't have time to look at others. I stayed in my lane. Besides, this place was near my school and didn't cost very much.

The first morning after leaving Elaine and the kids, while dressing, I discovered I had forgotten to pack my underwear—I initially thought. When I returned home to get them, Elaine told me, "Gavin ran to our bedroom after hearing of the separation.

Hiding your underwear, he thought, would make it impossible for you to leave."

Has the girl lost her mind? Has she gone completely insane? was all that I could think. *Did Gavin have more sense than her?* Beyond thought, I felt the torment of missing my children. I longed to rub lotion on their hands and feet, read them a bedtime story, and hug them, saying, "There's no limit to how much I love you. You're special. Now, good night." I never thought I'd ever have to experience misery worse than what I suffered while serving in Vietnam, but the hurting isolation of being separated from my loved ones was almost more than I could bear.

I nibbled at a 99-cent bacon and eggs breakfast in a casino each morning on my way to work and toyed with my food at the buffets each night. Already thin, I began to look emaciated—anorexic.

Sometimes I brought my children over to the Westside, where I lived. I figured they needed to visualize where their papa stayed. The homeowner had an under-fed, malnourished greyhound, which my sons immediately took a liking to. As they stroked and petted the dog, I put myself in the dog's place. I needed loving, too.

Eventually, the renters moved out of our first home, and I moved in. When we separated, I left everything with Elaine. All I took was my Volkswagen, my clothes, a large workbench, all my tools, and a few dishes. Oh, and the $10,000 debt we had incurred on our credit card, I took that, too. I didn't have any furniture—not even a bed. I was very comfortable sleeping in my sleeping bag on the plush carpeted floor. Whenever my kids spent the night, they used their sleeping bags, too.

I didn't need it, but someone later gave me an old, 1960s T.V., housed in a Maplewood cabinet and a high-back, course, burlap, floral printed sleeper-couch for the children's use during their visits.

I was miserable when my children weren't at home with me. I didn't go back to drinking or smoking cigarettes. I serenaded myself on my guitar. But that hurt, too. Each time I played, I thought of both my losing Elaine and of how I used countless hours of playing to drown out the hurtful rejection of my old girlfriend, skinny Brenda. Thinking Elaine would eventually come to her senses and take me back, I didn't move my antique, upright piano from her house to mine. Besides, it was far too heavy.

Sudden separation was the sharp blade of rejection. It cut away my comfort, nearly causing me to panic. *What would I do without my wife and kids?* "Good morning Blues. Blues, how-do-you-do?" I crooned on my guitar almost everyday. But I would not allow myself to play my guitar to the extent that I played it when Brenda left me. I vowed not to return to wallowing in that type of deep isolation and self-pity ever again.

One day, I came to my senses, deciding I'm not going to linger in despair. I declared, *Elaine is not God, no, not my everything; she's only a person. I will always have her friendship, and I'll never let go of my boys!*

Elaine and I decided we'd let the boys determine when they wanted to stay at her house or mine. As I saw it, they'd have two homes—both equally open to their coming and going, as they liked. I never said anything negative about Elaine to them to sway them in favor of living with me. Nor did she to entice them to live with her.

Looking back on our decision; however, I don't think it was a good one. Did we place too much pressure on our children? We could have told them, "One week with Mom, and then the next week with Papa." We could have established a number of possible schedules. Did we give them any guilt in having them make the schedule? Today, I like to think, *Oh, the innocence in our lack of experience.* We did what we thought was right.

That first night Elaine kicked me out of our home Gavin was in pre-school. Jemal was in second grade. Eventually, we discovered it was easier on the children to have a consistent schedule during school days. We all decided the boys would live with Elaine during the weekdays. I got them on most weekends and holidays.

Over a period of time, I reverted back to my old ways dating back to high school. Though not drinking to anesthetize the pain, or smoking to calm my nerves, I isolated. Probably lacking trust in others, I stayed within myself. I fell into self-pity. Sunken, I didn't take the time to find Ronnie. Instead of finding a way to also nurture my child within, I hid behind nurturing my children and my students. I didn't want to run away from Gavin and Jemal like my father had deserted his wife and children. When I didn't have my boys with me, school and work became my salvation. I found it very easy to substitute helping others rather than focusing in on me.

Somehow, on a teacher's salary, I managed to buy a new four-wheel drive SUV. Starting in the spring and all through summer, my boys and I would take back roads and wind our way through mountains to fish the many reservoirs and lakes of Southern Utah. Panguitch Lake was our favorite. We'd often spend our weekends there. During the long drives, I often wished I had a partner to help me with the driving. Nevertheless, I enjoyed spending time with my boys.

On several occasions, I'd talk my male friends into joining me on a fishing trip. We would take our children and other neighborhood kids their ages for a three-day fishing trip to Utah. We would sleep in tents and sleeping bags. I'd prepare all the meals, using the impressive camping skills I had learned from my backpacking buddy,

Bruce. Besides canned baked beans, grilled corn on the cob and fish, I'd delight the group by making a boxed cake, roasting it in a homemade, covered aluminum pan, above red-hot embers—something else Bruce had taught me. How fortunate I was to have found a beautiful surrogate family after moving to Las Vegas all by myself.

During one of those fishing trips I remembered stargazing, thinking how we, not knowing any better, complicated our lives. I watched the stars and thought about our beautiful children and that I was the one who messed up my marriage. I began to reflect upon the horrible things I had done to both Elaine and myself. Although I hadn't figured out why it failed, I intuitively knew I was the problem. *Why was I so destructive to our relationship?* With all of the fishing party asleep, I lay there in a sleeping bag, comfortably atop an air mattress, asking myself, *Why do some have the insight to keep their marriages together while others just can't get it right?* On the surface, I wanted to blame or attribute it to luck, but I knew better. With all those college courses behind me and with my educational background, I knew behavior runs much deeper than that. For a brief moment, I thought about Pavlov's dogs, how his hypotheses led him to train dogs to salivate merely at a picture of food. I continued to let my mind wonder. I asked myself, Why hadn't my parents or society better trained me to behavior more rationally? I thought back to a time when Elaine and I were together, relaxing in our bed. I thought about a story she shared with me.

Young men typically don't delve deeply into their feelings, and rarely would they have the sensitivity to discuss them with each other. Following that line of reasoning and protocol, the men in our Las Vegas family were no different. Not once did we express any emotions regarding our group's Black men-White wives' composition. Nor were Black women excluded from our group as there were some married to other Black men. We simply took our group's racial make-up for granted. We didn't dare ask ourselves what had brought us together—*Why we Black men married White women? Was there a certain comfort in banding together, being part of this group?* Back then in 1975, Black and White interracial American marriages were not as common as they are today. They were frowned upon, somewhat as being taboo. Just as the saying goes, "There strength and unity in numbers," without our having to discuss it, I'm sure we all felt some solidarity in being a part of our group.

However, as most women seem to talk about everything, Elaine did share with me one of our lady friend's racially motivated sexual curiosities. Yet, she did not reveal her name. Having to get it off her chest, Elaine said she had been told that while married to her Black husband, our friend had copulated with a young, attractive White male only to see if sex was better with someone from her same ethnicity. In addition, she wanted to test the myth that Black men have no sexual restraints. Having no hang-ups, they do it much, much better—animalistic-like, they go all the way.

"What?" I interrupted. What Elaine was saying, what I heard made no sense. I could understand why a person would be unfaithful for various reasons—not having sex often enough; not being able to perform in a pleasing, satisfying way; being sexually dysfunctional, okay. But throwing race into the equation? I simply didn't get it. *Did this lady want to personally test a lot of sexual myths and stereotypes—finding out for herself while running the risk of possibly putting her marriage into jeopardy?*

Elaine ended her bedtime story saying, " The lady in question brought her story to a closing by matter-of-factly saying, 'The White guy and my husband performed about the same.'"

Oh, there was a lot I could have commented on, but I kept my thoughts to myself—especially with that Black chic I had met the one summer I had lived with my brother. That sex was less than satisfying, I had learned because I wanted it to be with my wife. Instead, I merely responded, "What made her think that ethnicity has anything to do with sexual performance?"

Then, there was this other time that a different member of our "family" asked me to join a bowling team. She wanted me on her team to prevent this White guy on the team from outwardly flirting with her. She believed that since he knew me well and that I would be watching his every step, that he would stop his unwanted, offensive advances. She said, "Ronnie, I value my marriage too much. I'm not getting involved with some jerk, thinking the grass is greener on the other side."

With that, I joined the team and, like a watchdog, stayed close to my lady friend. As she had predicted, her suitor ceased his advances.

Falling off to sleep, I thought, *How can some people be so wise and others be so stupid?*

CHAPTER 40

I taught the same subjects my fourth year at Las Vegas High School—one A.P. Composition course, two Honors English II classes, one Basic English II class, and my Freshman Study Skills class. When I first took the department chair position I vowed to always teach at least one remedial class. That way, I would always remember how frustrating the job can be and not burnout any of my teachers by assigning them all basic classes. Besides, it kept me humble, not walking through the halls thinking I was anything special.

I could not smile at school. I didn't want to pretend anymore. Several of my Advanced Placement students confided in me, "Are you disappointed in us, Mr. Smith? Is the quality of our work making you unhappy?"

I told them, "No," but I didn't tell them the reason for my sadness. They were students and didn't need to know that much of my personal life.

On the other hand, once news got out that I was separated, single ladies on our campus brought me homemade breakfasts, lunches, and dinners. Though I never dated any of them, I never turned down one of their meals, not even the ones that came with a rose or carnation in a small vase.

During one of my non-smiling days, my supervisor made the comment, "One day, Ronnie, you'll look back and laugh about this time in your life."

I didn't show it, but boy, was I ever angry at her statement. *How could she make such a comment? She was happily married. How could she know the loneliness and pain I was going through? She wasn't going through it!*

I loved teaching high school, especially the juniors and seniors. Unlike elementary or junior high students, older students had experienced life long enough to engage in "meaningful," conversations while discussing different concepts. Instead of keeping it for myself, I gave them and my biological children all of my heart. I wanted to make a definite difference in their lives. For some reason a story that Elaine had shared with me kept echoing in my mind. She said, "One of my high school students shared that she had gone home one evening and discovered her mom, dad, and her three younger siblings had moved away, leaving her abandoned." How well we knew that kids have problems, too. And I always wanted to be there for all my "children," appropriately helping them however I could.

One of my biracial students, Allen, shared a story with me that shaped my life for the next several years. I mention biracial because I was always curious. *How did he feel, being Afro-American and White?* One day I asked him.

"Awe, Mr. Smith, don't be axing me somethin' stupid like that. How am I supposed to feel?" was his reply.

I left it there. After hearing his response, I was the one feeling rather stupid.

Allen shared with me that he was happy to be graduating—not only for himself, but also because of his mother. He explained that she had sacrificed herself for him by not getting involved in any serious relationship before he would graduate from high school and leave home for college. He was happy that she would soon be looking for someone instead of complicating his life with potential male problems while he lived in her home.

After hearing his story, I thought about the potential problems I could possibly encounter subjecting my children to females who were not their biological mother. I did not want a lady who possibly could be jealous of my relationship with my two sons, thinking I loved them and gave them more attention than her.

I, like Allen's mother, decided to put my love life on hold and to simply raise my children. While teaching study skills I found out how strangely the universe hears our desires and corresponds accordingly. I was in class teaching my students how to plan out their lives and how to goal set. I wrote on the board, "One year from now, I will own a fishing boat." Sure enough, one year later, my boys and I were fishing in Lake Mead and Panguitch Lake from my boat.

Goal setting works sometimes but not one hundred percent. I still haven't figured out why sometimes I'll make a resolution and then turn around and do the complete opposite. As soon as I vowed to spend time only with my children, life had a way of introducing me to Cheryl, an elementary educator who had never taught with me. I met her through a friend. She was divorced and had two boys the same ages as mine. Her oldest was also named Jemal. Initially, we connected. Her likes and wishes seemed to be the same as mine. I loved having a family to cook for again. Her boys loved fishing trips with mine.

When Cheryl's mother and father came to visit, it didn't take long for me to win their hearts—nor for them to win mine. Being who I am, my first look at Cheryl's mom, I noticed she looked the woman of her age— sweet, full face, but rather overweight. I continued with my juvenile thinking, *Some day, your daughter will look just like you.* But this time, her mother's physical appearance didn't matter. I wanted a woman who would be with me for a lifetime, not someone shallow, caring only about looks. What I didn't know was that Cheryl was dating several men. I was not the one she eventually chose to marry. Her dumping me had little to no effect on me at all. I experienced no anxiety, none at all. This furthered my assumption that those who are truly ready for marriage can accept it or leave it, with no trauma or drama whatsoever.

CHAPTER 41

To further escape having to focus on my issues, side-stepping myself, I continued doing what I do best—I took an additional teaching job. By doing this, I rationalized; I could earn the needed money to support two houses instead of one. I could afford making the payments on my new car, and I could pay child support. On Tuesdays and Thursdays three of us used a Clark County School District car to drive out to Indian Springs State Correctional Facility. One taught history and government. The other taught mathematics. I taught English to the inmates, helping them to earn their GEDs.

During my first night at the prison, inmates made catcalls from their cells, saying things like, "Here comes some new meat," as we walked to our classrooms. Primarily, I saw Hispanics and Blacks. *Oh, this is where all of the young Black males come when they drop out of life and school.*

I taught two one-hour sessions—one from 7:00 P.M.-to-8:00 P.M., and another from 8:00 P.M.-to-9:00 P.M. That first night I entered names into my roll book and had the students write a paragraph describing themselves. I wrote about myself. After reading my paper aloud, I asked for volunteers to do the same. At the close of the first session, one student asked if I'd bring him a bottle of suede cleaner the upcoming Thursday. Of course I told him it was against the prison's rules. Jokingly, a student in my last session asked if I would trade clothes with him. He wanted me to exchange my dress pants, shirt, and tie for his denim trousers and jacket and his off-white t-shirt. The entire class, including me, all laughed.

On Thursdays, we worked on sentence structure, spelling, and punctuation. At the end of one class session, I handed out a novella, and asked the class to read the first chapter by the upcoming Tuesday.

To my surprise, all of the students, in both classes, read the entire novel. I only expected a few of the students to have completed the assignment. "What's going on?" I asked. "Was the story that good? Why did you men read the entire book?"

"We ain't got nothing better to do," seemed to be the general consensus. From that evening on, I gave these students my very best teaching.

One night, while driving back to the school District parking lot, Larry, the math teacher, commented, "You know, I never liked prisoners. I've always viewed them in my mind as selfish, evil people. But I must confess, I like my students. Some of them have real neat personalities. I have to say, this teaching assignment has helped me to grow out of one of my misguided prejudices."

During one of my later sessions, one student blurted out, "Man, you do like this stuff!" He was referring to me.

All I could think was, *How sad, how unfortunate for him. Apparently, no teacher had ever shown him any signs of passion regarding subject matter.* The more I thought it, the more off-course I probably got. *Could it have been that he had never witnessed a young Afro-American male so passionate in teaching English?*

I quickly responded, "Do you think I'd waste my time driving all the way up here, twice a week, to teach a subject I don't care about?"

Without my saying another word, I thought, *Those unfortunate teachers who teach day-to-day, year-after-year without joy, just to earn a paycheck. I'm glad I'm doing what I love. The District wouldn't have to pay me. I'd teach in this prison for free.*

My captive audience—pun intended—demonstrated superlative attendance, written work, and class participation. Their grades on tests and quizzes, taught me not to judge them. Their behavior motivated me to teach them all I could. I believed all of my students wanted to improve their lives.

I was glad I was there to help.

"Mr. Smith, I want you to meet an inmate in here," a student announced one Tuesday evening. "I think you'll like him. His name is Ray-Ray. He's the smartest person I know. He's smart, like you."

Thank you for the compliment, and yes, I would like to meet Ray-Ray."

This guy, Ray-Ray, figured out a way to get into the utility company's billing system. He uploaded information into the system that would add extra money to his balance. Having surplus credit, the company would mail him money to balance out the account. At first, he would get checks for five or ten dollars, but then he got greedy. I want you to meet this guy. I think that you would like him."

Curiosity got the best of me, and again I replied, "You can bring him to class."

Thursday evening, long before the start of class, a new face, held high, purposefully, confidently walked into my classroom. He was short, somewhat unattractive, and skinny.

My student, Parrish, immediately introduced us. "Ray-Ray, this is Mr. Smith. Mr. Smith, this is Ray Anthony Ray."

Extending my hand to shake his, I said, "So, Ray-Ray, what brings you to my class?"

"God. He wanted me to tell you something.

Every student paused. Silence suffocated all sound. *What?* I thought. *What's this criminal up to?* I was a little uncomfortable not knowing what was going to happen next. Had I fallen gullibly for some set-up?

"See, most people think that in order to change, they will need to start by correcting their present-day situation. They try to will a changed life. But while doing my hard time, I've managed to figure it out."

I couldn't believe what he was saying. *Obviously, he was a one-of-those-too-smart-for-his-own-good guys. Was he trying to set me up?*

"Transformation doesn't work like that. I've had to start at the beginning— thoroughly examining my first thoughts and actions that eventually landed me in this joint. It's not working backward," he said. "Instead, it's taking a good, hard look at the initial thoughts and then behaviors, which gradually manifested into a changed lifestyle.

Wow, not all guys in prison are inarticulate and going nowhere. And this man only looks to be about thirty.

"Then I had to courageously process and possess those thoughts and actions before any real healing could occur. I'm telling you, Mr. Ronnie, I'm already out of prison because I've released those demons that led me here. I'll tell you something else. I'm not ever coming back."

My tears gathered, and I wanted to grab him and hug him. But that's not something done in a prison—especially between an inmate and his teacher.

Worse yet, and probably like all of the other students, I didn't fully get it. Although I heard his words, I wasn't ready to understand.

One evening, the lights unexpectedly went out. One student, Mr. Love, pointed to a storage room, which was located inside our classroom. He quickly whispered in my ear, "Mr. Smith, you go into that storage room. Lock the door. Don't let anybody in until the lights come back on."

Students were scrambling to exit the classroom. Not knowing what to do, I decided to take Mr. Love's advice. I rushed into the room, and quickly locked the door. Standing there in the dark, listening to the screaming and yelling sounds during this pandemic blackout, I wondered if I had made the best decision. I hoped no one was in the room with me.

A minute or two later the lights came on. I heard students re-entering the classroom, so I came out. I felt good that I had trusted the advice of an inmate. Telling me to, "Go into that storage room, lock the door, and don't let anybody in until the lights come back on." Mr. Love had shown me love.

Another night a student from my 8:00 P.M. class asked, "Mr. Smith, would you like to meet my brother, uncle, cousins, and father?"

"You want to introduce them to me when you get out of here?" I asked.

"No," he replied. "They are all right up in here with me."

"What? Your whole family is in here?"

"You can't beat it, Mr. Smith. Three meals and a cot," he said with a big smile.

I didn't make a comment. I felt sorry for the inmate. I only thought, *From the cotton fields to prison, generation after generation. Education can change all of that.*

I started thinking about my own life, as far back as I could remember. I thought about the hobos my brother and I saw on the streets of downtown Los Angeles as we rode the city busses with my father. I thought about the fear I've always carried, thinking, *I might one day fall to their level.* I thought about the violence—the shootings, the stabbings, the cussing and stealing, personally watching the Watts' Riots in my mother's neighborhood.

I felt sorry for myself, that Black boy, still tormented with fear—that young man who had not let go of his childhood impoverishments.

During the last night of classes, a student asked if he could come back at the end of my 8 P.M. class. "There's something I want to tell you," he explained.

"Yes, Obie," was all that I could say. Just before his return I thought, *Is Obie going to punch me? Is he going to cuss me out? Why did I open myself up to this upcoming predicament?* Obie was as big and burley as a lineman on the NFL.

I did not have to wait long. Obie returned to my classroom immediately after class had ended. "Mr. Smith," he said, in a deep, gruffly voice, "I love you, Mr. Smith. Not in a sexual way, but in a spiritual way. Thank you for helping me to pass my GED exam."

CHAPTER 42

Divorce terminated my marriage, and singlehandedly massacred my family—one by one. Like cancer, it ate away at the four of us and spread throughout my close group of friends, my social family, as well. As usual, both Elaine and I were invited to our friends' birthday parties, holiday functions, and other events. Knowing Elaine would attend these activities bothered me. Once together, now apart, it was awkward and uncomfortable being around her in a social gathering. But these were my friends, too. I loved them and was glad that they still loved me and wanted to continue being around me, too. After careful consideration on my first invitation, finally, I decided, *I'm going. It will be no different than the painful times I have to meet with Elaine, picking up or dropping off, exchanging custody of the children.*

Although it was stipulated that Ann and Billy would prepare the meats, we had our annual potluck at their home on Labor Day. Our biggest event, other than celebrating Christmas, was held at Curtis and May's. They had the largest house. It included a huge spa and swimming pool, which allowed us to view the golf course, running along their backyard. Curtis' specialty was spareribs. He grilled them, along with hotdogs and burgers every Fourth of July. Everybody came to swim, relax, and enjoy the large quantity of pulled-together fireworks we would set off at dark.

Generally, it's the children in a neighborhood that bring adults together. Ours was no exception. Betty and Phil had two children, who were roughly our children's ages. Rio and Pat had a son. Cindy had two daughters and a son. Janie and Jim, not only had their daughter, Stacey, but also had another daughter around the same time that we had had Gavin. With the exception of Cindy, every one of the wives in our group was a teacher in the district. Additionally, Bob and May and Allison and Greg lived in our neighborhood and partied with us. They had no children, but all of the females taught for the school district, too. As we all lived in the same neighborhood, we threw a block party at Christmas time and traveled from one home to another eating breakfast at one house, lunch at another, dinner somewhere else, and dessert at another home. Of course we invited our friends who didn't live in our immediate area.

Even after our separation, Elaine asked me to continue grilling a huge leg of lamb for our annual New "Tear's" Day dinner. Of course I agreed to do it.

CHAPTER 43

When people are in pain, they will do almost anything to end it. Such was the case for Elaine. Now, I had learned to satisfactorily live with our being separated, but Elaine, listening to all of her divorced friends, suddenly, in 1986, sprang papers on me, filling for divorce.

To save money and not complicate the situation, we both agreed to utilize the same attorney. Rather than contesting the divorce, I decided to follow a Biblical precept, one I had known all my adult life—"But if the husband or wife who isn't a believer insists on leaving, let them go."

She kept the big house. I retained our first house. We both had the only thing that really mattered—joint custody of our children.

"Elaine, Elaine!" I hollered while waking up out of a dream one night, shortly after the divorce.

I knew I had to do something to truly let her go. I wasn't about to live the rest of my life in the past—secretly worshiping, longing for the fantasized relationship we never had.

The next day, I purchased three helium-filled balloons. One by one I released them into the air.

Watching the red one rise into the sky I thought, *Good-bye, Elaine; I'm really letting you go.* The yellow one symbolized my not needing the crutch of alcohol anymore. Shimmying while trying to catch the other two balloons, I watched the blue one, representing my father, travel on its

CHAPTER 44

In my own maturing I've learned whenever tragedy occurs, I'm not the only individual who has traveled the road of malady before. Surprisingly, half of our social groups' marriages ended in divorce. Ann and Billy divorced shortly after Elaine and me. Then May and Curtis, Kathy and Michael, and Rosemarie and Allen went their separate ways.

With the exception of Ann and Billy, all of the other divorcees were in biracial marriages. Like mine, the ladies were White, and the men were Black. White May left Black Curtis. She eventually married one of her own kind. Black Michael divorced White Deborah and married a different White younger woman, named Miss Lovelock. Black Curtis and White Deborah united and have been together ever since. I don't know what happened to White Rosemarie, relationship-wise, but Black Allen, not that it matters, married a Black lady his second time around. However, one thing is certain; Elaine never ever dated another Black man for the rest of her life. I like to pride myself in thinking I had given her more than enough of the Black experience.

And I guess May had gotten enough Black culture from Curtis to last her a lifetime, too.

During the time of the divorces, I felt the ladies were tired. Tired of parenting the children, and in some cases like mine, tired of parenting their husbands—tired of holding the marriage together, and tired of being tired.

I believe they were tired of trying to be super-women, taking care of everybody and not getting any relief.

Not to take away or add to the attractiveness or unattractiveness of anyone in our group, but I felt like the ladies, all around age thirty-five, somewhat believed they were being short-changed. We husbands had become so accustomed to them, taking them for granted; they weren't being treated special anymore. They were no longer pampered or treated as queens. With as little as saying, "Baby, you look good in that outfit," or "Would you like to split my candy bar?" it didn't take much for another man to get their attention, making them feel young, worthwhile, and sexy. Although it was never as simple as that, perhaps, the ladies who divorced the guys fell for their pursuer's lines and wanted out.

I was glad to be a high school department chair, but for months I had been feeling a little less adequate. Jim and Jimmy were now school administrators, both serving as Dean of Students in their respective secondary school. Billy had risen to the position of assistant principal at the elementary level, and Michael was the principal of a junior high school.

Having earned my M. Ed. in School Administration, I had the necessary credentials to follow after them, but fear kept me from doing so. *What if I failed the required four-hour multiple-choice test mandated by the district? The district also required a written test as well. What if one of my friends while serving on the screening committee were selected to read my written portion of the test? My being an English teacher, how embarrassing if I failed.*

Yet something inwardly continued to slightly tug and nag at me. It was like looking through a lighted mirror, magnified ten times. I clearly saw my image reflecting my sadness's, regrets, and pain. Sitting and sulking and continually lying to myself no longer was working for me. Through instinct I knew that something had to change: I couldn't continue holding onto all of my self-delusion. Wrestling with the ideas of changing or forever remaining stuck, I asked myself, *How true was all this stimuli? How true was my world?*

I sensed that my mind was taking phantasmorphic breaks, using filters to color and categorize everything I saw and felt.

In spite of what one part of me was always demanding, *You better watch it. Now's not the time to change.* I decided to aggressively become more confident, more of a risk-taker. Refusing to listen to that censor in my head, I was ready to go somewhere. *I'm going to take the first step by doing something to change my life.*

The day I walked out of the testing needed to apply for school administration, I felt like a winner. I told myself, *Even if I don't pass, I'm a winner anyway—just by taking the exams!*

Several weeks later, I was eligible to apply for an administrative position.

CHAPTER 45

A dean's position became available at Kenny Guinn Junior High School where I had taught. I interviewed for the job and got it.

The students in my Advanced Placement Composition I class threw a "surprise" going away party for me in the classroom. The assistant principal lured me out of the room giving me some administrative department chairman work. The students decorated the room and when I returned, I had one of the best times of my life. While entering the classroom, Lulu's song played aloud on an old phonograph, and the students had draped a banner across the ceiling, which read, "To Sir With Love." All I could do was cry.

CHAPTER 46

The dean of student discipline, whom I replaced, spent one day with me teaching me how to do the job.

Each student referred to my office would have a disciplinary folder. I had to document each infraction and dole out the appropriate consequence, increasing the punishment for each misbehavior. I did not know the students, and I did not know the job. Initially, it took hours, long after school had ended, to enter the necessary information into each student's folder, adding to each kid's behavioral chronology.

To make matters worse, my principal insisted that I write out a detailed description of any major incident on campus—he'd send a copy to his boss, not leaving them in the dark. As something was forever occurring, it seemed my work was never done. This written work needed to be completed the day it happened to ensure my memory served me correctly.

I'd give a copy of each teacher referral to the student during my conference with him or her. My secretary would mail a copy home and place a copy in the teacher's mailbox, with the consequences marked or described. Sometimes I would have to meet with a dissatisfied teacher if he or she felt my consequences were not harsh enough.

Once a student had been issued several dean's detentions or cafeteria clean up, I'd place him or her on Request for Parent Conference, which meant the parent would need to call the school and make an appointment with me regarding their child's behavior. If the parent wouldn't make the appointment within several days after telephone reminders from my secretary, the child would be placed on Required Parent Conference. Whenever a student was placed on Required Parent Conference (R.P.C.), he or she could not return to school until the student, parent, and I met to discuss the child's misbehavior. Since the student body of junior high school was seventh, eighth, and ninth grade, the parents of seventh graders gave me the roughest times. They truly believed their child was right and the school had it out to unjustly punish their precious child.

In the beginning, I was unproductive and completely baffled in trying to solve mysterious crimes on campus. But after I botched things up, the principal would hand me documentation on who had done what, telling me to resolve each case.

How can he get the information so quickly? I'd ask myself.

Then the assistant principal added insult to my injury by saying, "Smith, if you can't find out exactly what happened on this campus, anytime and anywhere, don't call yourself a dean."

To not be outdone, I continued racking my brain, asking the question, *How do I get accurate information from the students?*

It didn't take long for me to discover the answer. I called it putting puzzle pieces together. I began learning that an effective school administrator had to truly know the entire school's community—the teachers, the students, and the parents. Moreover, each individual had to trust my judgment. If a child felt I wasn't going to rat him or her out, he or she was more inclined to provide information that helped me solve the crime.

If a parent truly felt I had their best interest at heart, he or she seemed more willing to agree with my disciplinary procedures.

If a teacher believed I did all I could to discipline their students appropriately, they were more willing to accept my consequences.

It didn't take me long to figure out that if a student believed the dean already knew exactly what happened, he or she was less likely to lie.

One of my favorite tactics during an investigation was to simply say, "Joe, you aren't in any trouble because you had nothing to do with this situation. All I need you to do is to confidentially tell me the truth." I would then take one piece of information, add it to another, and slowly build a case.

I learned a dean must be able to solve any and all incidents on his campus. He couldn't afford to let any student get away with any mischief. The more cases solved increased the efficacy of future cases being solved. I made it a point to stay at one hundred percent.

On the job training as dean of students taught me a lot—especially about human nature and using child psychology to my advantage. But I could never understand why one of my parents named his child Harry Butt Junior. With a name like that, with all the teasing and humiliation the child frequently suffered, no wonder he frequented my office.

The more I learned my job, the better it got at it. All the time, effort, and energy I put into working with parents of sixth-graders eventually paid off. I remember countless saying' " During your first year here, I was on your side. I used to believe it was the school against you, not giving you a chance. I don't believe it anymore. You're the problem. You need to fix yourself rather than blame these people at this school. I'm tired of coming down here. You're the problem. You're the one who needs to change."

Figuring the job out came easy. But when it came to my feelings, my fears, and how to face them, I had no clue. I dreaded going to our weekly administrative meetings. During these sessions, the principal utilized an agenda. "Dean of Students" was always on the list. Days before each meeting, I felt uneasy and didn't want to attend. *Why I'm I stressing over going?* I asked myself. *Does he expect too much from me? Do I expect too much from myself? Am I going to do something terrible? Will I fail and disappoint us both?* I never found an answer to my own insecurity, but managed to understand that in the workplace women sometimes feel this way, too—I have to perform better than . . . Although the anxiety ended immediately after each meeting, it always reappeared the following week, for as long as I stayed on my principal's administrative team.

CHAPTER 47

Early one Friday evening I went over to Elaine's to get the kids for the weekend. While entering through the opened garage, I noticed a dozen dead roses in a waterless vase. They were sitting on top of the washing machine. I don't know why they caught my eye, but they did.

I took the kids to a buffet, so they could eat whatever they liked and as much as they wanted. Traveling there, Gavin commented, "I bet we run into one of Dad's old students. They'll say, 'It's good to see you, Mr. Smith.' He'll call them by name, saying, "It's good to see you, too,--.""

After dinner, we decided to take in a movie. Jemal wanted to go to a new theater complex in my neighborhood. It was one of those places that had twelve movies showing within its facility.

Both the boys knew we lived in the same neighborhood where I worked. So far, I had been extremely lucky not to have any of my students seek revenge on me, as I was the one suspending or expelling them from school, but Thank God, they never vandalized my home. I think the students respected me. Perhaps it was because I never disrespected them—even when they were in trouble. *Dislike the behavior, not the child* was my rule of thumb. They never even toilet-papered my house.

"Jemal, I don't want to place you or Gavin in jeopardy of being harmed. I don't want a plastic cup of soda-pop thrown at the back of my head." Nevertheless, Jemal was very disappointed when I explained why we would not check out the new theater.

Going to a different theater, out of our neighborhood, worked just as well. Gavin was right. While standing in line, one of my former elementary students approached and greeted me. I called him by name, returning my regards.

While returning my boys back to their mother on Sunday afternoon, I noticed the dead roses still on the washing machine. This time Elaine said, "Why'd you give me the dead flowers? Is it your way of being cute?"

I told the boys to go inside before I answered. "Elaine, I did not put the flowers there. They are not mine. I have no idea where they came from." I didn't tell her, "Elaine, my seeing them, too, hurt my heart a little. I could have speculated a thousand scenarios on who gave them to you, but I didn't. I simply let all maybes and perhaps go."

Several days later Elaine asked for forgiveness. She told me Gavin had barrowed the dried-out roses from a neighbor's house. He sat them on the washing machine.

With the releasing of that red balloon, I carried no ill feeling. I harbored no remorse or contempt. My previous supervisor at Las Vegas High School was right, too. I even laughed, thinking that at one time in my past I couldn't see myself living without Elaine. I was glad I learned to not be so dependent, to live a better, more complete life, standing on my own.

CHAPTER 48

Within no time, word got around school, "Don't do it. Mr. Smith will catch you." Their believing I was gifted and talented, my insightful magical powers discouraged a lot of misbehavior. "No, I'm not doing it; he'll nail every one of us."

I was honing my craft, learning to be a top-notch detective. Solving each case became easier as I learned more about the school community.

After realizing the school had its manipulative instigators, its snitches, fighters, thieves, cigarette smokers, experimental and social drinkers, alcoholics, drug-users and dope dealers, and gun and knife-toting characters, the job became a cinch. After learning of an incident, I ascertained who was at school that day. I began by weeding out the unlikely suspects, and then I would conquer and divide. Taking the least bit of evidence, I added to it, building a case against the alleged perpetrator.

For example, I could take the empty cigarette package given to me by one student, and hold it in front of another smoker. Looking him directly in his eyes, I'd say, "All I want is the truth. I'll be easier on you if you give me the truth." These strategies helped me to put more puzzle pieces together until I determined the guilty party.

One day, a transmission came over my radio. "Two boys are making out in a stall in the 400-area boys' restroom." I went to the entrance. I removed my shoes because I did not want the tapping of the hard heels to give my surveillance away.

By the time I entered the room I could hear the loud panting coming from a stall. I tippy-toed up to the stall and hoisted my chest above the door. *Whew, it's only a boy and girl making out!* Although they were engaged in full intercourse, I was relieved. I did not have to tell their parents two boys were making out.

The dean's position was an excellent job for learning diplomacy and tact. For instance, I discovered it's much easier to have the mother of the daughter attend the Required Parent Conference than to have the dad whenever I had to tell I caught the daughter copulating with a male student on campus. In the reverse, I'd have the dad in to discuss his son's behavior.

I found a few guns and knives in lockers. Students concealed them on their body, in their purse, or in book bags. While in my office, I had the students remove them. I didn't want to wait for the arrival of school police. Too many things could go wrong. Seeing the policeman, the child could spook and quickly draw the weapon out in haste. I figured it was better if I received the weapon. It wasn't that bad. I was a buff ex-Marine. The junior high students were smaller than I. I figured with my careful watch on them, especially their hands, I could easily drop kick them or body-slam them to the floor and take the weapon away before they could use it.

Once, I was more concerned with the look on my secretary's face than I was with taking a pistol from a student. Each time I'd get a weapon from a student, I'd have an adult witness present, in my office. This was to prevent a child from lying, perhaps saying something later like, "That's not mine. Mr. Smith planted that gun in my book bag. He's making this story up."

After conducting a complete investigation regarding an alleged loaded pistol on campus, I escorted a male student to my office. Following my principal's orders, I didn't call school police back in those days—kids were more compliant to adult authority. Besides, I had a student-to-educator relationship with this child. I knew his personality well. Moreover, I knew I could easily over-power him and take the weapon away—before he got it out—if needed. Entering his classroom, I didn't go to the teacher. With my eyes permanently glued to his hands, I quickly approached from behind, leaned over and whispered, "Get your backpack, and come with me. Focusing on his hands all the way, I escorted him into my office and asked my secretary, Betsy, to come inside as we passed her.

Briefly looking him directly in his eyes, I demanded, "Take your thumb and index finger, nothing else, and slowly remove the pistol from the inside front portion of your waist." (This information I had gotten earlier from a student snitch—although, sometimes it came from parents.) I immediately shifted my attention back to his hands. "Now, ease the pistol out."

After quickly but carefully placing the weapon into my hands, I looked at Betsy. With mouth gaping, her eyes were bulging from their sockets. Once the situation was over, I apologized for the possible danger I had placed her in.

I don't remember how many guns, knifes, and brass knuckles I took away from students, but the count would have been alarming if the public had known.

Back then, school police were called in to take custody of the weapon, arrest the student, and transport the criminal to juvenile hall. Many times the police paraded the student in handcuffs through the cafeteria, especially during lunchtime. The officer wanted to demonstrate to other students the consequences of unlawful behavior.

I never shared any of the unlawful incidents in monthly deans' meetings within the district. I always gave the impression my school did not subscribe to any of that nonsense. We were, after all, the "best" junior high school in the district. Luckily, I didn't have to change the subject or lie. My colleagues never asked.

Betsy had an amazing talent for working her eyes—her expressions of insult, admonishment, or genuine care and concern complimented my style of discipline. Once, after I had met with a parent and child, the father held a set of false D-cup breasts to his chest. Although his son had worn them in a classroom, nowhere near Halloween or the beginning of November, his father sashayed in front of Betsy, smiling like what his son had done was no big deal—totally negating what I had said during the parent conference. Betsy's bitter eyes were a far better silent scolding than any counseling and consequences I ever provided to the son.

Long before the use of computers in the school, handwritten data was collected for year-end reports. I accounted for the number of suspensions by category, the number of expulsions, the number of arrests, and the total number of everything. To be in compliance with federal mandates, most of this data was identified by student ethnicity, as well.

At times I felt overwhelmed. Writing reports for this and reports for that, I saw myself writing for the rest of my life. In college, I knew exactly how many papers I would need to write based on each instructor's course syllabus. Relief flooded over me each time I'd knock one out of the way. But incidents continued, and so did the reports. Sometimes, I had to write a summary of an incident and submit it to my principal, who would present it to his boss by the end of the day. With reports for everything, I felt like I'd be writing un-ending, timely reports for the rest of my life.

As a busy person, my only salvation was that just as minutes ease into hours, hours slide into days, and days slip into months, I successfully survived my first year as a dean. Summer vacation was on its way.

CHAPTER 49

During summer break, Elaine decided to sell her house and move to Alaska. She had applied for and gotten accepted into a masters degree program in counseling at the University of Alaska. Although she told me it was too difficult to get into a program at UNLV, I choose to believe her real reason for leaving was to get far away from me. Ending a relationship when no children are involved is easier than the pain we chose to endure—constantly making decisions the best interests of the kids. Jemal did not share Elaine's enthusiasm for adventure. He did not want to run away. Gavin, the younger son, still needed his mother's closeness.

I pre-enrolled Jemal in Las Vegas Day School as it was relatively close to my house. He would not need to attend my school, and he could ride the bus to and from home.

I spent as much time possible with both boys over the summer, taking them both deep-sea fishing in Mexico and freshwater fishing in Utah.

We went to Disneyland, Knott's Berry Farm, and Magic Mountain's Six-Flags whenever we weren't fishing. I even took them up to Uncle Bruce's for a few days on his "Ranch." I wonder if Elaine ever felt a little jealous because I spent my time mostly having fun with the boys.

Summer finally came to an end, and Elaine took off with Gavin.

It must have been as equally hard for Jemal as it was for me, our not having Gavin with us. I don't think I ever discussed the pain of the separation with Jemal although he had an equal hand in making his choice of staying with me instead of going with Elaine to Alaska. Hearing her news, he said, "I'm not going. I'm staying here with Dad and finishing my eighth-grade year at Las Vegas Day School." My thinking was neither of us was ready for an honest discussion at that point in our lives. It could not have been one of the happiest years of Jemal's life—the separation coincided with the difficulty of puberty. Perhaps Jemal, like me, simply accepted that year as one of the bumps that happens in the ride of life. We both had to accept life as it was. It would have served no purpose for either of us to have speculated on what might have happened to our family if Elaine and I had remained married. Not knowing any better, I endured the separation by myself—but physically with Jemal.

Other than myself, I would have lost it all. I'm strong, but I don't know how strong. Looking back, I wonder if Jemal's wisely, but innocently, choosing to live with me kept me from a nervous breakdown.

CHAPTER 50

With a student population of seventeen hundred, I breezed through my second year as dean of student discipline. I had everything in order. It was the same old job, but with different faces. One of my biggest challenges was learning the names of those student faces. Calling a child by name did wonders for getting him or her to abide by my directions.

Each morning I greeted my students as they got off of the school bus. "Good morning, Sally. Good Morning Jim. I hope you have a fantastic day."

One student in particular would look at me with anger in her eye every time I called her name. I decided I would not allow her evil looks to keep me from greeting her by name. "Good morning, Gloria. I hope you have a great day."

A few weeks into the greetings I had become conditioned. I knew what to expect from her. Nevertheless, I persisted, "Good morning, Gloria. Have a great day."

As a second-year dean, I learned more daily about running an effective school and about human behavior.

I worked on writing a report that historically, chronologically showed a student's misbehavior immediately after each incident, and then I used that report while conferencing with all concerned.

Sometimes, like whenever a student had been suspended three times, for up to ten days within a school year, I utilized the chronology to prepare the student and parent for my next, future student consequence—my recommendation for Alternative School placement until successful completion of that "Opportunity School" program. Although it rarely worked, my job as a dean was to get students to change their negative behavior. Somehow, I intuitively knew misguided children needed serious, long-termed counseling to help "Pied Pipe," and guide their acting out away. Nevertheless, I started with a little admonishment—like a warning, and then increase the punishment upon each new infraction. I utilized logical consequences, each time upping or increasing the ante after each refusal to abide by classroom and school rules, or district regulations and policies.

One day the principal entered my office, angrily looked me in the eye, and said, "Oh, so I don't have any real power in this school, huh? Everyone knows the dean runs the school."

Where is he getting this information? God knows, I've never implied or communicated this information to anyone. I was scared to death.

Then he smiled and said, "A parent told me you're the one who actually runs the school. I'm just a figurehead. Ronnie, you are doing exactly as you should. An excellent dean knows how to utilize the power of mystic."

Boy, did I feel great. Although I had to take paperwork home with me, I was out of school each day, early enough to meet Jemal by the time he arrived home.

I enjoyed helping girls re-establish friendships lost over some stupid boy. I loved helping them retrace their behaviors leading to the destruction of their relationships. Watching them cry and then hug each other in my office always gave me a little joy.

One day I had an angry parent conference with me. She blamed the teacher for her son's disruptive, rude behavior in a classroom. "Mr. Smith," she said in anger, and gritting her teeth.

"I'm going to make you angry, just to show you it can be done."

She preceded shaking her index finger at me, and then giving me "The Finger."

"Mr. Smith, I think you are the most selfish asshole I've ever seen. You never give the kids a chance. You're a Black, racist, motherfucker."

I did not stop her. I allowed her to continue her rant until she grew tired of it. I gave her no indication of what I was thinking.

Eventually, she stopped and said, "The reason my barking at you didn't work is because you are trained in these types of situations. Kids are not. They can be pushed to bad behavior by a bad teacher, Mr. Smith."

I didn't mention her child might have learned some things from her. *Why light a fire? A wise administrator may think it but would never say it,* resounded in my head. I unemotionally disagreed with her and explained the student—her child—is responsible for his own actions. No one can make him do anything.

One of my biggest insights came when I understood that many parents could not comprehend that they were in my office for their child. Often while talking to me, a parent would revert back to their own childhood time when they were in the dean's office for some misbehavior they performed. Seeing the parent as a child gave me an additional task to perform. Getting them to come back to the present was a difficult chore. With all this psychological stuff, sometimes I failed.

On the last morning of school, I gave my final greetings. "Good morning, Gloria. I know you're going to enjoy this day." I expected her usual frown.

Instead, she hit me with a smile. "Good morning, Mr. Smith. You have a good day, too."

I felt as though I had been pushed backwards. The emotional force of Gloria's delightful comments nearly knocked me to the ground.

CHAPTER 51

In September, Jemal and I flew up to Alaska to watch Gavin play in a Pop Warner's football game. The weather was something like 40 below zero. Gavin was a linebacker. He did a good job, and not that it mattered, his team lost the game.

Elaine and Gavin lived in a two-bedroom apartment. Inside, the temperature was pleasantly warm. She allowed me to sleep on the living room couch. I enjoyed Gavin and Jemal's constant hugging, roughhousing, and joyously sharing each other's companionship. But my relationship with Elaine was strained and as uncomfortable as the weather outside. Careful not to evoke an argument, I watched and calculated every word I chose. The two days we spent together seemed like a week.

Flying home, I did talk with Jemal. I shared my pain in having to watch the two boys live without each other. At the tender age of thirteen, Jemal's wise words struck me, and I'll always remember them.

"Dad, life is suffering. Sometimes, all you can do is quietly accept and endure the pain."

CHAPTER 52

That December I was furious. So he could share Christmas vacation with his brother and mother, I put Jemal on a plane to Alaska.

Seconds after watching the plane pull away from the gate, I wanted to release my anger onto something, onto somebody—mostly Elaine. But God was there to help me.

I turned to leave, and there stood my friend, Rosemarie. She wished me a Merry Christmas.

"What's merry about it?" I replied.

"What's wrong, Ronnie?"

"I just put Jemal on a plane to visit Gavin and Elaine. I'm very angry at Elaine right now. She put all of us in this terrible situation."

"Ronnie," Rosemarie continued, "I've just put my daughter on a plane to visit her father, my first husband before I married Allen. Calm down. It's going to be okay. Shit happens, but it happens for a reason. You'll get through this and you'll learn from the experience. Now, go home and enjoy the time away from work. Find something to be grateful about. It's Christmas."

I took her suggestion and went to L.A. over the holidays to be with my family and friends.

When I went to the airport to pick up Jemal, I got the treat of my life. Gavin was with him. Later that day, Elaine called to tell me she couldn't bare to separate them again. I never had a negative thought about her not taking the time to notify me earlier. I saw it as a gift, a great surprise. Looking back, I wonder if her behavior was a sign of something ominous, perhaps.

I enrolled Gavin at Las Vegas Day school so he could attend the same school as his brother. All went well concerning our family of three.

School came easy for both of my sons. Intellectually, they were well above average. They had the academic grades to prove it. But one day I got a letter in the mail from Gavin's teacher regarding something of concern. The letter read, "Gavin received a HAM for not submitting his homework. When I, asked him to write the reason why he failed to turn his homework in, Gavin wrote, 'BLA, BLA, and BLA.' I've enclosed his written statement with this letter."

"Gavin, what does, 'HAM,'" mean?"

"Homework Assignment Missing, Dad."

Holding the teacher's letter and Gavin's explanation in my hands, I asked, "Why did you write, 'BLA, BLA, and BLA?'"

"Dad, I could have given her twenty different reasons why I did not do my homework. I found the situation to be an excellent time for me to teach her a lesson. The fact of the matter is, I simply didn't do it."

"Well, since you could have come up with twenty different reasons for not doing the work, I want you to find one good reason. Write it on the HAM form and give it to your teacher tomorrow." But I didn't stop there. "Gavin," I added, "You were most discourteous to your teacher. In addition to the explanation, write an apology letter to her, as well. I want to see both of your papers as soon as you complete them this evening."

Then shortly after, my perfect son, Jemal, got into a heated argument with his bus driver, which resulted in Jemal's consequence being a two-week lost of bus-riding privileges.

Initially, he thought his misbehavior would cost him nothing—that I would drive both him and Gavin to and from school.

As a dean, I would often tell parents and myself, *If my own biological son had done what your child has done, I'd issue the same consequences.*

How wrong Jemal was when it came to his bus privileges. I held true to form. I had him walk to and from school those two weeks.

There was a part of me that felt sympathy for him—watching him struggle, carrying a fully loaded backpack. But I never told him that.

On the other hand, I did ask him when his bus privileges had been reinstated, "What did you think about having to walk each day?"

Smiling, he said, "Actually, Dad, I rather enjoyed the experience. It provided individual, quality think time and a tremendous amount of exercise."

CHAPTER 53

My Principal left the building January 1, 1990, to open a brand new school, Walter Johnson Junior High, located in the Northwest part of town.

I was elated when I found out he was taking me with him as his assistant principal. My start date would be March 1, 1990. The new school was scheduled to open in August 1990.

Surprisingly, a new dean of students came in to replace me in January. Obviously, someone made a mistake. He was early by two months. But I spent my time training the new dean.

The school having two deans only lasted one week. The new principal called me into her office and told me to move out of my office. She gave me a different office to perform my new duties—writing teacher evaluations until it was time for me to transfer.

I started my classroom observations and writing right away. Boy, was I pissed. Writing good, meaningful teacher appraisals was somewhat like writing quality lesson plans—but much longer, more detailed. It was so much easier being a dean—especially sharing the job with Mr. Thomas Whitson, my replacement, two of us doing the work of one.

I unloaded upon my former principal as soon as he called. I wanted him to know my fate, how horrible she was treating me.

Telling him how horribly she was using me. "She's got me writing teacher evaluations!" I barked.

He cut me off midstream. "Ronnie, I suggested the idea of having you write the evaluations. As the assistant principal, you'll write half of them in our school. You might as well learn how to write them now."

While trying to balance what he was saying with the anger I was feeling, "Yes, Sir," calmly, controllably flowed from my mouth.

Just when I was riding high, elated with myself, life pushed a pin in my inflated ego. A parent and her son entered my office late one afternoon. The boy looked like hell. His face was swollen and bruised. Obviously, he had been someone's punching bag. *Oh, no! What happened?* I wanted to ask, but something told me to keep my mouth shut—just listen.

"Look at my son," the mother said. "It's all your fault. This never would have happened if you had not put my son's name in your police report. He did the right thing, telling you about the thug who had a gun in his possession on this campus, but you carelessly put my son's well being into jeopardy. He nearly lost his life."

I did not know what to say. *What words could I use to ease her grief? Come on, now. I have to say something.*

"You assured him his telling would remain confidential. When that thug went to court, my son's name was revealed. You used it in your report. The judge explained to me all alleged criminals have the right to face their accuser."

"Ma'am, I wish the courts had summoned me. I know our district's student personnel director blacks-out all minor's names in all documents released to the public. I do not know why it didn't happen in this case. Probably the police work from different procedures. But I promise you this; I will never put another student-informant's name in any written report.

"And how will you get around that?"

"I'll simply put, 'Student wishes to remain anonymous,' wherever the name should go. I'm so sorry, and I promise, because of what I've learned from you, I will never use another child's name again."

Both the parent and her child left my office satisfied and smiling.

On March 1, I got out of Kenny Guinn Junior High School after writing over twenty teacher evaluations.

Like my principal, who took his secretary with him, I did the same.

CHAPTER 54

As the new school was nowhere ready for move-in, we worked out of a portable bungalow stationed at a nearby elementary campus. The principal, his secretary, my secretary, one counselor, and I occupied the building.

The counselor and I traveled to our feeder-schools to give presentations to our upcoming students and their parents.

While the counselor pre-enrolled students and built schedules for them, the principal and I interviewed perspective teachers and support staff. We, out of ignorance, did a terrible thing. We gutted our old school by taking all of the finest staff with us. Leaving only the less-than-average and average teachers behind, the district had to instate a new policy, which stipulated that no school could take more than thirty-three percent of staff from one school within a single year.

The principal had me design and layout all of the information to be printed onto the Pee-Chee student folder, which listed all of the class periods and times and gave a full, detailed description of the rules and consequences for all the infractions. It was also my job to develop most of our school's forms.

My anxiety continued a day or so before our weekly administrative meetings. *What's wrong with me?* Likewise, I had not found an answer for this uncomfortable feeling—probably because I didn't dare look—fearful of what I might find. Playing it safe, I remained stuck. Since I never asked the question of how do I face this unpleasant feeling, there was no need to propose an answer.

Every Friday afternoon, we went out to lunch and visited the school to see how much progress had been made on construction.

At that time, our Clark County School District was building nineteen elementary, and two junior high schools every year, plus two senior high schools every two years. I was overjoyed with my new position because prior to the growth, deans stayed deans for as long as five to six years.

CHAPTER 55

It seemed that Elaine's timing in asking for Jemal and Gavin to join her in Alaska came at an extremely busy time with my job. Although I was sad and didn't want them to be separated from me, I put them on a plane in June and threw myself into work.

This gave me time to work myself to death. Ignoring my grief, I put one hundred percent of my time into the job.

Only one problem occurred when the boys first moved away. Shortly after they left, Elaine called me and sobbed over the phone. "Ronnie, the high school I've enrolled Jemal in placed him in all remedial classes. What should I do?"

In retrospect, this should have been an easy one for Elaine—another glimpse into coming problems?

I immediately thought back to the award and recognition Jemal received in seventh grade from an educational firm called Rocky Mountain Testing. The letter from the organization read, "We are proud to inform you that your son, Jemal Tee

Smith, academically tested in the top five percent quartile of all seventh grade students nationally."

"Did they look at his previous test scores? Did the school request cumulative records from his previous schools?"

"Yes," she said. "But they say he's appropriately placed. What should I do?"

"Elaine, I hate saying this, but I believe his counselor racially profiled and categorized Jemal without ever looking at his academic abilities. His counselor probably saw a divorced, White mom; a Black dad not living in the home; and a Black child, who obviously, must be culturally and economically deprived. Where better to place him than in all remedial classes?"

"Ronnie, oh, my God, I think you are right."

"Elaine you have the right to request he be placed in their highest academic classes. Tell them you want to challenge all of his freshman course offerings. Call me later, and let me know how it works out." A few days later Elaine called. She wasn't crying. Jemal's classes had been changed.

CHAPTER 56

We finally took occupancy of the school the first of August, 1990. This was my busiest time. I was in charge of facilities, which meant I had to account for every item being moved into the school. The cafeteria served as the staging area for some of the equipment unloaded from the trucks. Using my organizational layout, movers carried and placed new teacher and student desks, bookcases, tables, chairs, computers, file cabinets, wardrobes—everything onto the cafeteria floor. I inventoried every delivered item. I placed signage everywhere, explaining what goes where, so the movers knew exactly where to redistribute each piece of pristine merchandise. I even hired campus security monitors working around the clock to ensure none of the boxes, especially the computers, were stolen during the night.

Department Chairmen volunteered to work without pay. They came in early to stamp our school name and number in each of the textbooks.

By August 24th we were ready to start the year.

CHAPTER 57

We had fifteen hundred kids, and just as I did while being a dean, I began learning the names of all the students on campus. I learned at least five names a day. I found it to be most practical calling a child by name. It helped to build mutual respect, and knowing names did wonders for decreasing the likelihood of misbehavior on our campus.

After getting away from that dean of student discipline job, I felt like I had been pardoned from hell. Dealing with negative behavior day after day wore at my positive attitude.

Slowly, I began taking on more and more duties and responsibilities—especially those the principal didn't want to do. But the job was always fun, never a dull moment.

I was the dean's immediate supervisor, so I took care of any appeal hearings that disgruntled parents requested. While meeting with the parents, I learned a valuable administrative lesson. Let the problem end with me. A good assistant principal resolves issues so they don't move on to the principal and waste his time. Working with negative issues was never overwhelming because I had balance.

Much of my time was spent with rational positive students and their parents, those who had kids in the National Junior Honor Society, Bridge-Builder's Club, Math Club, and so on.

At the end of the school year my principal was promoted. He left our school to become support staff director of personnel.

I did not have enough experience to become principal of the school. The associate superintendent of secondary schools assigned the school to someone with more experience.

CHAPTER 58

Elaine completed her masters degree in counseling at the end of two years. She and the boys returned to Las Vegas. She had depleted all of her money she made from selling her home in Vegas by renting an apartment in Alaska. She decided to rent an apartment across the street from Cimarron High School. This would make it easy for Jemal to go to school and baby sit Gavin until she came home from work. She took a counseling job at Cheyenne High School.

The timing was perfect. After my principal left our school at the end of the 1990-1991 school year, I had all the time in the world to spend with my children. Unlike the first principal of the school, the new principal never stayed on campus after official business hours. Exactly at "closing" time, he left. Both the staff and I found it frustrating with a principal who knew nothing about our school philosophy or school dedication and pride. I remained on campus a few hours helping teachers with their concerns or doing whatever paperwork I needed to complete. But my time on campus was nothing like the hours I put in while working with the inaugural principal.

And with this new principal, I never experienced any uneasy feelings in my gut prior to any of his administrative meetings.

In the fall, I spent my weekends fishing and camping with my children.

They had learned to snow ski while living in Alaska, so in the winter they asked me to take them skiing.

We went to Mount Charleston in my four-wheel Jeep. While driving up the mountain, I clearly heard Gavin whisper to Jemal, "I hope Dad likes it. Then, he'll take us skiing all the time."

Eventually, I bought snow skis for Jemal, equipping him with all the fashionable accessories and the same equipment for Gavin, including boots, a snowboard, and a very expensive case.

I told myself, *I'll get my gear later—when I'm better able to afford it.*

We were either at Mount Charleston or Brian Head Resort every weekend during the winter. I always rented my gear.

In late spring, we either fished at Panguich Lake in Utah, or I'd drive an additional hour North on Interstate 15 to fish at a place called Puffer Lake, next to Elk's Meadow. As the boys were too young to get behind the wheel, I did all the driving during our trips. I longed to have someone help me drive, and I swore I'd never fall asleep while driving. I vowed to never doze off to sleep, and possibly run off the road, harming or killing any or all of us.

Jemal talked me into buying him a deluxe float tube for the small reservoirs near Puffer. It came with a rod holder, high-back backrest, and attachable duck feet rubber swim fins.

While I drove during one of our trips, Jemal said, "Dad, please get us to Puffer before the break of dawn. I want to paddle out into the lake, cast my line before sunrise, when the sky is still dark grey."

It was 3 A.M., and I was exhausted, pushing myself. "I've got to pull over at the next rest area. Just let me sleep for an hour, Jemal."

"No, Dad. I want to fish in my tube before sunrise."

I pulled over anyway and tried to sleep, but I couldn't. I got up and completed the drive.

I pulled into the lake while it was still dark—just at the perfect time.

"Jemal, get out and fish. I got you here in time."

He was sleeping like a teenager during a growing spurt.

"Jemal, get out and fish."

"No, Dad. I'll get up in about an hour."

"The heck you will. I pushed myself to honor your request. I wanted to make you happy. Now, get your bottom up, your tube into the water, and your line into the lake," I demanded.

On our return trip home, Jemal pronounced, "Dad, I've been thinking, driving to Puffer is as far as San Diego. You could drive us there instead of always taking us to Utah. We could take a chartered boat to Catalina and Mexico."

I listened to him, and we spent most of summer fishing from chartered boats out of San Diego.

****

I worked with the new principal for one additional year before I was reassigned to Hyde Park Middle School to start a new magnet school for gifted math and science students. I was told I could not be the principal. The district needed me to be the assistant principal.

When it came time for me to leave at the end of the 1991-1992 school year, I found it interesting that Thomas Whitson, the Afro-American dean who replaced me at Kenny Guinn Junior High School, would now be replacing me as assistant principal at Walter Johnson Junior High. With Whitson's new assignment I started thinking, *Did the district not have enough Blacks for easy replacements? Was someone like the associate superintendent of secondary schools carefully monitoring and manipulating administrative assignments? Did he do this independently or collaborate with others?*

CHAPTER 59

Miss Gladys Goldstock,, my new building principal, and I had been assistant principals the same amount of time. But I wasn't bitter or resentful that she received the principal-ship of our school. After all, I knew that prior to her being an assistant principal, she had been the reading consultant for the district and worked in central office with the associate superintendent of secondary schools as his personal assistant. Working in that capacity certainly gave her experiences far broader than mine.

I remember the first time she invited me to visit the school. It was on July 1, 1992, after the previous principal and assistant principal had completely moved out. Compared to the new schools that both of us were leaving, Hyde Park Middle School was tired and run down. With its yellow cabinets, turquoise refrigerator, and stove in the break room, it looked like what it was—something leftover from the past. The school was built in the 1950's. The rooms, offices, classrooms, hallways, cafeteria, and gymnasium were constructed out of cinderblock. The lockers were dented and in need of painting. Nothing was shiny and new.

Gladys and I worked all summer long cleaning up the school, trying to give it an immediate facelift. We wanted parents to visually see that positive changes were already on the way. After school hours, I changed into old clothes and painted some of the areas. As I was in charge of facilities, Gladys had me place work orders for repairmen to retrofit the school. But that amount of extensive work took time and lots of planning. Very little actually got done.

I knew it wasn't true when I heard the rumor that was spread by a teacher. "The previous assistant principal made out with his secretary, right there, on that mustard-colored couch."

It couldn't be true. I worked in high school with his wife. Unlike his overweight, uncaring, unattractive secretary, his wife was personable, gorgeous, everything fine. Besides, she was a school counselor. I trusted her judgment. I referred all of my students with problems like pregnancy, rape, or potential suicide to her whenever they disclosed their personal secrets to me. *This teacher's got it wrong. He would never cheat on his wife, on that mustard-color couch sitting in front of his office.*

That sofa was one of the first pieces of furniture Gladys had me throw out. While doing so, I thought, *Perhaps the good looking, young teacher who started the rumor might have secretly wanted to have an affair with the assistant principal. He was a most attractive man. Maybe, denied by him, scorned, she wanted revenge.*

****

My mind took me back to the time I taught high school English. My students journaled everyday, the first few minutes of class. Because they were writing what they knew instead of one of teacher's assigned topics, this methodology helped to improve their work, while it also gave me time to take attendance and pass out graded work from the previous day. It also provided them extra points, which improved their overall grade in my class.

Over a period of time, I stopped requiring this writing. Even if I didn't read it, it was something I could be sued for if I did nothing to communicate the information to the proper authorities. The evidence, the writing was there—with my points clearly marked on top of each day's work.

I found myself reading their most intimate problems—like, "I'm pregnant, but my parents don't know it." Once, I read, "I stole my father's private plane on a weekend he was out of town. I flew it to LA and back without being caught. My friends and I went 'joy-flying' for the weekend."

With cases like these, it was difficult to tell my students, "Either you tell your parents, or I will. And your parents will have to call me to let me know you've given them your confession." I felt like I had severed their trust in me. But I was the adult and had to do what was best for both the child and myself. I thought back to the poem, "I have to live with myself, and so . . ." In the best interest of my career, I decided to stop my students from handing in their journals.

****

Becoming one of the first schools in our district to house a magnet school—an academic school within a school—helped me to rush some work orders through. The old, outdated, walnut veneer paneling in the principal's office was removed and replaced with an updated plastic drywall. Gladys and I both got new, modern desks.

My new, modern desk did not change my heartache over the loss of my old office in my previous school, however. In my last school, I had drywall instead of cinderblock. The walls were painted mauve instead of canary yellow. New gray carpet lay on the floor, and an oak desk—with matching bookcases and a credenza—filled the room. I knew I'd eventually get a new set of office furniture—even a newly retrofitted office. But being temporally stuck in the old nurse's office filled my heart with despair. Instead of having a large mirror hanging on the wall behind my desk, there stood a large Formica counter with an old wash-sink. The only good thing I had attached to my office was my own private restroom. Often, I'd put my head down on my desk and quietly sob, thinking what I had given up.

CHAPTER 60

There were times when I did leave school early to watch Jemal participate in his high school's wrestling tournaments in the fall and his springboard diving events in the spring. I felt good he was a well-rounded student, involved in his honors-level classes, participating in leadership and community-service clubs, and athletics—wow, athletics, too! I thought of swimming class when I was in college and how his physical strength had to come from my genes. He was doing so much more than I did at his age.

Gavin didn't care too much for school, although Elaine and I believed he was the smartest in our family. Ever since kindergarten, his teachers always wanted to hold him back—not for any academic deficiencies, but for social immaturity. He was disconcertingly strong-willed.

Not that we ever compared our kids, but Jemal was always the compliant child. Gavin continually tested or pushed beyond the limits.

One day, Gavin wanted a pair of rollerblades. I said, "No."

He talked me into going to a department store to at least check them out.

"Daddy, please let me get them. I'm not asking for the most expensive ones."

"No, Gavin," I said, "I'll buy them in a couple of days." I wanted to teach Gavin the lesson of waiting, not immediately getting everything he wanted.

"Daddy, please, please let me get them," he repeatedly begged as we walked out of the store.

In the parking lot he decided to use a different strategy. "Daddy, am I adopted?"

"No, why do you ask?"

"Last summer, you bought Jemal a five hundred dollar deluxe float tube, but you won't even buy me a hundred-and-fifty dollar cheap pair of roller skates."

"Good try Gavin, but it's not going to work. Wait until the weekend." Looking back, I don't think Gavin learned anything about patience while waiting, but I tried to teach him a good lesson. I didn't give in and allow him to persuade me otherwise.

Gavin's tenacity paid off in sports. He was a natural athlete—excellent in every sport he tried. When he was an infant, he loved for us to fill the bathtub. He opened his eyes wide, held his rubber ducky, and roll over and over like a crocodile trying to drown its prey.

While playing tee-ball, he always slid to first base when his team was at bat. During little league, while in the field, his coach assigned him two different positions—first base and catcher. He put Gavin wherever he was needed.

At four, Gavin choose competitive swimming. He was on a team coached by the Olympics gold medalist, Rowdy Gains. Gavin swam the American crawl, free-style, and the breaststroke with five and six year olds. He never lost a race.

"I've got myself a future Olympic gold contender," exclaimed Rowdy, but Gavin decided only to swim for a year.

While playing little league baseball, Gavin would either play first base or catcher. He was spectacular at both. One day while throwing the ball with him, Gavin made the comment, "You are scared of the ball, Dad."

How did he know that sports were not my forte?

At about age eleven, he got involved in BMX bicycle racing. Unlike me, he never lost a single race the entire time he competed. (Although I came in close to last, I still proudly display my trophy, which reads: NUMBER 1 BMX DAD Participant Nellis BMX 06/17/92.)

Jemal stayed with wrestling and diving his time in high school while Gavin eventually exchanged bike racing for ice hockey. He had played a little of that while living in Alaska.

It was cute watching Gavin skate at the peewee level. I even took on the position of League Commissioner. But by the time he moved to the bantam level, the parents, as spectators, became angrier, and the game became more brutal.

We traveled all over California, Arizona, and Utah in our red team jackets. One time, and I don't know why, but Gavin got angry with me. "Take off that jacket," he said. "You didn't earn it. You are living off of my laurels. Go earn your own sport jacket."

Just because Gavin had intestinal fortitude, and no one intimidated him, he became the "goon" on his team. During a game, his coach would always say, "Gavin, go take that player out. Go knock him on his ass." And Gavin would easily comply with the coach's instructions.

I was glad at the end of the season, when Gavin gave up hockey.

CHAPTER 61

C olor had been added to the original concrete so that all of the hallways throughout the school were a worn rusty red. Gladys tried to get the district to paint them, to brighten them up. The director in charge repeatedly denied her request. That left us to do the work ourselves. Every Friday afternoon after business hours, Gladys and I donned our painting clothes, gathered our gloves, brushes, and rollers, and then went to work, coating the long hallway floors satin, battleship gray. Repeatedly dipping into the five-gallon buckets, we painted until dark and then resumed the task on Saturday mornings.

Trying to find some humor in what we were doing, I called out, "What we got here, Miss Gladys, is a fixer-upper. And it looks like to me, it's going to take a hell of a long time to complete this task."

When we finished, the floors looked so good, they spirited us onward to spray-paint the outside of each and every locker—although the job was delegated solely to me.

If that wasn't enough, we pulled weeds, planted flowers, and trimmed shrubbery, too. By the end of the summer the place looked entirely different—like a woman was now in charge.

The weekend prior to the first day of school, Gladys and I went into every classroom, leaving a small care package on every teacher's desk. Using a monogrammed pencil, a piece of candy, a card, and a small bottle of apple juice, we wanted to show our teacher appreciation. We also took the time to quickly observe the physical learning environment of each room. It was easy to assume which teachers demonstrated talent and dedication. Unfortunately, it was just as easy to determine which ones did not.

Once school was on its way, we spent much of our time planning for the new school within a school—The Academy of Mathematics and Science at Hyde Park Middle School, which would open during the 1993-1994 school year.

We focused on the objective of having 200 gifted and talented sixth grade students pre-registered for the next school year. This meant advertising, interviewing, and pre-hiring the most qualified math and science teachers in the district. Every qualified person was entitled to an interview—including the math and science teachers currently teaching at our school. Our students would take English, social studies, and their other classes with the general population.

But their math and science classes would be one-and-a-half-hours long, compared to the regular fifty-four-minute classes.

While running our regular school, we created pamphlets, posters, and flyers. We visited all of the elementary schools in the evenings soliciting fifth grade students and their parents.

Application after application poured in. Our magnet school teachers designed pre-tests to determine which students would be selected.

Recruiting for our school, we continued holding meetings in libraries, churches, and other public places.

Gladys worked me hard, I never had time to experienced that uneasy feeling in my gut during any of her administrative meetings. *What was the difference in her administrative meetings opposed to my previous boss?* It really didn't matter—probably very little. Both excessively drove themselves and me. Maybe, being a little older and a little wiser, I could no longer blame others for my uncomfortable anxiety. Yet, I still wanted to believe that uncomfortable feeling came in subtle ways—it had to be deeply buried somewhere, but I was too busy with work to recognize it. In the end, because my old way of reasoning no longer worked, I gradually let it go.

Finally, the district began to support our facility requests. New ceiling and floor tiles started to replace the old soiled and stained ones in the rooms designated for the program. District workers applied fresh paint to the walls. New science tables and chairs filled the science rooms.

One purpose for the creation of magnet schools was to prevent massive "White-flight" out of old neighborhood schools. With this in mind, our district would provide bus transportation to any student enrolled in the program.

Because of the new facelifts, we could now give presentations at our school. During each meeting, we played into parental dreams. They could visualize this newly found fantastic educational salvation for their children. I felt part of something big.

CHAPTER 62

With all the additional responsibilities, I did not spend much time with my boys. I drove home many nights crying—exhausted from the work.

One night, during a telephone conversation with a friend, I fell asleep on the sofa. Hours later, I awoke with the handset in my hand.

I tried to make it to as many tournaments as possible to watch Jemal wrestle or dive. I had the time because Gavin had given up sports. It happened when he was involved in a wrestling practice program offered by Jemal's high school. The purpose of the program was two-fold. It supported community partnership and subtly gave coaches a look at the wrestling skills and talents of the brothers and friends of their current team members—a creative way of scouting for potential, future wrestlers. During this wrestling program, Gavin lost several bouts. Although we never talked about it, I believed his being a natural jock—winning at every sport he tried without exerting much effort—and then performing horribly as a wrestler broke his stride and spirit. All he saw was that he sucked. Not realizing he wasn't good at wrestling because it was completely new to him, he quit. He gave up sports altogether. Perhaps I was too busy, lost in my own problems and concerns. I don't know why I didn't tell him that all he needed was practice, that practice, practice, and more practice would have improved his performance.

Elaine and I both insisted that our sons be involved in some kind of afterschool activity, just to keep them busy enough to stay out of mischief.

Gavin started learning to play the up-right contra bass. In addition to taking the class in school, I bought him his own instrument and paid for private after-school lessons. One evening, I attended his school's orchestral concert. The "musicians" played "Ode-to-Joy." I felt proud seeing Gavin dressed in formal wear. He looked so debonair!

I was extremely impressed with Gavin's orchestra teacher. After the concert, I had Gavin introduce me to her. Thinking our magnet students might be interested in taking orchestra as a class, I persuaded Gavin's teacher to interview for a teaching position at my school. It worked. She took the job for the upcoming year. But I never told Gavin what I had done.

I don't know if my putting in long hours at my school had anything to do with it, but my "perfect" Jemal got a Required Parent Conference summons. His English teacher caught him shooting staples into the ceiling with a rubber band.

During the conference I started thinking, *I wonder if Elaine's extra pressure on Jemal had anything to do with his rebellion?* She insisted that Jemal be a member of National Honor Society, Alpha-Beta Society, Key Club, and more—in addition to his playing sports. With her being a high school counselor and all, she knew he would need all the attributes possible to get a college scholarship.

After the conference, knowing bribery would get me everywhere, I promised Jemal a car when he turned sixteen. My only stipulations were that he earned As or Bs, and not get any "Unsatisfactory in Behavior" marks on his report cards.

Elaine and I discussed Jemal's RPC. I don't think she tried to bribe me. Elaine was always outspoken. If there is such a thing, she wasn't a manipulative woman. "Do you think apartment living is the cause of Jemal's acting out?" she asked. She told me she wanted to move out of the apartment complex and into a home. She asked me if I would loan her ten thousand dollars for the down payment.

I gave the money to her—not for her, but for a decent home for my children.

CHAPTER 63

Over the summer, Miss Gladys and I continued helping the custodians clean the school. Knowing parent satisfaction was a priority, it was essential to keep the facility sparkling.

Since the district still would not approve our request to re-paint and tidy-up the battleship gray hallway floors, Gladys and I did it again, all by ourselves. As this was a second-coat, the painting moved much faster.

Opening day in August came in no time. We were off to a good start.

Middle schools did not have a policeman assigned to their campuses. Supervising our campus monitor and our dean of student discipline, I was responsible for heading School Security.

One day, while Gladys and I walked a hallway, a short, extremely overweight sixth-grader came from out of nowhere. He mounted her back. I wanted to laugh as she twisted and bucked, trying to throw him off. *Ride her, Cowboy!* jumped into my mind. But I quickly looked at him with great disapproval.

"Don't make me take you off her back," was all I needed to say. He immediately dismounted.

Then there was a time I walked the hallways while classes were in session. They were as quiet as a cemetery in the middle of the night. At one particular spot, I heard the sound of ticking. I followed the nerve-wracking sound to the inside of a locker. *Oh, my God,* I thought. *It's a bomb!* For some reason the ticking seemed to get louder.

I calmly walked to the principal's office because I did not want to use the radio. *I'm not triggering off this thing.* Besides, I learned a long time ago never to run or act panicky. People seeing me could become frightened. As a leader, it's essential to always portray a demeanor of calmness and control—even if it involved a bomb!

After explaining the situation to her, we both walked to the emergency site. "What do I do, Miss Gladys? Do I call the police?"

"No, just take your key and open the locker."

As quickly as it took me to remove my keys from my belt-clip, I looked around and she was gone—nowhere in site. *Just be calm, Ronnie. You can do this.* I did not think about myself. War had taught me to do what I had to do. My only concern was the children and teachers in the immediate area. *What if the bomb goes off?*

I turned the key, opened the locker door, and there it was—a tape in a cassette player had run its course. The player did not shut off. The tape continued to turn, making the clicking sound.

Whew! Thank God. My blood pressure began returning to normal.

CHAPTER 64

It seemed like each year Miss Gladys would add more duties and responsibilities onto my job description. The 1994-1995 year provided nothing different. I was responsible for supervising half the teachers on our staff, most of support staff—the custodians, secretaries, cafeteria manager—and more. I was in charge of running almost all the operations of the school, managing student activities, creating the yearly course catalog from which students would choose their classes, the school-wide calendar, facilities, security, textbooks, teacher appreciation, school transportation, and more. She could have given me more duties. I would not have minded. I needed to learn everything, all school operations, so that one day I could be the principal. But she didn't.

Gladys supervised the other half of our teachers, all of the counselors, and the librarian. She constructed the entire school's student schedule, putting all of the kids' names and the classes they would need into a computer program called SASI—Schools Administrative Student Information. She took complete control over the school budget and wrote our annual school's improvement plan, which had to be submitted to her boss for approval.

We shared planning teacher training activities and parent advisory council meetings. Although I wanted to build the students' schedules, just so I'd know how to do it, I was glad she performed this task because it took so much time and demanded great accuracy.

Unlike my male principal who had hired me as his dean of students and his assistant principal, Miss Gladys taught me a lot of "womanly" things, like how to set eye-catching tables for teacher appreciation breakfasts and luncheons. She bought two stainless-steel champagne fountains—the kinds with beaded chains and angelic babies posing at the top. Not only did we utilize the fountains for teacher events, but we also used them for open houses. Gladys taught me how to crease the four corners of the ironed linen table clothes—the ones she bought boasting our school's colors. She taught me how to twist the center of the colored napkins, too, to compliment the pretty doilies. We never purchased packaged food. Gladys would have each affair catered. With her leadership, I learned a lot about petit fours and other Italian and French pastries. For open houses she would buy donuts from Chef Cain, the instructor at our Vocational High School. "Ronnie," she'd say, "I buy the petit fours to support the culinary program and because they look exceptionally good."

She was right about the looks. Chef would place white powdered doughnuts on a large, commercial baking sheet. Then he'd have his students pipe a dollop of pink crème in the center to cover the hole. Finally, they would carefully place a maraschino cherry on top. Chef would also have his students decorate brown, coconut, and crumbed doughnuts with a dollop of chocolate crème with a pecan-half on top. His last doughnut creation was a chocolate covered doughnut with a dollop of almond crème and a walnut-half on top. Yes, Miss Gladys was right. The doughnuts impressed everyone. But to me, the dough was tasteless and stale.

I remembered the life-lesson my company commander taught during the time I spent in the Marine Corps. "Pay special attention to the little things. If you don't, they'll get you into trouble every time. The big issues will take care of themselves. It's the little things that will bite you in the ass." To increase my leadership skills—my management repertoire—Miss Gladys added her keen insight regarding paying special attention to detail. She discussed my need to further focus in on the little things and add this tool to my bag of administrative strategies. It was with her that I learned the importance of managing with compassion and to have the courage to follow my visualizations through, until they become actualized.

One morning after learning that our dean's secretary had a dozen roses delivered to her front desk, not from her husband, but by a flirtatious bus driver, Miss Gladys came to my office, as she often did, and said, "Here, come follow me." With her heels clicking on the concrete flooring, she walked with determination.

When we arrived at the office, there was no one there except the secretary. "Where did you get these roses?"

"From a bus driver," replied the secretary.

"How well do you know him?" Gladys asked. "Is he a relative or a close friend?

Puzzled, she replied, "I don't even know him. I think he wants to get to know me."

"Not on my watch. Not while you are working with me." Miss Gladys scooped the roses from the vase, and angrily threw them into a nearby trashcan. "Young lady, you might not understand, but I'm saving you from years of future grief."

After returning to her office, she sat me down and stated, "Ronnie, change comes with a price. Even though they want to see it, the people directly affected by the change don't want it. They fear it. As you will one day lead a school, ask yourself, 'Do you have the courage to effect needed change?'"

Wow, I was learning from a lady, a pro. I followed her all the way—right into a funeral home.

"Ronnie, please understand the importance of leading with compassion. I'm ordering flowers for the deceased dad of our campus monitor. We'll attend the viewing this evening to show our respect."

We entered the mortuary early and went straight to the coffin. No one else was there. While looking at the body, we commented on how embalmment destroys any family facial resemblance after our campus monitor. "No, he doesn't look anything like Ernest," I said.

"So young, how sad his early, untimely death," Gladys remarked.

We were paying attention to the smallest details while reading the cards on the floral arrangements, searching for ours.

Finally, not finding them, we gave up and left—only to see Ernest entering the mortuary, as we were about to leave.

"Thanks for coming," he said, as we stopped to give our condolences. "Here, let me take this opportunity to personally introduce you to my family. It will only take a minute."

Gladys and I looked at each other—puzzled, but we played it off.

Once we got inside the "right" parlor, I was so dismayed at what Miss Gladys had taken me through. Our large splay of flowers was there, and the deceased resembled Ernest.

CHAPTER 65

As I continued developing my leadership skills, and having more work piled on me, the more I learned about how to cope with stress. I was on thought-overload one weekend as I drove my sons to Brian Head. *I've got to finish all of my teacher evaluations and write a grant for teacher articulation among the elementary, middle, and high school math and science magnet schools. I've got to box up and complete requisitions to have the outdated, antiquated textbooks stored in an unused hallway removed from our campus. I've got to plan and teach a lesson on staff development, teacher in-service training day.* While driving farther and farther down the highway, I continued replaying this tape in my head. Then, all of a sudden I thought, *Wait a minute. I'm not in school now. I'm going skiing with my boys. School is for school, and vacation is for having fun, living in the present.* Jemal was stretched out in the back seat, fully asleep. Gavin napped in the front passenger seat. As I drove past the splendorous, colorfully lighted Oasis, a magnificent hotel and casino in Mesquite, Nevada, I thought, *I wish I had someone to help me with the driving. I can't take a break to just relax and watch the view. How neat it would be if I, too, could sleep.*

I decided to spend some quality time with Jemal as we rode the chair lift together. First, I took time to compliment him on his ski outfit. I told him how cool I thought he looked in his matching colors. Next, I complimented him on his skiing form and technique—masterfully he moved his waist from side to side, flying down the mountain. Finally, nearing the top of the run, I asked him if he had anything on his mind that he wanted to discuss with me. "Let me put it another way," I even said. "Have I done anything lately to disappoint you, Son?" Although we shared a lift seat off and on all day I don't think we ever discussed one, single problem or issue.

While riding with Gavin, I complimented him on his courage. "Man, you'll never see me locked into snowboard boots. There's no binding. You don't pop free. Gavin, I'm proud of how you will try something new. I'm proud seeing you ride your snowboard." Likewise, I offered to discuss any issues or problems, but Gavin never took me up on sharing his feelings. It hurt me that I had taught my boys to be just like me—to keep their feelings buried deep inside.

And then, just when I thought I had done something good, spending time with my boys, taking them on the skiing trip, ugliness seemed to pop up its awful head.

Gavin was now attending Walter Johnson Junior High School. During his seventh grade year, he did something stupid and was issued a Required Parent Conference. Whatever he did was rather insignificant because I can't remember his infraction. My female principal, Gladys, had taught me a lot about middle-school-aged children. For example, they will cuss, not because they are vial or lowlife. "They are just young people experimenting with something new." I think this is why Gavin got the RPC.

During the conference, I was rather impressed with the dean of students holding the meeting. She seemed to have Gavin's best interest at heart. Then, while ending the conference, she said, "Thank you, Mr. Smith for attending. Gavin can return to school tomorrow morning."

"Thank you," I said returning her courtesy.

"Oh, by the way," she added as we were getting up to leave, "I only hear excellent things about the job you are doing at Hyde Park. I hope you will get your own school soon. You deserve it, Mr. Smith."

Gavin threw a tantrum in the office. "See, I hate this. It's always about you. You always get the attention, even when I'm in trouble. I wish sometimes I could be the one in the spotlight."

Not wanting to exacerbate the situation any further, I excused Gavin and myself from her office and left the school with Gavin as fast as I could.

I've always wanted my sons to walk with the rhythm of my being or stronger—to have a more confident, resounding beat. I never wanted to be the father my dad was to me. While walking to the parking lot and driving Gavin home, I said, "Gavin, that hurt me, too, when your dean started talking about me instead of keeping the conversation focused on you. She's got it wrong. The very day you came into my life both you and Jemal became the center stage of my life. I love both of my sons, and I put the two of you first in my life."

A few days later, I did something foolish. It wasn't that I was trying to buy his love. How well I knew I already had that. It continued gnawing at me that Gavin felt I was stealing his spotlight. One afternoon, after school, I took him to the music store and bought him a full set of drums. As he spent the weekdays with his mom and only weekends and some holidays with me, we took the drum set to Elaine's house. I told Gavin he could bring the drums to my house on the weekends because I wanted to fully support his musical genius, giving him every opportunity to explore his talent. After all, his private music teacher had told Elaine that Gavin had both the intelligence to understand complicated music theory and talent in playing not only the contra bass but other instruments. Elaine didn't see it my way. Boy was she ever angry with me and raised all kinds of Cain. "Ronnie, how could you do such a thing without first asking me?"

"What but for the child, Elaine? What but for the child?" was all I said on my way out the door. Despite Elaine's anger, I knew for certain that Gavin, while playing his drums, certainly got to be in the spotlight, on center stage.

CHAPTER 66

My students at Hyde Park Middle School, unlike my biological children, rarely kept their feelings to themselves. One day while standing duty in the courtyard during the kids' end-of-lunch period, one of them—a dark chocolate boy—purposefully said loud enough for me to hear, "That nigger thinks he's so cool, standing in his polyester suit."

Taking his comment personally, I moved over next to him, opened the inside of my coat and asked him to read the tag inside.

"One hundred percent wool."

"Read it again," I said. I wanted to teach him a lesson in respect. "Next time, don't assume anything about me. I'm always better than that." What got me was I didn't know why I let his comment get to me. Perhaps his negative comment triggered that deeply hidden feeling inside, that horrible, overpowering, energy-draining feeling that screamed, *I'm not good enough*.

I wasn't the least bit aware that when I know that I'm not this or that, the lengths I go overboard, trying to convince myself otherwise.

When the drivers from our district's warehouse came to pickup the hundreds of boxes I had stored in a locked, unused hallway, they laughed with one another. "Yep," one of them commented, "The last time I picked up this amount of books was about ten years ago. Some nut had boxed them up at Las Vegas High School. There were over a hundred and fifty cartons."

Remembering all the work I had put into gathering, inventorying, and filling out requisitions to have the books discarded, I didn't think his comment was the least bit funny. I wanted to tell him off. But instead, I took a softer approach. "Yeah, I'm the one who boxed up all those books back then at Las Vegas High School, too."

This was one of the moments in my teaching career I finally got it. I realized the importance of not taking any of my schoolwork personally. It was better just putting on an act, while wearing the many different hats. I learned whenever I took an incident personally, it usually ended in my disappointment—the more detached, the further I removed myself, the clearer I saw, the better the outcome.

I remember spending one Friday evening and all day Saturday painting the teacher's lounge. Sunday, Gladys and I arranged the new furniture she had purchased. In addition, to the new tables and chairs, she bought new sofas, coffee tables, love seats, end tables, and chairs and ottomans—complete living room sets.

I walked into the lounge Monday afternoon, a few minutes before the end of school, only to see bus drivers sprawled all over the furniture, with cigarettes hanging from their lips.

Since old habits are hard to break, I lost it. "Oh, no you don't," I yelled. "This is not your flop house. Get up and sit on the furniture right."

"Quit talking to us like we are your children," one of the drivers squawked. "We're not kids."

"Then quit acting like them," I replied completely out of breath and storming out the door.

Although nothing further was ever said about the incident that was the last time I ever took a school-related situation personally.

CHAPTER 67

L ife seems to always be filled with irony. Just when I felt at my worst, thinking I needed to have better judgment and more self-control, I found I was selected for the 1993-94 Assistant Principal Award for the State of Nevada.

Better yet, I got to spend a week in Oakbrook, Illinois, at the University of McDonald's, who cosponsored the award with NASSP—the Nevada Association of Secondary School Principals.

There was live music, fine dining, and sensational table settings everywhere I turned.

As I walked into the first session of the symposium, I thought, *Shoot, I'm going to enjoy this stay. I'm going to sit in the very back, take few notes, and do as little as I can. This is time for me to relax.* As I walked further into the conference room, my feet kept going—right down to the front row, in the middle of the room. I thought about my understanding of educational research regarding seat selection. *If a student can sit anywhere he wants in the classroom, the ones thirsting for knowledge will always choose center front row seats. It's because most traditional teachers unconsciously spend most of their lecture time in this general area.*

We witnessed excellent speakers throughout the week, including the National Secretary of State for the Board of Education. He presented us our certificates. Two young ladies, who worked in the human relations department on the McDonald's staff, gave an interesting account of the lawsuit with the lady alleging that she burned herself because the coffee was far too hot. I'll always remember Stephen Covey giving each recipient a copy of his book and asking us the question, "Where do we see ourselves ten years from now?"

There were bus rides and special tours all over the great city. We visited the Art Institute of Chicago, the Sears Tower, and for some strange reason, a place called Market Street. *Why in the world are we seeing Market Street? This area reminds me of the poorest part of a third-world community. Why show us this dire poverty?* It's no place to be proud of. I never found out why they took us there.

In my mind, the black tie event at the John Hancock building made up for Market Street. We had cocktails in the lounge on the 96th floor and dinner in the Signature Room, on the 95th level. With everyone socializing in formal attire, except Ronald McDonald, I ordered tonic water with lime. The ambiance made me feel a soft drink would not be enough.

If memory serves me correctly, McDonald's gave us one hundred dollar gift cards and a free afternoon to shop in Chicago. But the best parts of the experience were the lobster and steak dinners, the live music and karaoke, and dancing most of the nights. I had myself a ball.

CHAPTER 68

The first three days of the 1994-1995 school year I learned quickly how to deal with the news media. We had about thirty buses transporting our students to and from school. About twenty of those buses carried our magnet students to and from various locations all over town.

A few parents were upset at how long it took for the buses to leave the school at the end of the day. I had worked out a system with the drivers to increase their pick-up efficiency. Each bus had a large sign in its front window showing its bus number and the general area where it delivered students. Each bus parked in the same spot each day. The students and their parents were provided this information. Yet some parents remained extremely impatient. Some called the news media to voice their exaggerated complaint.

One afternoon, as I supervised the bus parking lot, I saw news vehicles, news people, and cameramen everywhere. One newscaster had the audacity to shove a microphone in my face. "Are you the assistant principal in charge of bussing at this magnet school?" she asked.

"Yes, Ma'am," I replied.

"Please take me to the bus that goes to Henderson."

All I could think was, *What if I can't find the bus on first try? I'm not going to make a fool out of myself. That's all the parents need to see on T.V.* I searched my mind quickly for a strategy. Immediately I said, "Ma'am, I'd like to do that, but I don't have time. I've got to help the children who are still having trouble finding their bus." I walked away and embraced the nearest "lost" child to me saying, "I'd love to help you, but my children come first." Since there was no sensationalism, no story, nothing regarding our bus issues ended up on T.V.

CHAPTER 69

The rest of the year went fairly easy. I had my routine down to a science. Most of my paper work with annual forms and reports consisted of my simply cutting and pasting information on the computer. The campus was sparkling clean. All I had to do was stay on top of the head custodian, making sure he kept his staff always cleaning. I had taught him to carry a small pocket notebook to remind him of special tasks requested by the principal and me. I had acquired a lot of excellent training from all of my administrators in "prior, proper planning," executing those plans and evaluating their results. I knew how to run a first-rate, quality school. I managed all of my duties and responsibilities the way a music conductor would "play" his symphony.

On the evening of May 4, 1995, I was surprisingly promoted to the position of Principal of Grant Sawyer Middle School. I didn't have time to pack. The job would start the following day. I told Miss Gladys I'd come by every night to clear out my stuff.

As a going away gift she presented me with a long, slender, golden pen housed in a glass-base holder; a name plaque saying, "RONNIE TEE SMITH," which was mounted on thick, clear glass; and a glass business card holder. In addition to a card, she gave me a solid glass heart. The card said, "Thank you for your service. Take this heart. You are going to need it. Hold it during those times when your administrative duties become lonely and difficult. Remember, you're appreciated. I'll always have your back."

CHAPTER 70

My first day at Grant Sawyer Middle School felt like I had returned home. The school was built in 1994 with the same construction plans as Walter Johnson, where I completed my first assistant principal-ship. Built with rough, brown brick, lots of glass, and copper siding, the building brought back pleasant memories as I drove up to the school. I wore my teal sport coat, the one I had purchased while at Walter Johnson, because it matched all of the exterior doors. I loved all of the soft, mauve and lavender pastel colors throughout the facility.

As I walked into my office, the new oak furniture brought comfort to my soul. I sat in the high-back swivel chair. Placing my elbows on the curved armrests, I thanked God for the promotion and the return to a familiar peaceful environment on my favorite side of town. My school was only eight blocks from my house.

I met the assistant principal, Mr. Bill Appleton. He gave me a tour of the school while introducing me to the staff and faculty. That's about all we did on my first day. *It's important for me to remember names and faces*, is all I thought about.

Although both schools were the same design, Sawyer was different from Johnson.

By 1994, the district was practically out of bond money. It didn't have the entire amount to construct a full facility, but needed a school in my neighborhood. Out of necessity, Sawyer rose—erected as a half school. As I walked the campus during each passing period, I marveled at its size. The classrooms were standard dimensions, but the library and cafeteria were reduced to half-size. Although the locker rooms were small, the gymnasium, with its sparkling wooden floor, was full-sized.

I was used to running schools with populations well over one thousand. Sawyer would be no different. The only exception was it was on a year-round schedule—something entirely new to me. One third of the students, teachers, and staff took their "summer vacations," every twelve weeks. This meant continuous schedule changes, having them rotate in and out of different rooms. *This must take enormous creativity and loads of careful planning to keep up with the location of everyone.*

Knowing that the one who is doing the actual work is the one who truly knows what is going on, my assistant principal was greatly relieved when I told him, "Bill, from now on, I'll take the responsibility for developing the year-round schedule—who teaches what, when, and where."

I also took away Bill's responsibility for creating the master schedule, building class periods, placing students in them, and assigning teachers to the classes. Since my previous principal had always done this work, I eagerly wanted to do it, thinking, *If I lose my assistant principal, who will train his replacement? I need to know how to perform this task. Besides, it's the best way to definitely learn the names of all students and faculty. I'll even know by heart where to find them without having to look them up in a computer program or on a paper document.*

As I began to learn the school, I discovered there wasn't one Afro-American, other than a male physical education teacher, on our faculty. *This will have to change,* I placed into the back of my brain. *Why is it that typically, Blacks teaching academic subjects like English and mathematics are rarely employed in affluent, suburbia schools? Oh, no, this has got to change*!

Not that I had any Black kids attending Sawyer.

There were only two. But from the time I first entered Clark County School District in Las Vegas, I started developing this notion that not only am I teaching students, but I'm also teaching multicultural education to teachers, parents, and everyone I meet. They have to first see me as a Blackman. They're kidding themselves if they say they don't. *What stereotypical thoughts about me first travel through their heads?* I wanted people to see me as a highly educated, articulate, confident, dignified, self-assured, atypical Blackman—if there is such a thing, like that security guard at the plane factory thought.

Anyway, loads of thoughts started occupying my mind. *I'll not let this community see me bring this school downward. I'll show them. This Blackman is going to greatly improve this school. No, they will not satisfy any stereotypical, racially based "less-than" first thoughts.*

Then I began thinking about Durango High School, a newly built school just down the street. Why is it the district placed a Blackman, one of the top leaders in my opinion, as principal at Durango. In fact, he opened the school in 1994. *Wow, two Black men were running schools in a neighborhood with homes worth fifteen million dollars or more. Why is that?* I proudly thought.

CHAPTER 71

As I assumed my new position at Sawyer, Jemal was just about ready to graduate from high school. My bribery, I like to superficially think, had gotten me everywhere. He was matriculating with mostly As and no Cs on all of his report cards. And as promised, I bought him a vehicle when he turned sixteen—an old, canary yellow, 1955 Chevy truck. It featured a rounded window in the back of the cab.

Thinking back about that truck, I had first discussed it with Elaine. Our family went to see it. We all agreed it would be a good purchase for Jemal. I liked it because of the price. The owner was letting it go for two thousand bucks. I also liked it because it gave me an opportunity to start moving past my pain. Risk-taking was still new to me, put buying the yellow truck was a good way to let go and grow. Like me, it had dents in it, but it ran like a champ. Elaine liked it out of concern for Jemal's safety. A truck built out of solid steel rode like a tank. It wasn't his safety I worried about. I didn't want him in a collision because that tank could totally destroy the other driver's car and maybe, possibly end their life. Both of our sons adored the truck. With this new privileged freedom came more responsibility for Jemal. Gavin, Jemal's special passenger, enjoyed riding shotgun. Both delighted in having transportation of their own.

****

Because of Elaine's persistence in demanding that Jemal remain an active member of many of his high school's leadership clubs, his chances of getting into one of the finer universities greatly increased. With her being an experienced high school counselor and having a post-grad degree in the field, she also made him apply for all kinds of scholarships.

How proud I was of my son. He earned a ten thousand dollar scholarship from the Golden Nugget Hotel and Casino, a scholarship from The Black Engineers' Association of Las Vegas, and acceptance into Yale University or The United States Army Academy, WestPoint, in New York.

Elaine took off from work so she and Jemal could visit both Yale and the Academy before he made his decision.

When they returned home, I remember him saying, "Dad, I know you don't have the money to send me to Yale, but that is where I'd like to go. Since you don't have the finances, I'll gladly go to the Army's Academy."

I knew he wasn't trying to con me with his statement. I knew he was genuinely sincere. How proud I was that my son had achieved an invitation to accomplish something that most people, especially Blacks, rarely, seldom got. I knew that education opens doors to a special quality of life that few will ever obtain. I was happy for Jemal and proud of the fact that Elaine and I had at least done something together right. "Son, I love you, and I'm proud of you, too. You are going to Yale. Financially, I'll do whatever I have to do."

As Jemal marched down the aisle during his high school graduation, he wore different colored academic and club chords, which I called ropes, draped all over his neck. The medallions clanked and sparkled, too.

As he paraded himself down the aisle, I thought about some of his teachers, the ones I had worked with at Las Vegas High. They, like me, were known for their high grading standards, their dedication to their students, and their passion for education. Jemal had made As in their classes. I also thought about the open house nights I had visited his school—how I saw only one or two Black students in his classes, compared to all the Whites. I thought about his tenacity in sports. He wrestled his entire time at Cimarron, but never earned a sports letter. It took winning so many bouts before he could be eligible for a letter to place on his letterman jacket. Sometimes he'd come very close to winning, but he never won enough matches to earn his letter.

I didn't feel all that bad for him because he proudly wore his letterman jacket with the letter he had earned from diving. I thought about the self-confidence he possessed to continue wrestling his whole time in high school.

After the ceremony, I asked, "Tell me, Son, why do you think you earned the great grades you obtained? I personally know most of your teachers, and they don't give grades away. They are hard as hell."

Jemal smiled and said, "Dad, I like school, and I like being challenged. School comes easily for me."

"I'm proud of you, Son." I wanted to say more, but the words wouldn't come. "I'm proud of you, Son." I never got up the nerve to ask him how he felt about not lettering in wrestling. I decided it might be best if I left that question alone.

I decided to borrow money from my tax-sheltered annuities to pay for his education

When it came time for Jemal to leave for Yale, Elaine, Jemal, Gavin, and I took a plane to New York and vacationed for a week. Riding the subway, we visited the museums, the Empire State Building, and went to the Apollo in up-town Harlem. (I had to see for myself what West 125th Street was like after reading about it so much in the novels and short stories of James Baldwin.) Although we rented a Town Car, which we'd used to drive to New Haven, Connecticut, we never drove it once while in New York. Downtown streets, without white line dividers, were something I wasn't used to. They scared the heck out of me.

We stayed one day at Yale, checking out a campus cafeteria, the bookstore, and Jemal's dorm before the three of us boarded our plane for home.

Jemal didn't want to come home for Thanksgiving, which told me he had successfully settled in, but at Christmas he commented, "You guys just dropped me off at Yale, leaving me to fend for myself."

I didn't respond, but thought, *One's eighteen, out on his own, and one more left to go.*

CHAPTER 72

As the two boys are four years apart, when Jemal was graduating from high school, Gavin was matriculating from junior high to his freshman year of senior high. He had continued playing the contra bass for three years under the teaching of his school instructor and his private mentor. Moreover, he was teaching himself guitar, drums, and piano. He sounded pretty good, especially on bass and guitar. Often, I'd fall asleep on the weekends listening to him practice. His private instructor frequently told me how much he enjoyed teaching Gavin, restating, "Gavin has both the intellect to understand complicated music theory, and he has the God-given talent to master the bass."

I told Gavin how proud I was that he had stayed with the bass. I also shared my disapproval with him taking my Bob Dylan complete book of songs without his first asking for it. He had somehow managed to lose my cherished, out-of-print book. But I was still very careful to express my pleasure in his ability to play the guitar. "Gavin, not that we are keeping score, but you can outplay me by far. I love the way you play." Often, he'd play a song, which caused me to smile with great delight for the length of the tune. And then I'd play and sing a piece I had played for him since childhood. I'd begin with, "What can you do with a drunken sailor?" which produced a wonderful childhood smile on his face, as well. Nodding up and down, while keeping beat to the music, I knew Gavin was filled with joy.

Gavin would now be going to the Las Vegas School of Performing Arts, a magnet school in the Clark County School District. Moreover, Elaine worked there as a counselor. (The school opened at the same time Hyde Park's mathematics and science academy opened.) I knew Gavin's orchestra teacher very well because she, at one time, had worked under my supervision at Walter Johnson Junior High School. In my opinion it was our school's second principal who did not value the orchestra teacher's musical accomplishments or her teaching talent. Here was a jewel he turned loose. He let her get away. *Good for Gavin!* was my thought in the end.

When Gavin wasn't practicing his music, he started taking Thai kickboxing from a coach named Master Toddy. Since I was now, in a sense, my own boss, I could leave school anytime I wanted after official business hours. I was free to take Gavin to all of his training sessions. I paid for them, too.

CHAPTER 73

My first month at Sawyer went nothing like I imagined. Not even my increase in pay. Both Yale and the IRS notified me saying, "More of your money will be needed by us since your salary has substantially increased."

I also learned that new funds from a recent bond election had produced new monies for the creation of more schools and the completion of Grant Sawyer's upgrading to a full-sized facility. *Why is it that I was in charge of facilities at Walter Johnson, a brand new school; in charge of facilities at Hyde Park while it went through a complete retrofit; and now I'm overseeing the building of the second half of Sawyer—while school is in session? This new school construction is quickly getting old.*

The builders would first extend the library by fifty percent, add onto the cafeteria another fifty percent, and increase locker rooms by fifty percent.

Upon getting the promotion, because of my genuine passion for education, love of children, and my wanting only to support good teachers and their quality teaching,

I believed my new faculty would adore me. I soon found out that was not the case.

The school's previous principal had opened the school. She and her assistant principal had created the school's vision, hired the entire faculty and staff, and were well on their way in pursuit of their long-ranged goals. My predecessor was a talented, strong-willed leader who knew exactly what she wanted to achieve. She had built an excellent group of teachers and staff who also embraced her educational dream. As I had frequent talks with the assistant principal regarding her vision, I quickly determined my school philosophy and vision were not the same as theirs. Because the kids in this high, affluent, upper-class community could handle the rigor of education, the staff was doing an excellent job of running a "mini college" as some parents on my Parent Advisory Council later expressed.

Various times I would overhear a teacher and the assistant principal talking. As soon as I approached them, they both put on looks of guilt. I would wonder if they were talking about me. I started feeling a little paranoid whenever this happened. Then—finally—I got it. They had created an objective for them to eventually self-actualize. It was theirs. I had nothing to do with it. Their leader, unfortunately for them, was so good at running a quality school, she had been promoted and transferred to the opening of a brand new high school. Unfortunately for her and her crew, she could not take her entire faculty and staff—only one third of them moved to the new high school with her. Accordingly, most of the others were left behind with me, hoping, right along with me, that she'd pick them up in subsequent years.

Miss Gladys, who had completed lengthy research on the subject, taught me volumes about the middle school philosophy. These kids were not in elementary or high school. Having profound hormonal swings, they were stuck in the middle. I didn't see it as giving them less academic knowledge. Based on qualitative and quantitative principles, I saw it as giving them more opportunities to apply skills and concepts to their lives, developing not just the mind but also the whole child. Although I knew I would be in a close-heat, competitive race with Gladys, my dream for them was to create the best middle school possible.

By the end of May, another third of my teachers signed transfer forms, which would allow them to join their previous principal. This was good. I didn't mind it at all. *Why have people working with you when they didn't want to be there? Now, I can replace them with new teachers and teachers who had previously worked with me.*

The hush-hush conversations, ending with my approach, eventually got on my nerves. It wasn't my paranoia. It was change for them, which they didn't want to do. I somewhat felt that they and the assistant principal wanted to sabotage everything I wanted to put into place.

That is when I realized what had happened at Walter Johnson Junior High when our inaugural principal left the school. The teachers came to me, discussing the different practices our new principal was putting into practice. We, likewise, with guilt written on our faces, must have shown him our frustration whenever he approached us.

Now, I understand. There's no way I'll be able to change anything in this school with my assistant present. We'll only work against each other, canceling out our efforts.

I asked my boss to ask his boss, the associate superintendent of secondary schools, to transfer my assistant principal and replace him with one of my own choosing. Strangely, I wondered, *Is that why I was moved to Hyde Park? And on a larger scale, is that why Thomas Whitson always seemed to be my replacement? What goes around certainly comes around.*

The parents on the Parent Advisory Committee expressed their lovely thoughts with having me as the principal. Many of them said I was certainly child oriented. They could tell this because their children came home sharing, "Mom, the new principal always calls me by my name."

CHAPTER 74

By July, my assistant principal and my secretary were reassigned away from my campus. The secretary joined her previous principal, and Bill, I don't remember where he went. I only knew his leaving left opportunity for change.

I did my homework while interviewing for an administrative secretary. I wanted someone with experience, someone with compassion, and someone committed to working beyond the designated, officially contracted time.

God gave me Linda, a cheerful, skillful, slender, six-foot redhead—not that physical attractiveness had anything to with my hiring her. What I truly was looking for was someone steeped in performing great customer service, someone who could keep up with my hyperactivity, or better yet, out-work me.

I selected the tall dean from Walter Johnson to be my assistant principal. In this case, her height played a little in my selection criteria—just a tad-bit. I wanted an administrator who could physically oversee the students, knowing height increases quality observation, and stature helps to create a strong command presence. Moreover, ignoring her "putting me in the spotlight," I liked the way she had treated my son and me way back when we attended his RPC.

One of the first comments my new assistant principal shared with me was her observation of our students. "Mr. Smith," she said, "the students here are different. They smile. They're polite to adults and to each other."

"Lorraine," I replied, "quality schools don't just happen; they are made. One of the reasons I chose you for this job is because of your up-beat, positive personality. I truly believe you want to help everyone in our school—the students, parents, faculty, and staff."

Although I hired a lot of teachers to replace those who had left the school, there were still instructors there who didn't like my leadership style. I had also gained enough experience to realize the important role of politics in school administration. Although I agreed with those principals who didn't like the fact that lots of political games exist in schools, I, unlike some of them, tried to use political astuteness to the best of my capability.

One day, one of my science teachers came to me and said, "Mr. Smith, I'm sure you are quite aware there are teachers here who are hoping you won't last long. They would love to see you fail."

I took a moment to look her in her eyes. "I'm sorry they feel that way," I replied.

"They asked me if I liked working with you, or if I was planning on jumping ship with them, too."

I did not ask for her response. She gave it anyway.

"Mr. Smith, I told them my air conditioning has never worked properly in this school, not since day one of my opening the school. I told them the minute I brought it to your attention, it was fixed in no time at all. No, I'll never leave him. He cares about us. He cares about us all. That's what I told them, Mr. Smith."

Another time, out of nowhere, a telephone call came from the press. The person on the other end of the line wanted to know why I wasn't allowing my teachers to use the copy machines in their departmental offices and why I would not allow them to purchase needed supplies, such as books.

"What?" was my first outcry. "What do you mean, 'I won't let them use their departmental copy machines or buy the supplies they need to teach.'"

I didn't stop to think, *Where are these ridiculous allegations coming from?*

The reporter continued, "One of your female students called us to report that as the new principal of the school, you are micromanaging your teachers to the point of ridicule."

That really set me off. I forgot and took the allegations personally. From my perspective, I started telling it all. "We have commercial off-set printers and a full-time graphic artist. What I want is for teachers to plan their lessons well in advance and give their printing to the graphic artist in a timely manner, so they will have it when they need it. Why burn out the small copy machines running a hundred or more copies when the off-set press is designed to do the job?"

Instead of thinking, I continued my rationalization. "Books I invite you to come and see. Each student has a textbook for all of his or her classes. We even have extras in stock because there will come a time when we will need them—the same edition or in the event the book is no longer available." I don't know all that I said, but I wanted the reporter to thoroughly understand the allegation wasn't true. "Supplies," I went on trying to plead my case. "We have supplies galore. My school is not by any stretch of imagination short on funds. I keep all the supplies teachers request or will ever need in abundance in the supply room. Come down and see."

The next morning, after reading the article the reporter wrote about me, I felt just awful. My pride, my self-esteem was flat—about as flat as a tarnished, thin dime.

To make matters worse, I had to attend a district-wide principals' meeting that day. When I walked into the meeting, I felt greatly embarrassed. Although they weren't and probably could have cared less, I felt everyone in the room was staring and inwardly laughing at me.

My old boss, Gladys came over, put her arms around me, and said, "Ronnie, don't worry. We've all been baptized and humiliated by the press. Everyone in here empathizes with you. We learn from our mistakes."

Later in the day, someone from our district's public relations office called me. "Mr. Smith, I simply want to help you. In the future, don't rattle on. Use short sound bytes. When the reporter continues pressing, trying to get you to rattle off, remember, short sound bytes. Repeat your short comment as many times as needed. Never give them any more than what is succinctly needed. The one good thing you did was not ever saying, 'No comment.' By saying this, it sounds like something is being hidden, like the interviewee doesn't want to tell the truth. Remember, nothing more than short sound bytes."

In the evening, before going home, I held my glass heart, the one Gladys had given me. I cried. Then, I tried to comfort and forgive myself for the mistake I had made. Even at this point, so far into my career, I hadn't taken my eyes off my goal—to gladly learn and gladly teach.

CHAPTER 75

After I had completely finished the next year-round teacher rotational schedule and ran the "final" school-wide teacher/student schedules for the upcoming year, I gave those two responsibilities to our new assistant principal, Lorraine. I figured I knew enough about them—all I wanted and needed to know to get me through in an emergency.

My dean decided to transfer, so I had to hire a new one. Instead of training a neophyte, I decided to select one with experience. She was short in stature, but I did not break any hiring policies or regulations. Even though I thought, *A short dean, one shorter than our students, how will she know who's about to get into a fight? Students "do-the-dance." They display attitude and shout personal insults before actual fisticuffs. How can she prevent the altercation when she can't even see what is about to happen?*

A few days after hiring our new dean, she came to me smiling. "The students here, Mr. Smith, they're so kind and polite. They are nothing like the students in my previous school. You are lucky to have such students, Mr. Smith."

I smiled in reply but said nothing in return.   Apparently, she hadn't learned about opportunity and expectation. In education, and probably in life, luck may be overrated while expectation rarely gets its needed acclaim. *If students aren't achieving great progress, a lack of expectation may be one of the causes. Minus all the fantasy and illusion, tit for tat, what we truly think, we create,* was at the forefront of my mind.

One morning, at the start of school, an angry parent stormed into my office demanding to speak with one of my students. "Where can I find David Bloodsaw? I need to have a word with him."

"Sir, I cannot allow you to talk to a student without his parents' prior consent."

He punched a fist into his palm and repeated, in a bitter tone, "I said I need to speak to David, and I need to talk to him now."

"Sir, I won't permit you to do that, and I'm sure you understand. You would not expect me to allow a parent to speak with your child without your approval, now, would you?"

He gritted his teeth and announced, "I'm going to speak to that boy, and I'm going to do it now. What room is he in?"

"No you're not!" I said.

"Oh, yeah, and who's going to stop me?" he inquired while poking his huge chest out. (In addition, his biceps looked like cantaloupes.)

Not being intimidated by his bullying, I poked my chest out, too, exactly like he had poked out his. "I am," I replied, in the same tone of voice as his. "Now, if you want to tell me what your issue is, I'll be glad to discuss it with you so that we can resolve the problem."

"Mr. Tough Guy" backed down. He explained that David had allegedly hit his daughter while at school. He just wanted to discuss the incident with David.

Our conversation ended when I shook his hand—squeezing it as firmly as he squeezed mine—thanked him for coming in, and said, "I will take care of the alleged incident and make sure it is handled in an appropriate manner, consistent with school rules and procedures and district policy and regulation."

After talking with the students, I contacted each of their parents and let them know the incident had been resolved to everyone's satisfaction. David never laid his hand on the girl. She knew her dad well, and admitted that she concocted the allegation to get attention from her father.

****

My biggest task came with working with the contractors expanding our school. Each day presented frustration for everyone on the campus. The noise from the jackhammers, the ripping down of rebar and concrete, and the constant shattering of glass made us feel we were in an insane asylum, not a school.

Attempting to prevent any physical injury to students, parents, faculty, and staff while on the campus, I spent a lot of time writing newsletters and flyers soliciting everyone's caution. I met often with our Parent Advisory Council, giving them updates.

The summer monsoons from Mexico came one afternoon. I had to close school early. The torrential rains washed out roads. Parents living in the Blue Diamond area in the South part of town were calling the school to find out when and how their children would be getting home. I was in constant communication with transportation and relaying the information to my concerned parents. One of my on-going sayings to parents was, "I will always treat your children as if they were my own." And this situation was no exception.

The rainstorm left sheets of plastic Visqueen sheeting hanging and blowing from the two dismantled exterior walls of our locker rooms. Both rooms resembled shelters that had been bombed by enemy aircraft. The howling, flapping plastic made both areas mystifying and creepy. Worse yet, three inches of rainwater lay on our hardwood gymnasium floor.

The contractors tried to no avail to save the hardwood floor. They took squeegee push brooms and forced the water outside. Gigantic fans blew day and night. In the end, the floor twisted and turned all over the place. Walking across the floor was difficult enough; playing basketball was totally inconceivable. The contractors, in trying to save money, insisted the floor could be salvaged, even if it took patching the floor in several places. All of this had to be worked out with the builders and our school district insurance agency. As to the floor being saved, I wasn't having it. Knowing what I know about working with wood, I knew the woods and the stains would never match. I wasn't about to have a sloppy, shoddy patchwork gym floor in my brand new school. I wasn't about to settle for second best. I called the district's facilities superintendent. I knew him well because of all the meetings I had with him in the past. I begged him to come out and take a look at the floor. "Just come out and take a look before you approve what everybody else wants to do." He did. And he agreed with me. "Ronnie, I'll see to it you get a brand new floor."

****

Once I took complete possession of our new facility, I had the task of hiring fifty percent new faculty. I also had to hire a new dean. My current one quit and retuned to teaching in a classroom. She resigned one day after telling me, "These kids. They're terrible. They've got no manners, no morals, and no nothing. They are just like the ones at my last school."

In contrast, I thought of my assistant principal, Lorraine. Her opinion of the students continued to match her spirit and expectations of the children.

Like magic, what we truly think, we create, again popped into my head, along with, *"Sinner man, you can't run, you can't hide. Wherever you go, you take yourself with you."* And once more I utilized the sound, administrative principle regarding good judgment: "Think it, but don't dare say it." But, who's perfect? I had to get at least two cents worth of judgment in. All I said after hearing her comment was, "My Dear Dean of Students, who made them that way? Do you remember what you said about my students when you first entered the school?"

It was pure joy interviewing candidates for faculty positions on our campus. I could now hire people who shared and would execute my teaching philosophy. I didn't conduct hasty interviews. I utilized a carefully thought-out, self-made questionnaire, which I collected after each interview. I did my best to ascertain if teachers that I hired enjoyed teaching students. Did they use mutual respect, were they competent in their subject matter, and would they employ the highest expectations for their students and themselves, and would they willingly model for students the attitudes and behaviors required for academic excellence?

And because of the fifty percent increase in student population, I also had the opportunity to hire, not one but two new deans. I decided to get two neophytes so I could train them my way.

With all going well, I decided to treat myself, something I rarely did. I bought a tie, a special tie. It was black with yellow smiley faces—small, medium, and large smiley faces. I felt happy wearing it from time to time.

CHAPTER 76

Jemal came home for Christmas. He, Gavin, and I spent a lot of time skiing, especially during my two weeks of winter break.

Rarely would we plan any of our trips. We'd just jump up and go. Driving now was easy because I had Jemal to help. We'd drive to St. George, Utah, spend the night in a cheap hotel, get up early, and proceed to Brian Head. We never packed food either. Whenever I tried to convince the boys the trips would be less expensive on me, Jemal would say, "But Dad, I don't like making lunches. It's easier to buy hot food from the counter."

"Well, put hot soup or chili in a thermos," I wanted to yell out, but I held my tongue with my children, too. I didn't argue or put my foot down. I felt good, just being able to spend time with my sons. Instead, taking Jemal's lead, I paid a fortune at the counter.

While the three of us were together we never talked about anything important or significant.

I could have pushed the envelope, asking about their worries, fears, or concerns, but I didn't—probably because I hadn't been raised that way. My dad certainly hid behind a bottle, too afraid to search or sift through his feelings. Mother had taught her children, by example, not to go looking for possible trouble. "Don't go there. Just work hard an leave well enough alone. Sometimes you might discover you aren't able to handle what you find," is probably what she would have said if asked.

Once Jemal returned to college, I continued giving Gavin a lot of my attention. I took him to all of his kickboxing training sessions, and I bought tickets to several local Ultimate Fighting Championship tournaments hosted in Las Vegas. When we weren't going to a live fight, we spent time watching them on T.V.

On evening, Gavin decided to attend an orchestra performance with me. My orchestra teacher and her students were presenting it. I think Gavin wanted to come, not to merely spend time with me but to see how much he had grown musically from his middle school training several years ago.

After the concert I asked, "How'd you like it, Son? What do you think?" Gavin never answered my questions.

"Dad, did you see him? He was at the concert."

"Who, Gavin? Who was at the concert? I don't have the slightest idea what you are talking about."

"Dad, one of the greatest UFC fighters was at the concert tonight. I thought you saw him."

Then it came to me. "Oh, that guy. Yeah, I know him. His daughter attends my school. I've talked with him before," is all I said to Gavin. I did not mention how he had tried to intimidate me and how I stood up to his physical threats.

CHAPTER 77

For some reason I thought back to a time when my brother-in-law, Edley, was a patrolman with the Tucson Police Department. It was during the time when I had settled into my job as a dean. "Does your job ever get mundane?" I asked. "There must always be something new—never a dull moment."

"It gets boring," he replied. "Same incidents with new faces."

My job as principal was starting to become predictable, with nothing new under the sun. I often thought and shared with my deans and assistant principal, "I do this job based on experience. The decisions I make don't just pop out of my head. They're based on prior knowledge—either a colleague's or mine. If the incident turned out positively, I will use the strategy. If not, I need to utilize something different."

Thoughts of all bad decisions made by administrators I had known, even my own few blunders, came to mind. *Boy, you really goofed when you rattled on and on to the media. Don't ever do that again.*

My thoughts, perhaps, conjured negativity into my world—situations that were entirely new for me. The first was a food fight in our cafeteria. Knowing this type of behavior occurs in other schools, I thought I was totally prepared for it to not happen in my school. All administrators, including our counselors and some staff, stood duty, monitoring student behavior in our cafeteria—all three lunches. But like life, this kind of incident erupts totally out of nowhere.

Without forewarning, Styrofoam plates full of food flew across the room. Large paper cups, loaded with red punch followed. Salad drizzled down my face. *How could this be happening? How do I bring it to an immediate end?* "Stop it. Stop it!" I screamed, trying to rush to the nearest cordless microphone being held by one of my deans.

The faster I moved, the slower I traveled. My feet got no traction on the slippery tile floor. With feet sliding back and forth, I did the food-fight-shuffle. I looked at my white shirt, now hemorrhaging from red punch.

Finally reaching a microphone, I calmly but sternly said, "Students, stop this behavior. You know that it is wrong. Anyone I see from now on continuing in this behavior will suffer from the consequences. Now stop it. Deans, counselors, all adults, start writing down the names of any students who are not abiding by my directions."

The pandemonium ended immediately.

Thank God it was the last lunch.

I went home, quickly showered, changed clothes, and retuned to school. Tracing down the instigators of this fight, I spent all afternoon doing detective work. By the end of the school day, I had identified the perpetrators—two eighth graders, who admitted they had planned the entire incident. One had brought a dozen rotten eggs, which he had concealed in his backpack. He told me that he had let them sit outdoors, in the hot, summer sun for weeks. He also freely confessed he had thrown them during the riot. *Whew, I'm glad I didn't get hit with any of those eggs.* Both boys were placed on formal suspension, arrested by school police, and transported to juvenile hall.

Several days later, one of my deans held the expulsion recommendations, which went through without a hitch.

CHAPTER 78

D ecisions, how do I use good judgment in making them? This thought invariably stayed on my mind. I decided to handle the case when one of my deans brought to my attention that the child of very affluent parents—one on my Parent Advisory Board—was caught selling marijuana on our campus. Not that I had favorites, and how well I knew the concept of equality, the importance of treating everybody the same. But in this matter, I also knew the need to not offend the parents of this child. They were far too politically influential and could ruin my performance as a principal. (I don't know if that is really true. One side of me says, *You'd do this for any child. Yet, the other side said, I knew that I hadn't.*)

I decided not to further question myself. Somehow, I knew exactly what I had to do. I called the child's mother, briefly explained the allegations, and asked for her to join me as I conferenced with her child.

The parent returned my call minutes later stating she would not be able to come; she would be sending her husband on behalf of their child.

Because of my training, I looked at the child's registration paperwork to see exactly what her father did for a living. *Oh, shit! He works for the F.B.I. Oh, my God. How do I handle this situation wisely?*

When the father arrived, I showed him all of the written evidence my dean had collected, even his daughter's written confession. I explained that I would need to place his child on suspension; and notify school police, who would take his daughter into custody, and transport her to juvenile hall

When school police arrived, the officer worked out an agreement with the father. Both agreed to allow the father to transport his daughter to juvenile hall since Dad was a legal law-enforcement agent.

I also had my dean place on school suspension all of the students who had purchased marijuana from the seller. I had them arrested for purchasing an illegal substance on campus. Then school police transported them to juvenile hall.

In the end, the seller and the buyers were all expelled from my campus. It wasn't what I had done. It was the way in which I did it that caused my soul to suffer. *Was I a hypocrite, a phony like so many others?* My differential treatment of my students caused me both headache and heartache. However, I could find some comfort in knowing why her father transported the seller to "juvy," as opposed to the others who were driven in the backseat of a common cop car.

CHAPTER 79

Dealing with non-compliance wasn't an issue restricted solely to the students; teachers were reprimanded, as well—even my father-in-law, Ed.

One morning before the start of school, a student came up to me and asked, "Mr. Smith, do teachers have a dress code?"

"Why, yes." I said.

"Do they get into trouble if they don't follow it?" she inquired.

I threw my hands in the air, smiled, and said, "What is it you're hinting at? What is it you really want to say?"

"Mr. Smith, apparently no one has bothered to look at the way my teacher dresses. Her mini-dresses stop at her crotch; they're way too short."

After finding out her teacher's name—Angelica—I had my assistant principal meet with her on a day the teacher was inappropriately dressed.

It's funny how after one set of behavior is brought to light, stranger eye-openers suddenly follow.

Non-compliance with dress code not only applied to Angelica but to my father-in-law, a sixty-year old man. A friend in personnel called me to inform me that Pampaw had walked into our district's office to apply for a teaching job. "Ronnie, here's this six-foot-five, unshaven man, dressed in denim overalls, and a brown pith helmet explaining that he wanted to teach."

"How did you know that we were connected?" I asked.

"Ed went out of his way, telling everyone in hearing distance how proud he is of you, 'Ronnie Tee Smith, Principal of Sawyer Middle School, is my son.' That's what got my attention. I invited him into my office. I figured I needed to call you, to give you a head's up."

He's laughing inside as we speak, I thought.

"Oh, by the way, I noticed the elastic string Ed uses for shoe laces. My eyes noticed the string when he pulled away from my desk and crossed his legs. Why does he dress like that?"

"Funny you should ask. After noticing it myself, I popped the question to him. Ed's borderline genius and crazy. He puts elastic string in the eyelets of his shoes to stretch them open. 'It's laziness and convenience,' he says. He never needs to tie them. Thanks, for the call."

I waited to see Ed that evening. I didn't want to talk with him over the phone. Although it was his behavior, not mine, I still felt embarrassed. Waiting gave me time to cool off, to let go of my humiliation, my disappointment in his judgment.

"Ed, don't ever do that again," I calmly, respectfully schooled him. "Most people wear a suit, dress shirt, and tie, with polished shoes when seeking employment." I didn't have the courage to tell him that he embarrassed me. I didn't want to use a put-down that would make him feel less-than. My ego wasn't that wounded. I simply didn't want him going places, telling people we were family whenever he was grossly unkempt and dressed like that.

He didn't get it. All he said was, "But Ronnie, I'm so proud of you. I want everyone to know you are my son-in-law."

He got me—stopped me dead in my tracks. *How could I be hurt or even truly embarrassed with a genuine, sincere comment like that, coming from Ed's heart?*

My secretary, on the eve of my fiftieth birthday, reentered the school late that night. She decorated my office—all in black. There were black balloons, black fluffy tissue paper stapled to the walls, and posters with Happy

Birthday wishes written in black hanging from the ceiling.

My teacher, Angelica, who loved dressing provocatively, pranced into my office the next day wearing too much mascara, outfitted in a tight-fitting dress and spiked heels. "I just came by to personally wish you Happy Birthday, Mr. Principal."

"Thank you, Angelica."

"Oh, Mr. Smith," she said as her long eyelashes batted and her eyes scanned my office. "I just love the energy in this room. Your black balls—I mean balloons sure look inviting. May I have one?"

Damn, I thought and utilized a controlled expression. What the hell?

"My pleasure," I replied while handing her one of the helium-filled balloons. "Shouldn't you be getting to your next class? I know you don't want to be late."

On her way out of my door and still batting her lashes, she waved goodbye and said, "I'm going to bake you a cake for your birthday." She added breathily, "You'll get it very soon."

The nerve, I don't want it, I thought. "No, you needn't. Your wishing me Happy Birthday is more than enough. Enjoy the rest of your day."

As soon as she left my office, I rushed out to my secretary, Linda, to share the teacher's Freudian slip. "Linda, Linda, Linda, what is wrong with this teacher? Her red ruby lips, the thick mascara and long eyelashes, Linda, what do you think?"

"She's got the hots for you. But obviously, she doesn't know you, like I do—that you would never sink to her level."

There was no need for me to say any more. Linda had that matter-of-fact quality for saying it like it is, of putting everything to rest.

The next day Angelica brought me a chocolate cake. After sampling it in our break-room, both Linda and I thought, *Angelica will never get a mate based upon her baking.*

CHAPTER 80

As a teacher I heard rumors about colleagues who were fired for being active pedophiles. Two taught in the same secondary school as I. I remember, I would never write the word "sex" on the chalkboard. In my judgment, there was just no need. During the time of one teacher being terminated, I had said to my seniors, "You know I love you all."

Their response was, "Yeah, but not the way Mr. Roberts loved his students." I didn't respond pretending I didn't hear them; yet, I thought, *How sad—a young, married-with-children pedophile, robbing even younger students of their joy.*

Then, there was one male student attending the same school who was molested by a male teacher. Although I never butted into anybody's business, I later found out the preyed-upon student was also a student of mine. He gave me hell in the classroom everyday, and he knew what he was doing. He never got to me. I showed him nothing but kindness and belief that he would rise to my high expectations. All of this was done without my knowing of his sexual situation. He passed my class earning a grade of B. The last day of school, he brought me a gift—a six-pack of beer.

After opening it I said, "Son, I can't accept this. Yes, you tried my nerves all semester long, and for that, I truly appreciate your gift. But I cannot take it. I'll make sure you won't get into any trouble.

Your parents will be able to pick it up in the dean's office."

Looking back, I guess I had been fortunate in all of my schools. As an administrator I never had to deal with any sexual misconduct pertaining to my teachers or staff. None displayed any pedophilic behaviors.

One day my boss shared a story with me about how a substitute teacher had brought a cassette VHS tape from his home, believing it to be something other than what it was. He started the tape for his students. They watched it a good three minutes. Then a student brought the movie to the substitute's attention. He had been playing a silent tape of him masturbating. Of course all of the students were most attentive, with no one speaking a word. With my supervisor telling me that story, in my school, she allowed the universe to present me with my first teacher pedophile, I'm convinced.

The very next day a parent entered my office and informed me that her daughter had been sexually abused by one of my teachers. This mother had lots of evidence—sexually explicit pictures and e-mails that had been passed back and forth.

I gave the computer information to school police, so they could conduct their investigation. Concurrently, I interviewed the child, with her mother present.

Eventually, the teacher was arrested—arrested at my school because the police prefer to take a person like this into custody in neutral territory, a place other than the perpetrator's home. (As a dean, I learned that police aren't too fond of going into homes of domestic cases because of the possibilities of surprise and violence. They prefer to control the environment.) But before the arrest, I had arranged for our district's legal counsel to meet with the teacher and me. Legal counsel convinced the teacher to resign on the spot. "If you choose to sign this resignation document, the media will be much kinder to you," he explained. "If you've resigned, you are no longer a teacher. You've taken the wind out of the media's sails. I'm sure you don't want to put your family through the horrific embarrassment brought on by the news media."

The teacher took the attorney's counsel to heart. He resigned on the spot.

CHAPTER 81

O fficers of the Metropolitan Police Department came close to busting me—a school principal. Several of my eighth grade female students approached me in the courtyard. "Mr. Smith, Mr. Smith," one of them said. "Some boys at Durango High School have been following us home and throwing rocks at us along the way."

"They've been bothering us after school for the last few days," another girl interjected.

"Who are they?" I asked.

The excited one replied, "We don't know their names, but we're sick of them throwing the rocks at us. Please help us, Mr. Smith."

I could see "a set up" all over their scenario, but I took their bait anyway. I knew almost all of the students who lived in the neighborhood. Most of the high schoolers had attended my school when they were younger. More than likely, I would know the names of the alleged rock-throwers. "Okay, young ladies. Here's the deal. Today, after school, I'll meet you in the front of the school. I'll be in my car. Once you get my attention, start walking home.

I won't be close to you, but close enough to see who's throwing the rocks."

A few minutes after dismissal, the girls and I were on our way. I drove slowly and let them get ahead of me. I waved at students who noticed me. As a matter of fact, I had a ball smiling and waving—kind of like I was in a parade. I got close to the girls and then stopped at a house. Two of my male students were playing table tennis in the front yard. I chatted with them briefly, and then started to catch-up with the girls.

Before I could close the gap, a white car raced in front of me and cut me off. Another car dashed up behind me. I was trapped, caught in their net. *What the heck? What are they doing?*

A man dressed in suit and tie rushed to my car. I don't know how I noticed his clothes. My eyes were focused on the pistol in his hands. The gun was pointed at me. "Hands in the air. Put 'em up. Put 'em up," he yelled rushing closer and closer to me.

My window on the driver's side was down. I heard him clearly. My hands flew to the roof of the car.

"Don't move. Don't move," he demanded as he quickly approached my window. "What are you doing? Why are you in this neighborhood? Don't you dare even flinch."

I didn't want to open my mouth. Without moving any other muscles than facial ones, I said, "I'm the principal of Grant Sawyer Middle School. I was following some of my students home. They have had problems in the neighborhood. I wanted to make sure they got home safely."

"Aw, damn!" he sighed. Lowering his pistol to his waist he explained, "We thought you were a child molester. My I see some ID?"

"I'm going in my wallet to get the ID, okay?"

"Yes, sure," the detective acknowledged his approval.

I gave him my driver's license and my district I.D., which indicated my title, work location, and expiration date.

"Mr. Smith, while watching you stopping and talking to the children, I told the other detectives over the radio, 'That's him. We got the son-of-a-bitch.' I was certain we had caught a pedophile red-handed, especially after you stopped at the house and chatted with the two boys."

He politely returned my identification cards a sent me on my way. I still had enough time to see that the girls made it home without incident. I laughed while driving back to the school. Then the thought hit me, *I wonder how the police would have treated me initially if I were driving a rust-bucket and was dressed in casual clothing instead of my white shirt and expensive tie?*

CHAPTER 82

My mother was born in Innes, Texas, in 1912, and had only gotten as far as fourth grade. Since my brother, Donnie, and his wife had recently purchased a six-bedroom vacation home on the golf course at Rhode's Ranch, I decided it would be a great idea to have Donnie drive Mom to Las Vegas for a weekend. She could learn a lot about her sons—experience the kind of lives we lived. We could all go early to a fine-dining restaurant and then attend a drama production my theater teacher was presenting at my school. This would give my family, especially my mother, the opportunity to visit, briefly live in the manner Donnie and I are accustomed, and to see my new school.

As they entered town, they drove straight to my house. Mother hadn't visited since she first came to see my first-born's arrival to this world. (Elaine and I always took the boys to see their grandma in L.A.) I was glad that my mother could see my home. I knew she would be proud of me, seeing that my quality of life far exceeded hers.

How I wanted my mother to say something about my house, to compare it to the farm where she lived and picked cotton when she was young, about my age. How I craved hearing her express some type of raw emotion. But she never did.

Then we went to Donnie's palatial estate, so they could all dress for dinner. Mother rode with Gavin and me, in my car. As we pulled up to the guarded gates, I thought, *Now this will certainly be the place where she has to let something out, where she will release at least a little emotion.* But no, I was wrong. She continued holding her feelings in-check. Yet, I understood—suppression is a survival trait acquired by those living in the ghetto or by those immersed in emotional conflict or pain.

Although I did not ask, I wondered what she was thinking. I know every time I drove through these gates and along the golf course by myself, I thought, *With Donnie being vice president of operations of a high-tech startup company, damn, life for Donnie and Joyce must be exceedingly good.*

As Joyce gave Mother the grand tour of their home, Mother whispered in my ear, "They renting or buying?"

I broke out in laughter. I whispered back in her ear, "They're buying, Mom. They own this place."

It isn't much, probably the best that she could do, but something, as little as it was, finally came out. How can I be expected to show my emotions when my parents never did my entire life? Could it be they were repressing all the hurting, disappointment, fear, and pain they had experienced all of their traumatized lives? Could it be that if they expressed their true, pent-up feelings, releasing them as easily as pushing the button on a pressurized can of spray paint, exploding anger, ugly retaliation, and unforeseen revenge might uncontrollably gush out, causing destruction to the nearest things around? Is this why, by holding in resentment, some Afro-Americans seem to be cruel and disrespectful to each other, including themselves? Does this type of repression create built-up anger that comes out in other destructive ways? Is that why most old-school Blacks have been taught by Jesus, their church-going parents, and grandparents to love those who persecute them?

After dinner, we went to my school to watch the play. During intermission, I took my family into my office. Mother sat at my desk, in my high-back chair. For some reason, the room got quiet. I heard weeping. Searching all the faces, I found my mother crying. Her tears broke my heart. She saw my nameplate, ink pen in its stand, and business card holder. Perhaps, it was the glass heart. Something touched her heart, but she didn't say a word. She sat in my high-back office chair and cried—

keeping her thoughts to herself.

Being a parent myself, I knew she was crying tears of joy. How proud she was of both of her sons. How proud she was they had captured the American dream. I bent down, wrapped my long arms around her and my chair. "I love you, Mom. You can be proud of yourself for raising your children right."

CHAPTER 83

B y late spring, Jemal was ready to graduate from Yale.

When the time came Elaine, Gavin, and I flew to New Haven, Connecticut, and stayed in a classy hotel—the Omni. Jemal gave us grand tours of the small city and the university. He introduced us to his roommates. We met with their parents one evening for dinner in an exclusive restaurant—fine dinnerware, crystal, glassware, and all. I felt good that I could hold my own in decorum and conversation—no licking my fingers or anything.

Later that evening, Jemal shared with me separate stories of his three roommates. He explained how the four of them had remained together the entire four years at school. One was on his way to medical school; another, to the Massachusetts Institute of Technology for graduate school. The third roommate would soon be entering a masters program, working on his MBA at Yale.

"Dad, you don't get it," Jemal said, at one point in his conversation. "These guys come from money, and you have no idea how much money—money far beyond your understanding and imagination. They have it made for the rest of their lives."

"And so do you, Jemal," I interjected. "With your college degree in engineering, and your graduating from Yale, you'll have no problem making it big in this world. You're going somewhere. I'm so very proud of you, my son." I could not stop myself from putting my arms around him and giving him a healthy hug.

I've always wanted to be a serious scholar. What I was unable to do, my son has finally been accomplished. I feel terrific!

Jemal showed us his fraternity house. He was a member of the Wolfpack, or something like that. Members of this organization had a private chef, paid for by alumni. There were secret passages throughout the house and shrunken, human heads displayed in glass cases. What took my interest were the old, rare, hardbound copies of medieval and renaissance literature. These books were covered in dust. I found Milton, Chaucer, and Shakespeare. Flipping through the pages made me sneeze. What a treasure, what a find. *These privileged kids of today don't realize what they have. Better care should be taken regarding these fine, extraordinary books.*

We attended three graduation ceremonies while at Yale. One was for the graduates of the College of Engineering. While sitting in the sanctuary, I marveled at the veteran members of the audience. How impressed I was at their ability to lip-sync the dean's graduation speech. They mimicked his presentation word for word.

The second ceremony the following day was for all undergraduates getting diplomas from the university. This program was conducted in Latin. I overheard one lady sitting behind me ask, "What are they saying?"

Being smart, I looked over my should and replied, "They are all speaking in Pig-Latin." Those around me laughed. I felt proud, knowing that my own education had placed me in a category above the masses. I somewhat felt uppity, "better" than the crowd.

The final graduation ceremony was for recipients who had earned their doctorates, masters, and undergrad degrees. This was the program filled with pomp, pageantry, and ceremony. Filled with long speeches, it took forever to end. Several times during the program I thought back to the time Elaine and I selfishly did not attend our undergrad ceremony. I thought back to the times she and I, after having children of our own, tried to make up for our ignorant behavior by having our mothers and her dad attend our post-graduation ceremonies. Looking back, I wondered why I didn't have my dad attend my post-grad celebration. *Probably because of his physical handicap. He was suffering greatly from diabetes and was in a wheelchair.*

Besides, I told myself, who wanted to chaperone and care for a dysfunctional, old drunk especially at a graduation ceremony?

CHAPTER 84

G avin, being exactly four years younger than his brother, was ready to graduate from high School—the Las Vegas Academy of Performing Arts. All the way though grade school, behaving nothing like his brother, Gavin fought hard against education. He was an extremely strong-willed child. Consequently, he wanted to do everything his own way.

As far back as kindergarten, his teacher recommended retention. I asked, "Academically, is he that far behind his classmates?"

"Oh, no, quite on the contrary," his teacher replied. "Gavin is probably the smartest student in my class, in fact, one of the smartest I have ever had. The problem is, he's socially immature. Retaining him for a year might correct his deficiency."

"Oh, no," I rallied, in Gavin's defense. "Gavin, since birth has followed his own mind. Elaine and I think he's so damn smart, his mind and courage often get him into trouble. He's always been one who is stubborn and insistent on finding his own way. I will give him that, and I won't agree to keeping him back—especially in kindergarten."

I was smart enough to realize that I couldn't change anyone. Until truly ready, I couldn't change myself. Likewise, I'd have to let them change themselves. I thought it strange, our having this conversation. I always believed Gavin would be the one to excel in education, that he'd be the one in our family earning the Ph.D. As far back as three, I remember Gavin saying, out of the blue, "When I go to college."

I remember thinking, *Hmmm, where did that come from? No one has ever suggested or demanded he go to college—especially at the age of three.*

Then there was the incident with his writing, "Blah, blah, blah," on his homework assignment missing form way back in third grade.

In sixth grade, Gavin had received a top-ranking award from Invent America. He was the first-place recipient of the school-wide science fair. As our family sat around the restaurant table, celebrating his accomplishment, Gavin smugly smiled and commented, "I don't see why anyone would be proud of a middle school principal receiving a sixth grade science award. Dad, you did the work; that's really your award."

In ninth grade, Gavin convinced his algebra teacher that he need not attend her class, stating he, she, and his other mathematic classmates would be better off if he could use the library each day to self-teach. Probably because he was so rude and disruptive in class, probably catching her and pointing out her mistakes in class, she consented to his request. Gavin's final semester grade was a B, in academics and a U, for "Unsatisfactory Behavior," in the class.

Elaine called me one day from her school, the Academy of Performing Arts. "Ronnie, someone stole my car. It's not in the faculty parking lot."

"Where's Gavin?" I asked. "Is he with you? And your car keys, do you have them in your purse?"

"I have my keys, but the car key is missing. Gavin's not with me either." Seconds later she said, "That little devil. Ronnie, Gavin's taken my car."

I picked her up from school, drove her home, and waited with her—we waited and waited for Gavin.

Gavin called about seven. He explained he had driven to Henderson, to his girlfriend's house. "Mom, I don't want to drive home. I'm afraid I might wreck your car. Would you and Dad come and get me?"

At a later date, Gavin stole my car, too. He kept it for a week while he lived on peanut butter and jelly sandwiches and resided in caves in the Westside mountains. I called the cops, but they never caught him. They did pull me over one day without incident because I had not called them to report that my car had been returned.

Finally, Elaine, Grandpa Ed, Jemal, his private music teacher, and I sat in the audience, attending Gavin's high school graduation. He had finally made it—in spite of him one day calling his orchestra teacher a bitch. Unlike his older brother, there were no honor chords or medallions draped around his neck as Gavin marched in the procession and across the stage, but I was relieved that he had made it through high school.

When Gavin was a freshman, Elaine counseled him to join service clubs and do his very best, like she had successfully done with Jemal. But no. Gavin had to do it his own way—which he did.

Because Elaine did the work—applying for Gavin's colleges—by submitting all of the necessary essays, reports, and forms for him, he received a full-ride music scholarship from Juilliard to play his contra bass.

Gavin turned it down. He settled for UNLV instead. I told him I would pay for his college and would even pay for a dorm if he wanted to move from his mother's home.

My reason for suggesting the dorm was to provide Gavin an opportunity to live on his own, as his brother had done. It was not to demean his mother in any way.

Perhaps Gavin took my offer the wrong way. "Here take your damn bass. Keep it, sell it, do whatever you want. You forced me into playing it since sixth grade, but I'm not playing it anymore."

I didn't argue with him. I merely took the bass, case, and stand and stored it in my home.

After his first semester, Gavin brought home a report card filled with Ds and Fs.

"Why, Son?" I foolishly asked. "I know the work's not too hard for you."

"Dad, I'm late for class all the time." With tears in his eyes, he continued, "Sometimes, I don't even get to class, driving Jemal's old, broken down yellow truck."

Even though I bought Gavin a brand new car, and myself one as well since I got a super deal, his grades never changed. At the end of his first year, I said, "Gavin, you are on your own. I won't fund your college education anymore—even if the university chooses to allow you to continue your schooling."

At that point, I decided to honestly speak my mind. "Gavin?" I asked. "Why didn't you accept the schooling at Juilliard? Was it because, in your mind, your brother had already sewn up all of the university glory and praise from your mother and me? Was it because he had successfully graduated and you feared that perhaps you would not?"

"Yes, Dad," he returned.

I did not question him any further. I felt sad—but not sad enough to pay for any more of his schooling.

CHAPTER 85

"It's easy to be nice to people who are nice, but better to be nice to those who are cranky," is another life lesson my mother taught me well. This lesson, added to the saying my father-in-law often quoted, which was, "Hell's bells, you can catch more flies with honey than you can with vinegar," Those adages got me far in school administration. I always strived to help pull out the best behavior in people—not only during my teaching days but also as an administrator. I clung to Chaucer's character, The Cleric from Oxford, in *Canterbury Tales*. Like him, I always wanted my teaching to be to the point, honest, without blemish, wholesome, and sweet.

It's rumored Buddha said, "Be careful what type of energy you release into the universe. Karma will return the same type and amount back to you."

I don't know if this is true, but three of my teachers one day made me feel like a king. My sister, Charlene, a.k.a. Lulu, had died of breast cancer at the age of forty-seven. Elaine, Gavin, and I drove to L.A. for the funeral. Minutes before the start of the ceremony I looked around the church only to see three of my teachers attending the service. How good I felt inside seeing them there to support me in my time of grief. *They must truly think highly of me to drive all the way from Vegas to be here with me.* I don't think I cried during the service because of my sister's early death, but I sat there and bawled like an infant because of the three teacher's love shown to me.

During my final year as principal of Grant Sawyer Middle School, I received Principal of the Year for the State of Nevada. This recognition came completely as a surprise to me.

The big celebration was held in Washington, D.C. Once more, I sat in the middle of the front row, taking good notes during every session of the symposium. One of the guest speakers' presentations changed my life. The United States of America employed him. I don't remember his job title, but he worked for the National School Board of Education. He began his talk by asking, "How many of you have had a bad day?" Every person in the room raised a hand. "I'm going to ask you again," he announced, and then repeated his question, "How many of you in this room have had a bad day?"

I looked around again to see if the hand-count had changed. It had. *I think he now has everyone's attention—even those who sat in the back.'*

"NO YOU HAVEN'T!" he yelled. He continued shouting, "In fact, most of you don't know what a bad day is!"

Now I knew for certain that the had captured everyone's complete attention. *What arrogance. What nerve. I thought. What gives him the right to be so bold?*

"Put your hands down. Put them down," he demanded. "Unless you've had teachers and students killed by gunshots on your campus."

Then I got it. *Thank God I have never experienced this type of incident. And I hope I never will. Tell me more, tell me more; you've certainly gotten my full attention.*

The speaker went on to explain he was principal of a high school when the shootings occurred on his campus. Six students and one teacher were killed. One of his students with very low self-esteem fired the lethal shots. The speaker told of the many on-going lawsuits that would probably never end for the rest of his life. He spoke of the guilt he'd probably endure for the rest of his life—his continual questioning himself, asking, "Why didn't I see this coming?"

By the end of his presentation, he had thoroughly convinced me that I haven't had a bad day. From that day to the present, I've never said, "I'm having a bad day."

CHAPTER 86

During my fourth year as principal, a new middle school was under construction a few blocks from Sawyer. The next school year half of my students would be transferred to the new school. With the reduced number of students I would also be losing half of my teaching staff.

Knowing me and my high expectations regarding students and staff, the new principal of the new middle school was excited to be getting my children. In addition, she also hired one-third of my faculty.

With the reduction in students and faculty, I also lost one-twelfth of my pay. I had been reduced to an eleven-month employee. My school was no longer a year-round school.

The lost pay troubled me a little. Once I got used to having the extra money, I continued spending what I no longer made. Besides, I still had Jemal's college loan to pay back from the money I had borrowed against my tax-sheltered annuities.

Looking over my track record pertaining to length of time in any school, I typicality lasted about four years. After four and a half years at Sawyer, I applied for a high school principal-ship. Besides, it was a twelve-month position, which would give me more pay.

CHAPTER 87

On February 2, 2000, I became principal of Clark High School. "Mr. Smith got this job because he's the nephew of our regional superintendent." Like the game of telephones, this busy comment buzzed in the ears of everyone at Clark—everyone except me.

Perhaps the rumor started because my regional superintendent met me at Clark my first day on the campus at 6 A.M. He introduced me to my new secretary, and she gave me my keys.

Wow, all these keys and their weight—I feel like a warden with a key to every prison cell. This is different compared to Sawyer. I guess there will be a lot of differences. I only had a few keys on my ring at Sawyer. That's probably because the middle school was smaller and new. Clark was twice the size and opened in 1965. My master key did not open every room. I guess because so many of the rooms had been used for specialty functions from time to time and had been re-keyed by special request. Although happy to be principal of a high school, and pleased with the furniture arrangement in my office, I was a little annoyed at having to carry a wad of keys as big as softball on my waist belt.

My boss walked me around the campus and introduced me to many of the teachers, as he had been principal of the school at one time in his career. On his way out, he commented, "Improve the school, but don't have people calling me. You're in charge. Handle your school."

Walking back to the office, I started thinking, *I'll have to get my hands on all the school's documents to learn the strengths and weakness as quickly as I can. I've got to read the teacher's handbook from cover to cover. Darn, I'll have to start learning new faces, names, and positions, in conjunction with student and parent names.*

I asked the one person I knew, Norma, my new secretary, for a bell schedule and teacher assignment list. By the end of second period, I was busy standing hall duty and ready to learn some names.

I contacted the local contracted school photographer and had him bring framed pictures of our entire faculty and staff. "Use the pictures taken for the yearbook," I advised. I talked him into providing the frames free of charge, suggesting that I would be deciding who would get the contract next year.

I had my secretary place their names, highest educational degree earned, and the subject or position they currently performed at the school, neatly centered under each photo. I hired an artist, one I had been working with for years, to paint a caption on a front-office entrance wall, which read, "Clark's Personnel Provides Excellent Customer Service." Starting with mine, a picture of all my administrators, faculty, and, staff hung proudly on the wall. I studied those photographs daily to help me learn faces, positions, and names.

CHAPTER 88

While doing my research, learning all I could about the school, I discovered that Ed W. Clark was a culturally diverse high school. Built in 1965, over the years, student population changed. Clark grew from a student population of 1200 in its opening year, to a population of over 2500 students by the time I arrived. As the size of the population changed, so did the surrounding community. From a sparsely populated area of primarily upper middle-class, White, single-family homes, the neighborhood became a diverse community of older homes and burgeoning apartments with an ever-growing population of immigrants from all over the world. Growth of the district and rezoning in 1993 were partly responsible for the population shift in the school, and by 2000, Clark had become thirty-three percent White, twelve percent Black, thirteen percent Asian, thirty-seven percent Hispanic, and five percent Other.

I continued my fact-finding, confident my newly acquired knowledge would help guide me in creating my educational long-ranged goals for the school.

During each of the passing periods, I'd leave my office a minute or so to monitor the students who would be leaving one class, going to another. Sometimes, I'd leave my desk at various times during a class period to simply see who was out of class. Once

I spotted a student carrying a toilet seat. *What, what is she doing, carrying the seat and the lid?*

I moved in for closer inspection. "Hello, and what is your name?"

"Jaclyn," she said with a smile.

"What's that you're carrying? Exactly, what's that you got? I don't understand."

"It's not what you think, Mr. Smith. I wouldn't steal a seat from the restroom. In fact, I'd never steal anything. It's my hall pass, Mr. Smith."

Reaching for it, I said, "Here, let me see it."

Sure enough it read, "HALL PASS, ROOM 204."

I walked Jaclyn to my office, wrote out an official hall pass for her, filling in her name, where she would be going, and the time of leaving my office. I signed it and sent her on her way—keeping the toilet seat and lid. Shaking my head I thought, *Did some attention-seeking kids sometimes proudly strut through the hallways wearing that seat as a laurel around their necks?*

Long ago, as a teacher I learned not to reprimand an entire class for the misbehavior of an individual student. There was no need to discuss this type of behavior in our next faculty meeting. Instead, during the next passing period, I took the seat to the teacher and told her to remove it from the school. I handed her a pack of standardized hall passes and instructed her to begin using the forms right away. I ended the conversation by saying, "Discontinue utilizing the seat immediately," but I wanted to say much more. *How humiliating to treat a child this way,* I thought.

I focused my attention on the information regarding Clark's three magnet programs, which were instituted in 1993, during the same year Gladys and I opened the math and science program at Hyde Park. As most of Hyde Park's students transitioned into Clark High School at Grade Nine, I knew a little about the Academy for Mathematics, Science, and Applied Technology (AMSAT). But I knew nothing of the other two magnet programs at Clark—the Academy of Finance (AOF) and the Teacher Education Academy at Clark High (TEACH). I learned that the 804 students in those programs attended both magnet and comprehensive program classes. I wrote a note to myself stating, "Our comprehensive program will need to be upgraded. I need to create more opportunities for all students to find a place that fits their particular educational needs." Looking back at my own educational journey, I knew the importance of high school, and that most students could achieve much, much more if they understood, too.

A new process in the business world hit education about the same time I received my high school principal-ship—becoming data-driven. I remember saying to one of my assistant principals, "Gerrie, I don't know what data-driven means, but we need to find out. Based on my little knowledge, Clark has the components to become one of the best schools in the nation. While I'm here, I want to reach that goal. Start learning about data-driven and trend-data. We are going to become a data-driven school."

CHAPTER 89

I nitially, what I enjoyed most about being a high school principal at Clark was all the additional help. I had three assistant principals, two deans of students, and a full-time magnet school coordinator. One assistant supervised our counselors and managed everything having to do with curriculum. Another managed all student activities, which also included facilities and supervising all P.E. teachers and coaches. (I stayed as far as I could away from sports. However, I supervised all of the English and performing arts teachers. Being in their rooms provided entertainment and relaxation during the day.) The third assistant's duties and responsibilities consisted of doing everything I did not want to do, mostly writing reports and completing required documents.

During my first year, Gerrie was in charge of curriculum. She was the most senior administrator regarding time spent at Clark. I felt I could trust her with student courses, grading, and graduation. I left my entire administrator staff with their current responsibilities, wanting to make as few changes as possible.

CHAPTER 90

Having personally taken the journey, I feel confident in saying many teachers at the elementary level are as gullible as their students. They innocently accept what their principal says. Teachers, working at the middle level, are somewhere in the middle themselves. Some things they'll accept, others they won't. High school teachers seem to want to be treated as adults. "I'll allow you, Mr. Principal, to tell me, but I will make my own decisions." Like older adolescents, they say, "I don't need you to tell me what to do."

After my spending a few days on the job, one of my teachers came into my office to learn more about my leadership practices and me. Linda announced his presence. "Mr. Smith," she said, Mr. Rob Petacheck is here to see you."

"Send him in," I responded through my opened door.

"Mr. Smith," he tactfully announced, "I came in because you said you have an open door policy. Is that right?"

"Yes, that's right," I replied, leaning forward, drawing a tad bit closer to him while at my desk.

He leaned in, closer to me.

This guy's good, I thought, and probably as smart as Satan.

"Mr. Smith, I came in to find out exactly where you stand on teacher preparation time. I usually go off campus to get myself a smoothie or something during my prep. Is that alright with you? How do you feel about that?"

I leaned backward and maybe slightly scooted my chair a little backward, too. "Thank you, Mr. Petacheck, for coming in to chat with me.

It's always good for us to know where each of us stands. I believe teacher preparation time is meant exactly for that purpose—it is your hour of non-student time, for you to spend planning your teaching lessons. No, I do not want you leaving campus at that time. It is part of your contracted time to remain on campus, planning for your students." I looked at him with a pleasant smile and added, "Besides, how do I allow you to leave and not let others go for different reasons? I have to hold all of my teachers to the same standards."

"Well, thank you, Mr. Smith. I'm glad we got that straight."

A few minutes later, Gerrie, my assistant principal, came into my office to inform me that Mr. Petacheck had come to see her. "He's putting in a request to transfer out of our school."

"Aw, Gerrie," I said, all the while shaking my head. "I like his style. He knows we won't get along; my philosophy is far different from his. I'm glad we won't have to fight each other. He is choosing to transfer rather than fight with me."

During my first week on campus, I discovered one of my special education teachers regularly switched teaching assignments with the substitute teacher whenever a male physical education teacher was absent—especially when it was the weight-training coach.

I called my special education teacher into my office to discuss his switching practice. After first clearly establishing that this was the case, I simply said, "But you are specially trained. You know your students and how much they need you. Why would you give your students away to a substitute when you can better serve them?"

"That's it, Mr. Smith," he rationalized. "I can do a better job teaching P.E. than the substitute. And when it comes to weight-training, we wouldn't want a kid to get hurt, now would we?"

I cut him off and went straight for his throat—so to speak. "Your special education students need you more than the P.E. students. Besides, you are legally contracted to teach special education, not P.E. From now on, you will remain with your special education students. You will no longer switch positions with substitutes." I concluded our conference by saying, "I'll provide you a memorandum summarizing this meeting."

His hands started shaking. He turned an angry red. "Yes, Sir, Mr. Smith. I know you're

the boss," is all he said as he got up and left the room.

Gerrie entered my office again saying, "You should have seen him, Mr. Smith. He stormed into my office demanding a teacher transfer request. 'That arrogant asshole. I can't work for him,' is what he said to me."

I smiled at Gerrie and asked, "Did you give him a transfer request?"

She, returning my smile and probably sensing my leadership style, replied, "Of course I gladly did, Mr. Smith."

Mattie, who had taught reading for me at Hyde Park and was my reading strategist at Grant Sawyer, presented a lesson on staff development training day. I wanted all of my teachers to learn the two-column note-taking technique, a strategy that asks a question in one column, and then answers the question in the next column. (I had learned this technique from the teachers at Sawyer and saw that it helped students retain knowledge better than by taking simple notes.)After Mattie's presentation, I stood in front of my faculty and preached until sweat pored from my forehead. "You gotta believe all students can learn." They looked at me like I was crazy. Yet, I'd continue my altar call. "Kids will work at the teacher's expectation level. Want more, expect more, believing you'll get it, that they will aspire to your true expectations." Like Tinker Bell and Walt Disney, I, too, had learned the power of belief. I wanted my teachers to accept these words, which would open up their teaching imagination and creativity. Boldly I shouted, " You got to believe. First believe and your desired student results will follow."

CHAPTER 91

My ex-wife, Elaine, was also working as a counselor at Clark High School. She's the one who informed me of the faculty's rumor, "Ronnie is the nephew of our regional superintendent. Nepotism—that's how he got the job." Elaine also had told me she did nothing to correct their belief.

Like not permitting a principal of a newly constructed school to hire more than one third of his faculty for the opening of his school, the district also had policies and regulations governing employees. One regulation states, "To prevent any possible conflict of interest, no family member of an administrator can work in the same school location with the administrator."

I never said anything to my boss about Elaine being in the same workplace with me. After all, we were no longer married.

However, after about two weeks of our being together at Clark, she, my two boys, and I attended my promotion ceremony one evening at the district's boardroom meeting. I felt like every eye in the room zeroed on Elaine, not me, when I stood to be recognized as the new principal of Clark High School. I felt the stares appeared louder than the applause. After sitting down, I could sense my bosses' thoughts. I nudged Elaine. "Elaine, I'm sorry, but I think you and I will receive notification tomorrow morning stating that you will be transferred. I'm so sorry, Honey."

While driving Elaine and the boys back to their home, Elaine asked, "Ronnie I like my job at Clark. It's a special place. I don't want to leave my friends and my students. You won't ask to be reassigned, will you?"

I took a moment to answer. *Elaine, you don't get it, do you? I don't call the shots. My job pays twice as much as yours. I'm not going to jeopardize losing it by requesting to be moved.* Without saying any of that, I replied, "I feel sorry for you, Elaine, but I won't. I'm going to stay at Clark."

Once I got the understanding, I began thinking, *A good administrator is able to make accurate predictions.* Sure enough, I was correct. Elaine and I were informed the very next morning that she would be transferred that day. The district gave her the choice of moving to one of three schools. She chose Palo Verde High School, down the street from where she lived.

CHAPTER 92

I happily lost myself in my work. I attended all of the athletic games, even cross-country, tennis, bowling, and swimming. I wanted students and their parents to know that I cared about them. While cheering for my students I often thought of the English teachers I taught way back during my teacher days. Many of them would not attend the school's theatrical performances. *How could I tell kids to get involved in the excitement of literature and not attend a school performance, especially whenever they were in it?*

One night I came home late and cried on the phone while talking to my friend, Arcola. "I'm tired, Arcola. I'm tired. I can't do it all. I cannot go to every activity, as much as I would like."

She changed my life. "Look at it this way, Ronnie Smith, you've got your own teams. How many people can say they have their own basketball teams, their own football teams, their own soccer teams, their own...?"

"I got it, Arcola. I got it!"

Since attitude is everything, after my conversation with Arcola, I never felt my time was wasted going to a game or any school function. In fact, I felt honored.

CHAPTER 93

Never changing my style or belief in striving for a goal, visitors on my campus who didn't know me probably would never correctly guess my title—especially after business hours. Often, I'd change out of my business suit, replacing it with denim jeans and an old long-sleeve shirt. People would see me using a roller brush, painting a wall inside or out, or using shears to trim shrubby. It isn't that we didn't have personnel to do these kinds of jobs, but if something looked bad or out of place, I wanted it fixed as soon as possible, and I didn't want to take them away from their work. Clark was my home, and I took great pride in it. Perhaps I also took on many quick fixes—physical jobs—as therapy. Most of my professional work did not produce immediate, positive results. But by keeping busy, running from my inner fears and demons, lots of satisfaction came from completing tasks that showed immediate external results.

Naturally, the custodians liked me because I did a lot of their work. It was also very easy for me to demand exceptional campus cleanliness from my head custodian for that very reason. *If you see me doing your crew's work, I've earned the authority to expect the best, for you and your subordinates to follow my lead.* Although I never vocalized it, this was my way of thinking. And I practiced it with everyone in the workplace. *I'll show you how to do it, and I'll do it better than you.* I figured this concept kept my subordinates from hanging onto any traditional, out-dated educational beliefs.

I wanted them to see and to follow me into the making of a nationally recognized first-rate, quality school.

I was talking to my assistant principal over athletics and school events one day in his office. He interrupted our chatting as he saw the head custodian passing. "Hey, Barnie," he called out through his opened office door. "Please bring me two reams of eight-and-a-half by eleven, white copy and print paper. I need it for my computer."

Although I didn't say a thing, I hated what he had done. *Why take the custodian away from his duties to fetch paper for you—a job you can do yourself?* But I didn't say a word because I didn't want to offend him. I had to stop and think, everyone is not like me. We all see situations from different points of view. I learned a long time ago to pick my battles carefully.

Norma, my administrative secretary, also saw things her way, completely different from me. I often thought her customer service skills were awful. Parents coming in for help were frequently put on hold so that she could take her contracted fifteen-minute break. She would send parents away at the exact moment of closing time.

It did not take me long to determine I had had enough. I wanted to reason with her. " Norma, many of our parents are poor. They do not have the luxury of having their own transportation. Many of them have to take off early from their work just to get to our school. I can't demand that you work beyond your contracted time, but, I believe we are here to service the students' and their parents' educational needs. They come first."

"I don't feel that way, Mr. Smith. If they can't get here on time, they can wait or reschedule their appointment."

"You could reschedule your break."

"I deserve my breaks, and I'm not working any unpaid overtime."

With that, I started watching the lot as it pertained to her. I watched her every action, making sure her every action was in accordance to her contracted time.

It didn't take long for her to transfer out of my school.

Now, I could hire my old secretary, Linda. But first, I would have to convince Linda to leave Sawyer, a newly constructed, affluent, stellar school. "First, I will have to discuss your proposition over with my husband," she said to me. "He doesn't like the neighborhood. He feels it's unsafe."

"Linda, you know I'll take care of you," is all that I could offer.

Thank God she came, on the same day Norma left. I felt terrific, knowing Linda would have my back, and that I would not have any secretarial opposition. We could start putting everything in order.

CHAPTER 94

Jemal was home, living with his mother. It wasn't his being a Yale graduate that baffled me. This was my son; I had known him all his life. Something was wrong with Jemal's thinking, but I never asked him about his irrational behavior. Instead of applying for an engineering job, he only wanted to be a busboy, lifeguard, or valet attendant at one of the local casinos. He ended up selling knives to Elaine, our friends, and me—but only for a short while. Eventually, he got a full-time job as a lifeguard at the indoor municipal pool near Bonanza and Las Vegas Boulevard.

Gavin was living off of his mother, not applying himself to anything. He had never taken me up on my offer to pay for a dorm room on the UNLV campus even though it was much too late now.

I remember one day, after growing weary of Gavin's lifestyle, I made the comment to Elaine. "When will Gavin come to his senses and discover school is worthwhile? When will he get it? If he wants a good life, he'll have to acquire it through education?"

"Don't you start," she said. "And how long did it take for you to 'get it?' For you to find your way through school?"

I thought back to how long it took me to graduate from college. All I could say was, "Touché, My Dear."

By now, I had sold my home and purchased a two-story house in Summerlin at the baseline of the mountains.

One morning while getting dressed for school, I heard deep-breathing coming from somewhere upstairs. This noise wasn't steady. It came from time to time. Sometimes I had to ask myself if I truly was hearing it at all. It sounded like Darth Vader's loud, guttural, deep breathing, but I could not pinpoint its location in my house. Each time it erupted, I worked my way closer and closer to its proximity. Finally, I traced it to the closed, sliding, mirrored closet doors in one of my bedrooms. I went downstairs and got the largest, sharpest butcher knife I could find—one I purchased from Jemal. Then, standing in front of the closet doors I said, holding the knife at the ready, "Come on out, or I'm coming in."

Nothing happened. I was mortified. The inconsistent groaning caused my hairless skin to temporarily break out in Goosebumps. "Come on out, or I'm coming in," my voice crepitated.

Something had to be done, so I got the courage to separate the doors. I saw Gavin, sleeping on his back, snoring up a storm. Sometime he had entered during the night. Instead of sleeping in his bedroom, in his drunken stupor, he had chosen to sleep in the closet—in a completely different room.

I left him there on the floor and went to work. I never confronted him, telling him, "if it had not been for my controlled restraint, he could've gotten stabbed with a knife Jemal sold to me.

CHAPTER 95

I continued reading incident reports, faculty and staff investigatory summaries, and other documents on file at the school, as Linda, while reorganizing her files, brought them to my attention. More important were the latest evaluations. I read and approved each new evaluation written by my administrative team. I did not take supervision and the writing of teacher evaluations lightly. I wanted and insisted on more than fair, accurate appraisal. Since I believed the performance evaluation was an important motivator for teacher improvement, I taught my administrators to thoroughly discuss last year's appraisal, the new evaluation, and the new listed directions for improved instruction. I expected a good half-hour spent on quality conversation instead of having each teacher merely read and sign his or her document. As I held conference after conference with those teachers I supervised, I often thought back on Mr. Twitchell and the mentoring he gave me. Over the years, I had added the positive educational mentoring tools in his bag of teaching strategies to my repertoire. It wasn't anything special coming from me. All I used to coach my people were common sense and the skills I had learned from others. I wanted my administrative team to thoroughly understand that if we didn't hold our teachers to high expectations, we would never get high results from them or their students.

Driving everyone under my command to pursue his or her personnel best, I felt an energy-draining notion that very few liked me. Yet, I knew, I wasn't there to be liked—although it helped. I felt even my administrators talked about me behind my back.

Thinking back to a time in my childhood, when my siblings and I would talk behind my father's back, he would often say, "I can hear what you are saying. Quit your syndication." I found some comforting solace in believing that my staff probably syndicated in the pejorative sense regarding me because I pushed them the hardest.

I thanked God for Linda, for she understood and believed in my mission. However, one day she directed me to go to my mailbox, located in the teacher's mailroom. "I wanted to take it out, Mr. Smith," she confessed. "But it gave me the creeps. I just could not remove it for you. Go to your mailbox and get it out."

I didn't know what she was talking about, but I trusted her. *If Linda wanted me to see what was in my box, that's exactly what I needed to do.*

I arrived at the box and I noticed a brown, large envelope placed inside. I took it, opened the clasp, and looked inside. I saw the largest, dehydrated bullfrog sealed in a clear, plastic bag. I could tell it must have reeked with formaldehyde.

I further inspected the inside of the envelope, hoping to find some kind of clue, some kind of explanation, but there was nothing. I then examined the outside of the package, hoping to gain some insight. Again, there was nothing—no written markings of any kind.

Hummmm, I thought. *This has to have come from the science department; I'm really reprimanding their actions. I know that they don't like me.*

Standing by my box, I thought back to a time, one of my first encounters with a science teacher at Clark. This science instructor had actually burned a female student's arm while he used her to model a garment claiming to be flame retardant. While she stood in front of the class, he used a small, handheld blowtorch to set the material on fire.

During my conference with him, I explained that her parents were most upset with him, even though she had only received minor, first-degree burns on her arm. I sensed he did not like taking criticism from a Black man and resented even more my being his boss. "Mr. Smith," he replied, "I have a Ph.D. in science. I know perfectly well what I'm doing. Do you have a degree in science?"

I didn't mention anything about disrespect or comment on his question. All I saw was anger—pure resentment in his eyes. "Her parents called you incompetent and wanted to call in the police. I've spoken to our attorneys regarding this matter. The district will pay the medical bills. With that, the parents are thoroughly satisfied. Please know, all of this will be included in your evaluation and placed in a special conference of summary document." I wanted to tell him, *Be glad that your arrogant ass is not being suspended, terminated, or hauled off and going to jail. You think you're as smart as Einstein, but it's this Blackman who saved your behind.* But I didn't. The way I saw it, he had not intentionally harmed the child. He didn't know the fabric would catch on fire. And all of us make mistakes.

As I stood holding the bullfrog, I also thought of the evening when a custodian came to my office and said, "Mr. Smith, I've been cleaning the science department office. There is something in there I think you need to see."

"What is it?" I asked.

"Oh, no. You need to see it for yourself," he replied.

I thanked him for bringing the matter to my attention. What could it be? I thought as I walked to their office. *It must be serious. After all, the custodian came all the way to my office to point it out. What will I find?*

I walked through the back door instead of marching straight through the front door. (Standing there, in the present, holding the dead, gigantic, green frog, with outstretched limbs, I thought, in retrospect, *Why had I entered through the back door? Was it something apocalyptic? Something ancestral?*) After opening the back door, I could not help from being distracted from my primary mission. The science supply room looked awful. It wasn't dirty—just totally disorganized. Beakers, flasks, petri dishes, Bunsen burners, microscopes—there weren't two of anything sitting on a shelf, side by side. The place looked like a hoarder's paradise. There was no organization anywhere. *I'll have to buy more shelving to get this place in order,* I noted in my mind.

Finally, I walked into the office area. At first glance, everything looked fine. There was row after row of teacher's desks. Half of them were cluttered. I saw nothing out of the ordinary. I looked in the refrigerator, expecting to see a dead cat or something. But no, there were leftover lunches, bottled water, and canned sodas. My eyes began scanning the posters and charts affixed to the walls. Then, on one end wall, with no teacher desk underneath, I spotted the problem. Someone had taken a portrait of me from a parent newsletter, enlarged it to an eighteen-by-twenty-four inch poster, and stapled it on the wall. Who knows who had drawn circles with a fine-tip, black marker around the portrait so that it resembled a target board—with points and within "Ronnie's eyes," two darts were hanging in the board.

Seeing my picture displayed in this manner filled me with rage. My first reaction was to go over and rip it down. *How could they? These ungrateful, arrogant assholes. How could they be so hateful, so blind? Was it the White men, those who all their lives grew up being privileged, thinking they are the alpha males, the ones at the head of the food chain?*

As I started towards the dartboard, eager to rip it down, I noticed a caption written in bold black letters. It was centered at the bottom of the board. "OUR BOSS, RONNIE TEE," is what it said.

How could they? How could they be so mean? I thought I had had a "strong back," that I could take the "slings and arrows" of ridicule and unwarranted insults, but this was painful—probably the most hurtful experience I had endured as an educator.

As I walked over to snatch the poster down, my out-stretched arm and hand delayed their execution.

"OUR BOSS," caught my attention. *No, don't rip it down. Every day, they will see "OUR BOSS," which will let them know they are not the leader, the one in charge of this mutinous department.*

****

As I stood there at my mailbox all I wanted to do was to find gummy-bears, soft, rubbery candy to place in each science teacher's mailbox. I wanted to attach a brief note, saying something like, "You're Special. I'm glad you're on my team. Ronnie Tee."

As I knew I wouldn't be able to find any frog-shaped gummy bears, I let the idea go. I took the dehydrated bullfrog to my office and threw it in the trashcan.

CHAPTER 96

A lthough Jemal stayed committed to his lifeguard job, he aspired and dreamed for much, much more. In addition, to his work, he opened up a non-profit diving school for children, wanting to give back some of his talent to others.

To spend time with him, I would pick Jemal up after his work and coaching. We'd get Gavin and go out to dinner at least once a week.

Gavin drove for a pizza company—adding extreme mileage to the new car I had recently purchased for him. *How he's tearing up his car delivering pizzas instead of going to college, something so easy for him.*

I worked myself into unhappiness watching my sons doing little with their lives. I had expected so much more. Gavin had the potential of becoming a great professional musician or athlete—even a scholar if he wanted. Having the natural talent, all it would have taken was for him to put forth the discipline and the vision. And Jemal, being perfectly content settling for the titles of "lifeguard" and "coach." Both had settled for so much less.

Although I had never asked them, from my perspective, *How could they be happy with what they were doing?" How come they couldn't or wouldn't be like me—striving to be somebody, pushing, always going somewhere?* But I said nothing. Instead of voicing ridicule—my constant admonishments regarding their lack of ambition—I settled to keep my anger, disappointment, and resentment silent.

CHAPTER 97

By June, Elaine decided to run away once more, selling her home and returning to Alaska. Both boys were satisfied with their jobs, so she moved by herself. Perhaps she thought now, with the boys being older, she could spend her time working on herself; she could find a new life, escaping her troubled past.

I let Jemal and Gavin move into my house since I bought a new, much larger home for myself as far west as I could. With both boys working, I only charged them three hundred dollars a month for rent. This covered the mortgage payment.

We never discussed feelings—my feelings for them, their feelings about me, their feelings regarding each other, or their feelings about being separated from their mother. The best I could do was to keep tabs on them. I continued taking them out to dinner once a week. Hoping they would soon get it together and find their way, I kept patient and quite regarding their non-pursuit of upward mobility—their apparent lack of aspiration.

Soaked, saturated with shame regarding my own life, I headed down Interstate

15 during the summer to repair some damages to my sister, Betty's, rental property located on 78th and the notorious Crenshaw Avenue in South Central, L.A. She had informed me that her tenants weren't paying the rent. They were squatting for several years. "The only way I can legally get them out," she said, "Is to sell the property."

I patched and painted, using plaster on the interior and stucco on the exterior walls. I re-screened several windows and replaced some pipes and faucets. The job took about a week. Most nights, I stayed at my mother's. But to escape the anxiety brought on by my past experiences of ghetto-living, some evenings I would drive the thirty miles from L.A. to Chino and stay with my brother, Donnie. Listening to the conversations of the bums living rent-free in my sister's house while I toiled away on repairs often wore on my nerves. Getting away to Donnie's helped.

I frequently revisited some of those conversations while driving from the "rental" to Donnie's. The drive was long but easy. I worked hard trying to block out my observations of the men in my sister's home, dressed in nothing more than their underwear and the women parading around in baggy house coats, slippers, and rollers in their hair all day. "Honey, fry up that rabbit we got in the freezer. It'll be some good eatin'" I overheard one day.

I presumed they had gone hunting somewhere on the outskirts of town or bartered with someone who acquired the meat somehow. I thought of the children in the home. *I'm sure during school-time, they don't even attend.*

Continuing my drive, I reflected on my work. *I'm making this house look so good! But if Betty doesn't sell it fast* . . . My anxiety accelerated. *I'll do whatever it takes. I'll get more education. I'll do whatever it takes. But I'm never living here again,* I confidently vowed, without tears.

Out of nowhere, puzzle-pieces started connecting. Betty's daddy is not my daddy! Vernon Sparks is her father. That's why whenever he came to visit when we were young children, he gave Donnie and me buttons and Betty and Charlene money.

I remembered him saying to Donnie and me while dropping buttons into our outstretched palms, "One day, you'll be men. I'm teaching you now to not look for handouts. Go earn for yourselves."

That's why Mr. Sparks always bought cars for my mother—so his daughter . . .
Arriving at Donnie's, I raced into his house, shouting,
"Donnie, Donnie, Betty is only a half sister. I've figured it out!"
"Ronnie, I don't want to hear it, whatever you're talking about."
"But Donnie—"
"Ronnie, I said I don't want to hear it."

He was so emphatic; I stopped mid-stream, wondering why he could care less. *Maybe he had had a bad day? Maybe he wasn't emotionally ready to hear what I had discovered?* Nevertheless, I let it go and kept those connected puzzle pieces to myself. I didn't call Betty either. Information like this was far too valuable to be announced over the phone. I decided I would wait until I saw her to deliver the news.

During our annual Thanksgiving family dinner at my mother's house, I seized upon the moment when Betty and I were in the kitchen—alone. "Betty, I have something to tell you, and YOU KNOW WHAT IT'S ALL ABOUT!"

Her eyes opened wide. Her lips puckered, and then she snapped back, "No, I do not know what you are talking about. And I certainly don't want to hear it!"

She replied in such a way, I had nothing else to say. *Hmmmm, both Donnie and Betty must be comfortable keeping and living with family secrets.*

I talked with one of my friends about my discovery, and she said it this way, "Ronnie, you ain't no psychiatrist. You cain't be messing with people's heads. There's some things they may not be ready to deal with. You could trip them up real good just by delivering the news. You better check yourself. Don't be gettin' in people's heads when they ain't ready."

I thought about it. Not how she said it, but what she said made good sense. I decided never to bring up my findings with family again—certainly not my mother. I didn't want to send her in a dizzy spin. I didn't want to break her heart.

CHAPTER 98

Even though I was no longer responsible for facilities because I had a subordinate to do that, being principal still made me ultimately in charge of everything having to do with the operation of the school. Over the summer, I learned that thirty-four million dollars of old bond monies would be spent retrofitting Clark High School over the next few years. The purpose of the remodeling was to bring Clark up to the standards of the new high schools. This job was far too important to leave totally in the hands of my assistant principal.

One bright and hot morning, a crew from construction came to my school to enlarge the head-in room (the room that holds routers, servers, and all kinds of modern technological equipment). One of the workers said, "Mr. Smith, we're here to expand this room in your library. We are going to make it twice its size."

"And you are going to add a new, larger air conditioner, as well?" I asked.

"No, that's not in the plans."

"How can you double the size of the room and not replace the air conditioner? As you all can plainly see, this room is currently way too hot. The current air conditioner isn't doing the job. How can you not replace it with a larger, more efficient cooler?"

I added, "When are you planning on starting this job?"

"Tomorrow morning," one of the workers replied.

"No, don't start. I need to research this project more.

Do not start tomorrow," I added.

Later that afternoon, a new group of workers sought me out. "Mr. Smith, we are here to install a new telephone system into your school. It will entail a complete rewiring of your telephones and intercom system. We plan on placing this system in one of the supply rooms in your library."

"Wait. Hold on," I insisted. "You've discussed your project with the men who are installing the new add-on to the head-in room, right?

They all looked puzzled. "No, our work is completely independent of theirs. There isn't a need to discuss anything with them."

"Oh, yes there is," I barked. "Before any of you come into my school wanting to piece-meal your work, there will be a meeting to plan, coordinate, and design a system for the upgrades that will be added to my school. Do not come into my school and start anything without first discussing your planned work with me." I got on the phone and repeated the same thing to the leader of the crew wanting to start work expanding the head-in room. "If you start any work without first having a meeting to establish organized, coordinated plans, I'll rip out any of the work you will have done."

Later in the week an architect and an engineer stopped by my office to thank me for not letting the right hand work independently from the left. "Thank you, Mr. Smith, for bringing unity to our ambitiousness. A hodge-podge of our work would have made no sense at all."

Back then, I could not see it—that perhaps I was God's "building," undergoing rehab. Foolishly I silently asked, *What is it that I have done, oh God? Why do You keep putting new-school construction on my plate?*

CHAPTER 99

Afer three months of not paying the rent, I had to kick Jemal and Gavin out of my rental. "That's okay, Dad," they said. "We'll just come and stay with you."

"Oh, no you won't. Go get an apartment. Go and do whatever you have to do, but you can't stay here or with me." *I'm not having it because they will still be living with me at forty.*

They found an apartment. It was located on the corners of 15th Street and Carson—one of the most notorious crime and drug infested neighborhoods in the city. Prostitutes, both male and female, lurked on and near the complex.

I had second thoughts, *For their safety, should I go against my belief—what my mother had instilled within me at an early age? "The only one who is there to help you is you," she would often say. "If you want something, go and get it, no one is stopping you, but you." For their safety, should I abandon my mother's precept? Should I allow them to come and live with me?*

I thought of all the times since my beginning days of administration I had told parents, "The consequences I'm giving to your child, believe me, are the same ones I'd give to my biological son if..." *Have I lied to them all this time?*

Do I let my boys come and live with me?

The answer came on a day I took them out to dinner, on a day Jemal asked me to pay his rent.

"No, Jemal, I am not going to pay your rent. I am not going to let you and Gavin come live with me either. The two of you have the resources within to make it in this world. I'm not going to cripple you. I will not have you dependent upon me—living with me at age forty.

Whatever you guys want in this world, it's out there. Go and get it. Do not rely on me."

Jemal had had enough of my barking. Being grown and angry, he decided to let me have it. He cautiously fired back, "Dad, I don't mean any disrespect, but you have to be the most critical bastard I have ever known in my life."

I was stunned. I had no words to fire back.

CHAPTER 100

Somehow I convinced the faculty into dressing professionally, modeling the kind of behavior we wanted to instill within our students. I switched back and forth from wearing a sports jacket to dressing in a full suit—sometimes with and sometimes without the vest. But I always wore a tie. And boy did I have ties—over three hundred of them. I especially liked wearing my educator ties, the ones with small handprints, school buses, apples, pencils, or the ones with either Snoopy and Charlie Brown characters, or Disneyland characters on them. Some were cartoonish while others were eloquent and dignified. My shoes were always shined. No one could say, "You are looking neat, but what about your feet?" a statement I had learned while walking past a shoeshine stand in an airport while on my way to a national conference.

The students in our Academy of Finance Magnet Program dressed for success most days, as they had learned the adage, "Someone is always watching you," all too well.

Members of our Student Council and National Honor Society took the lead in modeling excellent, well-mannered politeness on campus. It was the type any parent would want their child to exhibit. Student-made banners and posters hung all over the school, praising club after club for a job well done. Whenever I held a principals' meeting or a special meeting of some kind, visitors would always comment, "Your school looks like an elementary school because of all the banners and posters." Someone would also say, "Yes, but unlike most secondary schools, the displays remain up."

Sometimes, I'd have the parent of a thug meet with me, requesting that I allow a special zone variance for their child. "This school is too boring. There's not enough action. I need a school where the kids aren't so nerdy."

I got it. I understood him fully. No child wants to be where his peers do not welcome or embrace his behavior. What I didn't get was why his parents didn't want their child in a quality school. Why they would support him in wanting less. Although I knew his reasoning didn't warrant a variance to a different school, I found an effective strategy to grant him his wish.

"There are people who unfortunately lose their apartment out of hardship and are forced to move in with relatives," I explained. "Two different utility bills with your name on them and their mailing address, plus a signed letter from your relative stating that out of hardship you have moved in with him or her usually does the trick. As soon as you get those three proofs of residency, your child can be transferred to a different school."

Did I tell a White lie, or did I suggest to the parent to lie? My previous years as Dean of Discipline, coupled with years of administrative experience, had taught me that I'm not going to save every child. In some cases, "One rotten apple..." For the good of our school, I didn't want a student hell-bent on going nowhere to pollute any of my kids' minds or behavior. In my mind, I did what I needed to do.

From time to time I would get on the school intercom and praise the students for their positive, adult behavior. Accentuate the positive was my style. *Expect the best, you get the best—capitalize upon it.*

One evening I spotted a student-made poster stapled on the wall in the social studies wing. "Respect the 'C,'" is what it said. ("C" stood for both Charger and Clark.) "Respect the 'C,'" was printed in black, on yellow poster board.

Hummm, pretty good, and using our school colors. I like this, I thought, shaking my head up and down with satisfying approval.

It didn't take me long to compliment the poster's creator during our next school assembly. I loved how I held off on reciting the actual words written on the poster until the end of my praise. "I thought this person's poster was super cool, but what I loved most was the passion and care obviously this person feels about our school. And the poster reads," I finally announced, "Respect the 'C.'"

"That's mine!" a young female voice shouted from the audience.

"Come on down," I replied from the gymnasium floor. "I want to see who you are, hug you, and tell you once more I love your heartfelt work regarding our school."

The next morning, repeating the first and last name of the artist, I gave an additional announcement on the intercom pertaining to the poster. I also said, "Anyone who would like to submit a poster about our school can give it to one of our art teachers. We'll have a monthly contest. I'll have the winning posters professionally printed. We'll display them on our corridor walls."

Tons of entries flooded the art department. I loved personally presenting the winners with their own creative copy of their posters.

It didn't take long before our student council club advisor asked if I knew the school's spirit song. I had to confess that I didn't, so I was ordered to learn it right away. I went to our choir teacher for lessons, and soon was able to sing it like a pro.

From that experience I learned and fully understood why the principal of Eastside High School in the movie, *Lean on Me*, insisted that all shareholders of his school learn the spirit song. I discovered that singing the song evokes school pride, esprit de corps.

Many times I would use it to easily rally and solicit a consensus whenever I needed everyone to pull together—like the time someone sprayed pepper spray into the intake system of one of our air conditioning units.

During the actual time of the incident I was in a principals' meeting at Fertitta Middle School, way on the Westside of town. My boss came up to me and whispered, "Ronnie, you need to get to your school immediately. Your school is on lockdown, but I don't know why."

I dashed out of the meeting and drove down the city streets doing seventy miles an hour. *What could it be? What has happened at my school?* While stopped at a red traffic light, I called Linda, my secretary from my cell phone. She did not answer hers.

Oh, My God, What can it be? When the light changed to green, I punched the gas pedal. My screeching tires took me from zero to eighty in seconds. *If the cops stop me, I'm sure they'll take me to jail, but I have to get to school. Maybe they'll provide me an escort. I've got to get to school.*

As I raced down Pennwood Avenue, nearing the front of the school, I saw ambulances parked in the middle of the street, with their emergency lights flashing. Abandoned cop cars, with both doors opened, crowded the eerie-looking street. *Oh,*

My God, what on Earth has happened?

I roared up to the curb, screeched to a halt, and barely got in park before bailing out of my car at the front of the school. I saw Linda standing near the flagpole with several officials. *Thank God she's tall. And with that red hair, I could spot her anywhere.* With knees and elbows flying I dashed towards her. Bypassing children and their teachers, my eyes focused on Linda. Before I got to her, I recognized the captain of our local fire department and the deputy sheriff of the Metropolitan Police. I did not know the men in black suits, but I sensed they had to be important higher-ups—maybe members of the FBI.

Gasping for air, I frantically asked, "What's going on?" Linda gave me a walkie-talkie and introduced me to one of the men in a black suit, saying he was in charge. He briefly told me someone had sprayed pepper spray into one of the intake units of one of our air conditioners. One student freaked-out, and when Hazardous Materials, (Hazmat) arrived on the scene, they stripped the female student of her clothing, in front of all the other children—no curtain, no shell or shield, no privacy of any kind. I didn't have time to think, "Lawsuit." My mind was on the welfare of my children.

I immediately called my boss from my cell phone. "Mike, pepper spray, sprayed in an air duct. You better get out here fast. It looks worse than it is, but I'm sure it's going to make the news."

Within minutes, Pat, a director from our district's public relations department, arrived on the scene. I briefed her on the situation. She broke out her cell phone and called the superintendent of schools. "Mr. Garcia, you will need to come to Clark. There's a situation here that requires your presence."

By the time she hung up, my boss, Mike, was using his phone, talking to his boss. "Allen, you need to get over here. Pepper spray in an air duct. A lot of people are overreacting."

I wanted to use my walkie-talkie to check with my assistant principals, to ascertain if there were any additional problems. But I knew the media would be listening in, monitoring our frequency.

I didn't want my voice broadcast on the news, so I kept quiet.

I must have placed the thought in the air. The universe must have welcomed it. One of my assistant principals came over the radio saying, "Mr. Smith, most of our students are assembled on the football field. One female student's asking for you. She says, 'Mr. Smith, I need him. He can help to calm me down.'"

I looked at my boss. He looked at me. We both knew emergency protocol. The building principal, not being an expert in all things, relinquishes leadership and clings by the side of the head official in charge whenever there is an emergency of this magnitude.

"Go ahead, Smith, go to your student. I'll stay at the command post in your place."

By the time he completed his sentence, a custodian had arrived on a mobile work cart to transport me to the field. While traveling the short distance, I saw ambulances everywhere.

When we got to the hysterical student, I called her by name. "You are going to be alright, Mary. Calm down. Take deep breaths. You are going to be just fine." I explained the problem to her while holding her hand. I told her once this ordeal was over, I'd let her use my phone to call her parents. My strategy worked. She didn't need an ambulance.

By the time I completed my session with Mary, my boss' boss told me we could re-enter the school.

I went into the press box, high above the football field and used the microphone to orchestrate the re-entry. It took no time to get everyone's attention. I explained the situation, thanked everyone for being on his or her best behavior, and ended by singing the school's fight song. All the top officials were awed by my students' compliant behavior—especially their joining me in singing the fight song—"Fight on, fight on, fight on 'til we have won..."

As kids have to talk—there is no need doing something if others don't know that you did it—the perpetrator who caused the school disturbance was caught, arrested, and expelled from the school.

On the other hand, one victim wanted silence. The mother of the child who was undressed by the Hazmat crew initially wanted a lawsuit. But because of the unsolicited counseling provide to her daughter, funded by the district, the mother finally decided not to pursue her original intent.

CHAPTER 101

When he looked me square in my eyes, I knew something serious was about to come. Gavin had stopped by my house to visit one Saturday afternoon as he often did. We sat at the kitchen table drinking coffee and eating apple pie. "Dad, how much money did you spend in total, paying for Jemal's college education?"

Humm, where's he going with this? I could see beyond his calculating eyes. "I don't know," I replied. "About $150,000, not counting airfare and extras." I paused and then asked, "Why?"

His face beamed like a lighthouse. He smiled like a fisherman on an excellent, lucky day. Oh, oh, here it comes, I thought. He's thrown his line out, and I've swallowed Gavin's bait. He knew the hook was firmly set. Instead of

reeling me in, he toyed with his catch. "How much did you say?"

Annoyed with his game, I sternly asked, "Gavin, what do you want?"

"Dad, if you spent well over $150,000 bucks on Jemal's education, would it be too much to ask you for only two hundred for mine? I want to go to community college and take a truck-driving class. It's a short course. I will get my certified driver's license, a C.D.L."

No, you'll end up dropping out of the class. You'll say your instructor was full of crap. You'll find some excuse for dropping out. That's what I thought—my expectations had soured. Although I didn't voice my thoughts, I returned his satisfying smile, thinking, *You really know how to play me.* I wrote a check—made out to the community college.

CHAPTER 102

When it came to academics, our school was off the charts, but as I refused to take the leadership in sports, my football team couldn't have been any worse. It got to the point my fellow principals, community leaders, and parents frequently ribbed me. I decided to write an editorial, letting stakeholders know exactly how I felt. The newspaper article went like this:

Principal Reflects on Clark's Football Program

Because I was attending an educational conference in Washington, D.C. with several of my teachers, we, unfortunately, were not able to attend Clark High School's last Varsity football game of the year. Moreover, this game was Homecoming and our final chance for a win.

I was standing at the Vietnam Memorial the evening I received the dreaded news. Our team had lost its Homecoming game to Bonanza High School—twenty to twenty-four. Worse yet, I learned several of our senior players lay on the ground after the game sobbing because of their loss. While staring at the bronze statues of the three Marines, located at the front entrance of the memorial, how quickly my mind shifted back and forth to Clark's football team and my youthful days, serving with my Marine Corps teammates in the jungles of Vietnam.

I know what it's like to lose. Suffering from profound loss, and as the principal, I felt an enormous urge to share my thoughts regarding Clark's program with our players, parents, coaches, fans, and the Las Vegas Community.

Though our student population is over 2,700, I have always said I will always treat students at Clark as though he or she were my very own daughter or son, which is why I want to take a brief detour from football at this juncture. I want to talk about my biological son—some of his accomplishments both in the game of life and in high school sports in Las Vegas.

Jemal, of whom I am most proud, was born and raised in Las Vegas. He graduated from Cimarron-Memorial High School and then from Yale University, with an engineering degree in 1999. Although he participated in every wrestling match for his weight class for four consecutive years of high school, never missing a match, he never accumulated enough "wins," to earn an athletic letter in this sporting category.

During many of Clark's football games, I've often reflected upon Jemal's tenacity— his will to never, never, never give up but to always continue to strive for the goal.

In fact, I've often thought about one of the wisest, most insightful observations Jemal shared with me about life, which came when he was at the tender, precocious age of four. The conversation went something like this.

"Dad, I've figured it out." he said

"Figured what out, Jemal?" I asked.

"Life."

Chuckling to myself, I said, "So exactly what have you figured out about life, Jemal?"

"It's all opposites, Dad. It's all opposites," he said.

I have to admit it took until age fifty or so before I was able to comprehend what Jemal had discovered at four. It took that long for me to discover that what hurts me helps me. What helps me hurts me. Life, what a mixed up ball of opposite confusion!

But give or take a few years, this year, while watching our Varsity football team lose every game—a losing streak of forty consecutive games—I have often pondered over the statement, "Dad, life's all about opposites."

In my eyes, Clark High School's Varsity Football team can never be categorized as losers or defined by the points displayed on scoreboards. A team that consistently refuses to give up, one that has each teammate routinely attend practice, suit-up for game after game, and repeatedly strive for improving one's personal best, certainly demonstrates winning characteristics. Jemal was right. The line between winning and losing is life's twisted game of opposites—the scoreboard opposing character.

To each of our football athletes please know how proud our Charger Family is of you for the gains you have made academically at Clark and for the courage each of you have shown repeatedly on the gridiron. Know this, in the real world, in playing the game of life, it's easy to keep going when everything happening to you seems to be in the winning mode. But, ironically, only true winners have the intestinal fortitude, the heart, to keep "Charging" forward, time after time, when their expectations and hard work continuously result in losses or setbacks. Personally, I can now remember the struggles my teammates and I endured in Vietnam, the jeers and insulting comments made by unfavorable audiences as we returned home to the United States, and the fact that we "lost" that "conflict" back in the day when I was all but nineteen years of age.

To our juniors and underclassmen, who will return to Clark's football program next year, I say continue to strive for the "Big W's" on the scoreboard, for with your tenacious sprit, your ultimate refusal to quit, and the leadership from Coach Don Willis, I am confident you eventually will prevail in reaching your goal. Don't ever think our family has ever or will ever give up supporting your efforts in the classroom, on the practice field, at all of your games, and in whatever you do for the rest of your life.

Seniors, thank you for your continued persistence throughout the football season. Let your ceaseless participation in football throughout your years at Clark always serve to remind you to stand tall, and always give your best, no matter what setbacks may arise throughout your life.

CHAPTER 103

G avin proved me wrong. He completed truck driving school, passing all tests and getting his state certified driver's license weeks before his classmates. When he shared his good news with me, all I could think was, *That boy is so damn smart. There's so much he can do with little effort.* Of course, I did not voice my opinion. I simply said, "Gavin, I'm so very proud of you."

Gavin got a job with a trucking company that transported merchandise throughout the Southwest. I felt he was in good hands because he worked with a mentor. I bought him a cell phone and told him to use it only for emergencies. Giving him my blessing, I watched him drive away.

One month later, the phone bill arrived. Eight hundred dollars, and he had only called me twice. When I finally got a hold of him, my only question was, "Why is the bill so high?"

"Dad, I'm lonely. Driving is such a lonely job. I call my girlfriend every day to keep her and me happy."

"Well, get your own phone now that you are working. I'm going to the phone company and cancelling this account."

He ended the phone call telling me he'd be home on December 18th. He wanted to be here for Christmas.

I got a call on December 15th, about 2 A.M. It woke me out of my sleep. "Ronnie, drive over to our house, and check on our daughter. See if she's all right."

"What?" I asked into the phone, trying to wake up and make sense of what was being said. "Why do you want me to drive to your house?"

"This is Rena's dad."

"Yes," I said. "Gavin's girlfriend, Rena. You are her father, George. I got that, but why do you want me to go to your house?"

"Rena just called," he explained. "She's hysterical. She said, 'Gavin has driven his rig through the front of our house!' We are in Phoenix, visiting family for Christmas. Please go and check on our daughter."

"Damn it, damn it, damn it!" was all that would come out of my mouth. *Gavin has really screwed up now.*

I jumped in my car and started towards Rena's house. *What the hell was he thinking? He'll never get another job.* It was like my driving to Angelo's house, when he thought he had shot and killed a man—except the driving distance was much farther. I envisioned a Mack truck and part of its trailer lodged in the house's entrance. I could see the top of the rig with a new wooden roof. *Oh, God, what the hell was he thinking? He'll never get another job again.*

As I arrived, I saw two police cars parked in front of the house. Both had their red and blue lights flashing. I did not see a tractor and trailer rig partially impelled, rammed into the house. I didn't see a rig. Instead, and to my relief, I only saw a mini Ford pickup truck sitting on the front grass. It was nowhere near the house. I saw turned-up grass, where Gavin had "burned rubber," leaving deep tread marks in the lawn. Apparently, he had tried to make a statement. But, thank God, he had stopped long before touching the house.

I introduced myself to the policeman, explaining that I was Gavin's father.

One policeman began to laugh.

What? He can't be finding any of this funny.

"That son of yours," he said. "He's tough. It took four of us to take him down. We told Gavin he should have become a cop."

And then another policeman interjected, "The irony is we would not have arrested him since we were not here at the scene to see what actually happened. Gavin's mistake was he tried to flee the scene. Then we had to take him down and place him into our custody. We are going to impound the rented truck. Sorry, but you can get it later."

I went into the house to see Rena. She was with a girlfriend. They both were calm. Since no harm had come to the house—no gaping, largely exposed open area with a Mack truck sitting in it—I suggested she spend the night at her girlfriend's house. I called her parents and explained what really had happened. Rena's dad told me they were on their way home.

Driving home I thought, *I'll get the truck out of impound, but Gavin will have to get himself out of jail.* Both of my sons knew very well the repeated tape I had played in their ears. It was the same my mother had recorded in my mind long before I became a teenager. All the way home, I replayed that tape in my head.

If you ever go to jail, you will need to get yourself out. I didn't put you in there, and I'm not getting you out!"

Jemal's the one who put up the money to bail Gavin out of jail. Big Brother sought the assistance of our attorney, who actually got Gavin released. And as a good friend, the lawyer didn't charge either son a fee.

CHAPTER 104

I f it didn't work the first time, what made her think it would be any different during the second try? That's exactly what I thought when Elaine called me one spring Sunday afternoon, telling me she was leaving Alaska. She told me she had an interview for a headmistress position in a boy's home in Northern Nevada.

A few days later, Elaine informed me that she had gotten the position and would be starting within the week. I congratulated her and ended the conversation saying, "Now you will be able, from time to time, to fly down from Reno to visit with the boys." I also told her I would be more than happy to purchase airline tickets for them to fly up on various weekends to spend time with her.

Two weeks later, I learned Elaine was in Vegas, living with our friends, Jim and Janie.

"What? Why did Elaine come back here?" I asked Janie during a phone conversation. "I thought she had taken a job in Carson City."

"She did," Janie answered. "But I think Elaine is suffering from a nervous breakdown. She's not the same, Ronnie. Elaine is not the person we all knew. She's broken and as jittery as all get out. I am going to take her to get some medical help."

I couldn't let it go. I couldn't let Elaine's condition go. I started thinking, *All of this started shortly after Elaine's mother's death. That's when Elaine began her crazy thinking. That's about the time she wanted the divorce.* I felt bad for Elaine, but a long time had transpired since our separation. Elaine and my own inefficiencies had caused me enough pain. I did not want to get close to Elaine. I did not want to share her pain.

Eventually, Elaine and her father moved into Donnie's six-bedroom vacation home located in Rhodes Ranch. But that did not last long. Ed, in his absent-mindedness kept letting one of the upstairs bathtubs overflow. Elaine had to ask for him to leave and to return back to apartment living.

Soon after, Elaine called me, asking to live with me. "Ronnie," she said, "my psychiatrist doesn't think it's good for me to live by myself, especially in a house as large as Donnie's. May I come and live with you?"

"I don't know about this, Elaine. Give me some time to think about it." I immediately thought back to the time my mother allowed my alcoholic father to live with us long after they had gotten a divorce. Her request helped me to better understand why my mother probably took my father into her home. They had once been the best of friends. They had children together, which joined them together for the rest of their lives—married or divorced. Even though I pretended both to Elaine and myself that I wasn't sure and didn't have an immediate answer to her question, I knew. I knew that if I told her, "No," and that if she were to kill herself in her confused state of mind, I knew that I would never be able to forgive myself.

Later that same afternoon Elaine called. "What's the answer?" she asked. "Are you going to take me in?"

I thought about the large house that I gave her when we first divorced. I thought about the second house that I had paid a large down payment on when she left Alaska the first time. I thought about my mother and her taking care of her ex-husband. Then I said, "Elaine, I thought I asked you for some time."

"You did," she replied. "And I've given it to you. Are you going to take me in or not?"

"Yes." I said. "When are you coming?"

"Right away. Thank you," Elaine returned.

When Elaine arrived, I sat her down at the kitchen table. "Look," I explained, "we're not going to have sex. This relationship is purely platonic. Take one of the guest bedrooms. You're here solely as a friend and as the mother of our children."

Elaine looked me in my eyes and then asked, "Ronnie, do you think we'll ever get back together again?"

Immediately, I told her, "No. Elaine, please understand I will always cherish what we had, but that marriage is long gone. I've moved on in my mind and in my life." While speaking, I somehow knew I wasn't just saying the words. In my heart I meant them.

Often our sons would come over for dinner primarily to spend time with their mother. I'd invite them out to a movie, just to get Elaine out of the house. But Elaine always turned the invitation down.

One weekday morning about 1 A.M. she woke me up, saying she needed to go to the hospital.

"What's wrong? Why do we need to go?" I asked.

"I don't know," she'd reply—twitching and shaking like a junkie desperately needing a fix. "Perhaps the doctor will be able to tell us when we get there. All I know is I need to get to the hospital."

After arriving at the hospital, it took hours before seeing a doctor. I did the best I could explaining the problem. Elaine decided to help. "Call my brother in Virginia. He will know exactly what is wrong," she wailed at the doctor.

He looked at me. All I could do was to shrug my shoulders.

After calling Elaine's brother and learning nothing about her condition, the doctor called me to his side and explained that all he could do was to give her Benadryl, let her sleep for a couple of hours, and then for me to take her home.

By then I was so worked up, I probably could have used the Benadryl and rest as well. I decided to walk my frustration away. I walked the streets until sunrise, returned to the hospital, picked up Elaine and took her home. I showered and went to work, thinking, *How am I going to get through this day?*

A few days later, Elaine arranged for our friend, Ruby, to bring a certain cosmetic to our house. Ruby showed up at the time I was ready to leave for work.

The front doorbell rang. I answered it, with Elaine looking over my shoulder. We greeted each other. I saw Ruby hand Elaine a bag. Elaine slammed the door in Ruby's face.

I immediately walked outside and begged Elaine's forgiveness. Ruby looked shocked. "I don't know, Ruby, but Elaine is not the same. Please forgive her. She is not in her right mind."

Before getting in my car, I walked Ruby to hers and watched as she drove off in a state of disbelief.

Elaine must be far gone to have treated Ruby that way, is all that I could think while driving myself to work.

Off and on, I'd frequently take Elaine to a local mental healthcare facility for checkups. She stayed for a couple of hours and sometimes over night, but never for any length of time.

CHAPTER 105

When cars are on empty, drivers fill them up. At school, I was running on fumes. I'm sure there were occasional times I might have stalled out or jerked a little, but my faith pulled me through. When I had completely run out of effective strategies and motivational techniques to improve and move the school forward, God sent Charlotte, an employee with the Nevada State Department of Education. She had applied for and received a two million dollar grant for a federally funded educational program called GEAR UP, which stands for Gaining Early Awareness and Readiness for Undergraduate Program. The program sparked my interest as soon as I discovered it would provide my low-income students an increased opportunity to prepare to enter and succeed in postsecondary education. My school would be receiving additional funding of seventy-seven thousand dollars per year, for four consecutive years. There were no stipulations. The grant money just had to be spent on services designed to raise the expectations of my low-income students and families and to increase college attendance and success. I could spend money on programs like motivational speakers that would impact every student in my school.

GEAR UP's beliefs matched mine to a T—all students deserve an equitable education, one that provides the knowledge and skills to choose and be successful in postsecondary education pursuits. I believed students must master rigorous academic standards to successfully progress along the pipeline from middle school to high school and into and through college. In order for students to plan for college they need to see themselves in college.

I wanted to get started right away on GEAR UP.

Charlotte invited me to attend the eighth-grade awards program, which would be held at my primary middle school feeder school. She wanted me to begin developing my relationship with my future freshmen and their families early. She also invited me to attend the meetings of the GEAR UP advisory board governing her specific program. I accepted both invitations.

The awards program at Cashman Middle School was cute. It reminded me of being principal at Sawyer Middle School several years prior. I made it a point to learn a few names of students and what awards they received. I used my cell phone to take their pictures. I jotted down lots of notes. I would use this information the next time I saw these students, when they came to my school for freshmen orientation. What a surprise it would be for them and their parents to see the principal already knew them by name. That would certainly start our relationship off in a positive way.

During my first GEAR UP advisory board meeting, I was in awe of the members—such muckety-mucks, higher-ups, and prestigious people in my eyes. For example, there was big, old, overweight Dr. Bill sitting at the oval table, with his fat fingers interlocked. He was dressed in a tight black suit, skinny black tie, and heavily starched white shirt. This Black man, with balding gray hair, looked like an aged, retired NFL lineman. My respect, first and foremost, probably came from his being Black. Tucked deep within the child inside of me is admiration for educated Black folk—especially Black men who rose above adversity, poverty and ignorance. Through education, they became somebody. Dr. Bill was one such person. He was the director of a student outreach program, called Upward Bound, at UNLV. All of GEAR UP's beliefs were the same as mine. *This program was a Godsend.*

CHAPTER 106

Life is a constant juggling and balancing act. The timing and emotional agility has to be just right. Elaine said something profoundly wise to me one evening, while going in and out of her struggle with rational thinking. "Ronnie," she said as she looked at me, putting her fingers to her cheeks, and smiling. "The only things that are black and white are cop cars, you, and me. Although you want to control everybody and everything in your world, to reduce all social issues to the lowest denominator, which for you is black or white, life doesn't work that way. You are not in the ghetto anymore. All things are blended shades of gray."

I didn't know what I had done to prompt her to make the comment. *Was it something going on in her own mind?* Not wanting to exacerbate her anxiety, I never discussed my work with her anymore like we both used to do when we were young. And I knew for sure she couldn't read my mind. *Why did she make the comment?*

Perhaps her mind had slipped back to one of the few times I had felt trusting and comfortable enough to share my fears and frustrations of growing up Black, poor, and in the ghetto.

Maybe she had reverted back to how she always saw me—driven, putting my education and work before her and everybody else. Who knows what was going on in her mind? I don't think she was cognizant enough to compare my way of coping with my gut-wrenching fear of living a life with a dream deferred to her present state of insanity or instability.

CHAPTER 107

As Edley's wife, Noboko, had recently died from breast cancer, Elaine had talked him into taking her into his home in Virginia for a while, possibly to give me a break. And during this break Charlotte, our local GEAR UP director invited me to attend the national GEAR UP conference in Washington D.C. during the summer. She wanted me to see in full detail how the program worked. I had one full week of five-star hotel accommodations, great conversations, meeting new people and dining on gourmet cuisine. How pleasurable it was, getting away from the Vegas heat and snacking on fresh fruits and special treats during session breaks throughout the day.

Principals, pompous coordinators, and directors of all kinds, from all fifty states and the federal government, filled the conference rooms. Mixed in with "common folk" I felt like muckety-mucks dominated the place. All were highly educated, including me. But many were pretentious, sagely strutting sophistication and rarified airs. I easily entertained myself watching their bourgeoisie affectations.

Ironically, I thoroughly enjoyed a speaker who gave a presentation about children of poverty. She spoke on how the filthy rich live their lives and how the poor struggle through theirs. She described how the rich could spend thousands on a painting.

And how the poor would sell it if they were lucky enough to miraculously get their hands on it. "Sadly," she said, "that person in dire poverty would spend all the money obtained by selling the painting in no time, having nothing to show how the money was spent. "The person in poverty could do no more than simply raise his hands and say, 'All gone. The money is all gone. I don't know where it went, but I had a great time spending it.'" This speaker also talked about overcoming the challenges faced by low-income, first-generation, and college-bound students—how it requires the continued engagement of school leaders, families, and communities.

Several speakers got me all jazzed up. *Okay, this is all good, I thought, but I'm not the one who needs motivation. I need to bring my teachers to this conference, and they need to bring their students. We all learn by doing, so I need my teachers and students to present a session at the annual national GEAR UP conference.*

I presented my idea to Charlotte. She said she would work to make it happen.

Utilizing my counselors and administrative staff, we rethought our methodologies for freshmen orientation. We used GEAR UP monies to purchase three thousand t-shirts to distribute to our incoming Class of 2007. We handed out a t-shirt to students and parents—all who attended the introductory high school breakfast. We also bought large fresh fruit platters; chocolate, blueberry, apple-cinnamon, and poppy seed muffins; juice of every kind, and coffee.

During the program, a counselor explained grade point averages, class rank, and the importance of being ranked at the top of the class instead of in the middle or at the bottom. The band played, the cheerleaders cheered, and our ROTC cadets—both armed guards and drill team—performed. We talked about high school being merely a stepping-stone. "The end of the journey is lifelong learning. Education will change the quality of your life," I preached. They could look to me. I would be their role model. "Don't do as I say, but follow my footsteps. Do as I am doing." My assistants passed out Clark candy bars, note cards and pencils—all paid for by GEAR UP funding. We had the students set a goal and write an affirmation using their own wording. We wanted their affirmation to emulate the one I wrote on the overhead projector lighting the large silver screen. I wrote, "Today, I will begin my journey to graduate not only from high school, but also from college."

Paid for by GEAR UP, we fed everyone a good lunch consisting of sandwiches from Subway, chips, and soda pop before ending the program.

CHAPTER 108

On August 13, 2003, Edley called me, telling me Elaine had committed suicide. "While I was out of the house, she used my handgun to shoot herself in the throat."

"Oh, Edley," was all that I could say. "Let me make sure I heard you right. Her shot was fatal? Did I hear you right? How are you, Edley? Is there anything I can do?"

"Go tell my dad and then tell the boys. I'm all right," he calmly said.

I decided to drive to Jemal's and Gavin's first. I felt the need to separate them and tell them individually. *If Jemal handles this with composure, I'll be all right. If he completely falls apart, I don't know what I will do. Oh, God, how I need Jemal's strength.*

When I arrived at their apartment, Jemal was outside, standing against the railings, waiting for me.

I had him join me in my car. "Jemal, brace yourself. I don't know how to say this, but . . ." I don't remember exactly what I said. All I know is that I looked directly into his eyes.

After I had told it all, Jemal looked at me in awe. It was almost a look of disgust. I waited for what seemed forever for my son to say something. I waited for his downpour.

Continuing to present his quizzical look, he calmly said, "Dad, Mom's been dead for months. What I don't get is that I thought you knew this. Apparently, you didn't."

I grabbed him and hugged him hard. *Oh, thank you God. Jemal has given me the strength I need.*

We went into his apartment. I gave the news to Gavin. However, I've blocked his reactions out. Gavin is a lot like his mother, wearing his emotions outwardly, loaded with lots of drama, which is why I probably blocked out his reaction, so that I wouldn't loose my composure.

While driving the two boys to Ed's apartment, I continually asked myself, *How do I tell a father he has lost his daughter?* I don't remember what I said to Ed, but I remember well his appearance and response. He was sitting on a small stool, unshaven, ungroomed, and in his white underwear. Ed was in his own world—no house robe, no slippers, not much of anything. "Oh, no," he calmly said. "Elaine has always been temperamental, spirituous, so rambunctious. She acts without thinking." Tears filled his eyes. He lowered his head and said no more.

I tried to imagine how he was feeling, having recently lost his wife and now his daughter. I wondered how I would be feeling if I had lost one of my sons.

Gavin went to Ed, hugged him and said, "Pampaw, you still have me. I give you all my love."

CHAPTER 109

I spent the next few days planning Elaine's memorial service. One of Elaine's friends, who was on the board of trustees at her church, got me the use of her church. My secretary, Linda, got the Minister who had buried her mother to officiate the service. I paid a professional cater to provide the food and service at my home for the repast. Gavin and I practiced "Ode To Joy" to get it perfect for the ceremony. He played his bass, which I kept at my house. I played the piano. I ordered an enlarged portrait, which would rest on an easel placed up front, by the podium. I took the poster to a florist to have a special arrangement of small roses and baby's breath affixed to it. Linda sent out an email to everyone in the district announcing the date, location, and time of the memorial service. Edley contacted his family. I contacted my family and friends. I don't know how the local newspaper got the information.

While making the arrangements, I felt great animosity towards my boss, his boss, and the associated superintendent of secondary education.

I did not want them to attend Elaine's going-home event. Perhaps, in the back of my mind, I somehow wanted to blame them for her death. They were the one's who had forced her to leave Clark High School. I adamantly did not want them to attend the service, smiling, shaking my hand, and mendaciously offering their sympathy. I did not want them there, but Linda reasoned with me, convincing me that I could not decide who could and should not attend the send-off.

CHAPTER 110

Elaine's brother, Edley, spoke at the service. My two sons gave eloquent, articulate speeches. I knew Elaine would have been proud of them. I certainly was. I don't know why, but for some reason, I felt my dignity rested in how well my offspring spoke. Donnie told the story of how all of Elaine's and my male friends were taken aback that day at the lake when I was trying to water ski on one ski. He spoke of how Elaine thought that I was drowning when I went underwater. How she charged into the water to rescue me. He described how all of our male friends jealously longed to have a girlfriend like that. One of Elaine's dearest friends spoke of how Elaine could meet a stranger on the street, and then within twenty minutes of conversation, they could become friends for life. Gavin played his upright bass flawlessly, but I botched our duet. I was too nervous to play the piece in public—the piece I had practiced a thousand times. Big Ed, Elaine's father, came appropriately dressed. I figured one of his family members had supervised his dressing. But he stood at the podium and spoke for over five minutes about the health benefits derived from drinking fresh carrot juice. He spoke of how he had tried to encourage Elaine to drink lots of fresh carrot juice.

Throughout his presentation, all I could do was lower my head, bring my hand in front of my face, and think, *The man is definitely in his own world. He has screwed this whole program up.*

As I stood in the foyer greeting guests, I felt relieved that none of my bosses attended the ceremony. As a tribute to Elaine, and to use her term, I wanted her service to be genuine—no "bullshit" included. Big Ed certainly played his part in keeping the ceremony real. Other than his horrid presentation and my terrible piano playing, everything went well. That is until one of my friends came over, shook my hand, and said, "Man, your kids sure can speak. I know you are proud of them. I sure hope they have your genes and not their mother's."

How dumb can you be? I first thought. *There was no reason for him to say something as stupid and as inconsiderate as that. I guess the world is made up of all kinds, and I have to be accepting and perhaps a little less judgmental.* I wasn't upset or angry. How could I be? Deep down inside I knew he genuinely cared for me, and I felt the same for him... *I guess some people have a difficult time finding words of comfort during times of trouble,* is how I wrote it off. His comments lead me to thinking, *I've never gone out of my way to broadcast Elaine's suicide, but I've never denied it either, whenever I was asked.* I frequently told myself, *Something must have been mentally wrong with Elaine for her to kill herself. In her right mind, she never would have placed that guilt and affliction upon her children. In her right mind, she would have had the courage to endure going through menopause. In her right mind, she would have had the tenacity to fight against all of her psychological torment.*

Much of Elaine's family gathered at my house for the repast—including Aunt Patsy and her husband, Fat-Pat-The-Democrat. I felt good being with them again.

After the guests were mostly gone, Edley gave Gavin and Jemal urns filled with Elaine's remains. He told them that he had three—one for each of them and one for himself. Although I thought about it, I didn't say, *What about me?*

I guess he was thinking, "Ronnie really isn't attached to Elaine anymore."

Later, Jemal took his mother's ashes to Yosemite and released them to the wind. Gavin scattered her ashes on the beach in Santa Barbara.

CHAPTER 111

With most of the naysayers transferred, our school was running smoothly—practically "playing" itself. I had one full-time guitar teacher, one full-time theatre educator, one full-time choir teacher, two full-time band instructors, two full-time orchestra instructors, and two full-time art teachers. One taught Advanced Placement Art, where students could get college credit for high school work. Not that I was comparing my school to any others, but the only high school in the valley that surpassed us was the Las Vegas Academy of Performing Arts, the magnet school my son, Gavin, attended for four straight years.

How I cherished our humanities program. Even when our football team wasn't playing so well, our marching band attended every game—even the away games, right along with me. Sometimes, we would have more supporting fans sitting in the bleachers attending the away games than the home team.

At our home games, I felt great pride whenever our band played our fight song.

Sometimes, I would stand before the musicians, at the teacher's request, and conduct them as they played our fight song. But best of all was when they gallantly marched on the field at half time and used their bodies for signage, spelling out "C L A R K," our school's name.

Many times, I'd think to myself, *How can a Black man who loves the music of Dylan, Baez, Seeger, and Beethoven's musical setting of "Ode To Joy" not have a stellar performing arts high school program?*

Knowing talk is cheap if it's not followed through with action, I dreaded spending a few days before New Year's traveling on a bus with our band to the Fiesta Bowl, in Phoenix, Arizona. Marching with our band in a downtown parade was joyous—especially when the band played "Viva Las Vegas." But chaperoning two hundred kids wasn't my kind of fun, especially on New Year's Eve. The hamburgers, fries, sodas, and pizzas wreaked havoc on my healthy, nutritional eating routine. Knowing the gross penalties for leaving a child unattended, the counting and recounting of every student on my bus each time we loaded was difficult enough. The room checks and placing a strip of masking tape across the outside door and doorframe of each room housing our students made the job of chaperoning that much more non-enticing. Each morning before sunrise, the teachers would inspect the tape to see if it still remained attached to the frame and door. All the students had been threatened with bad consequences if the taped seal were to ever be found broken.

I shall never forget the miserable feeling of being trapped with our two hundred students, plus high school band students from all across the coast, in a huge sports complex, on New Year's Eve, in Phoenix. What a miserable night for me. Not because anything terrible happened—just because I was there, with thousands of kids instead of selfishly enjoying my time and peace at home. But my way of thinking was, *If my teachers could do this and without any extra pay, I, too, could give them my full, personal support.* Nevertheless, was I ever so happy when the busses finally returned us back to our school.

I fully appreciated the dedication my teachers gave to their profession—all of them, in every discipline. So much so, I began writing grants, applying for teacher-recognition awards, unbeknown to the teachers. I filled out numerous applications for special teacher scholarship programs. Many of which my teachers received, and I always gave them the credit. I didn't need it. I had more than enough recognition plaques and certificates hanging on my office walls.

CHAPTER 112

" Mr. Smith! We've been invited to play at Carnegie Hall. You've got to come along," my head-orchestra teacher shouted in my office, begging me to join our symphonic orchestra, our choir, and our band on a trip to New York.

Oh, no, I thought. "And you say the trip will last five days?" I could only think back to Phoenix.

Six weeks later, we were at the airport, ready to board three airplanes on a red-eye to New York. "Yes, we got three planes, mostly dedicated to us—and our musical equipment, Mr. Smith, my orchestra explained. Can you imagine how much space it takes for six hundred kids and their instruments? We're bringing the chimes and loads of contra basses. We've got our gong, harp, and tubas. Good God, what luggage. But the airline's given us a discount."

While there, we stayed in one of the luxurious hotels in Upper Manhattan. We toured the Empire State Building and rushed through Central Park. Unlike our trip to Phoenix, we dined at Carmine's and other fancy restaurants. We even took a special dinner cruise on a ship around New York Harbor. I was overjoyed as the ship passed the Statue of Liberty, and music of Ray Charles singing, "America The Beautiful," played over the intercom. Mixed in with our rehearsals, we also spent time at Julliard. Some of their teachers coached our students. Listening to the music and instruction, I could only think of Gavin. *Why did he turn this opportunity down? Too bad his fear of not possibly being able to pull graduation off, like his brother, Jemal, kept him from trying. Fear kept him from pursuing this incredible journey from the start. Fear boldly robbed him. Oh, if only . . . It would have been so life-changing good.*

From Julliard, we took a grand tour of the Metropolitan Opera House. While there, I could only think of our poor, "misrepresented" students, predominantly Black and Hispanic, who, had it not been for their passionate music teachers, would not be attending this trip. I thought once more about my solicitous fundraiser opening, my schmoozing to politicians and affluent business partners. Many times I preached, *In order for our students to be . . . they have to first be given the opportunity to see. Please, please, generously support our cause.*

The concert at Carnegie was a showstopper, especially for the senior-citizen audience when our band played a series of military marches. Everyone stood clapping long after the music ended. I was delighted that our conductor took the time to mention that I, the principal, spent time in Vietnam serving our country. But my biggest surprise came when I looked at the program and saw that our head band teacher's wife was listed in the program. She had been a former chorus teacher at our school until giving birth to their second child. That's when she quit teaching and became a full-time homemaker. Anyway, the eye-opener for me was when my band teacher's wife walked out onto the stage and sang a solo.

Shame on you! I thought. *That should have been one of our students singing instead of you.* In the back of my mind I knew she was going to do this—good principals are never surprised. Making accurate predictions is the name of the game. However, I liked entertaining myself with the thought that her singing came as a surprise. *Yeah, she has always fancied herself singing at Carnegie Hall, and this was her chance to do it.* Neither her husband nor I, were going to tell her, "NO!" Some battles are better left alone, and I believed this was one.

CHAPTER 113

Since my trip to New York was so much fun, I decided to take one more with the orchestra, band, and choir. This time it was to Disneyworld. Each group had their own separate performances. Included in the trip were special workshops put on for our students by Disney musicians.

I marveled at how the workshop teachers coached the students into improving their playing. "Imagine, you now have the opportunity of playing this piece for the President of America. What would you do? After practicing it a thousand times, you'd have the confidence you could play it to perfection. Let's pretend that you have practiced and are now ready to play for the President. You are now going to give it your greatest effort. Let's

begin," he said, counting. "And a one, two, and three." Bad, greasy fast food, but excellent instruction.

Hummm, I like his approach, I thought. *I've got to utilize it with my teachers.*

Along with the workshops, the students played their gigs at Disneyworld.

During the orchestral performance, the teacher announced how appreciative he was of my traveling everywhere with them. And during that time he had me stand for a special piece the orchestra wanted to dedicate to me. They played "My Girl," which left me crying. After all, it was my favorite old-school sound. It captured the best of my high school memories, which were far apart and few. The sweet harmony of violins, violas, cellos, and basses, playing especially for me—nothing could have touched my heart more.

CHAPTER 114

Because of his diving skills and working as a lifeguard, one experience led to another. Through Jemal's world of contacts, he somehow landed a full-time job in the pirate show, *Sirens*, at the Treasure Island Hotel and Casino.

"How'd you land the job?" was the first thing I asked.

"Dad," Jemal replied, "one of my friends told me to audition, and I told myself, 'I'll impress them with my double pike gainer, a dive I've done more than a thousand times.' It worked, Dad. I got the job."

Jemal told me he would earn fifty thousand a year, working five days a week, doing three shows daily.

I'd see the show often, just to let Jemal know that I was proud of him. Additionally, doing each performance, I'd tell everyone near me, "The diver, the pirate on the highest mast, that's my son."

One evening while Jemal and I were out to dinner, he shared with me, "Dad, I've got pictures. I'm standing and talking, one-on-one, with Michael Jackson. Entertainers visit with our cast all the time." He also said something I took to be more significant. "Dad," he said, "this job is the only one I've had where I don't have to lie."

Hummm, I thought. *Was he idealistic? Did he carry that wonderful trait, like Elaine and I had done in our early adult lives? Did he ever use the words "bullshit" or "mendacity", or allow falsehoods or calculating lies to upset him?* He had only had a few jobs, but after hearing him make that remark, I thought back to the time he worked as a lifeguard at the downtown municipal pool. During one of our dinner conversations, Jemal had told me how the city wanted him to lie about a shower stall that was always wet. Some patron had slipped on the slick titles outside of the shower and was pursuing litigation. The manager of the pool wanted Jemal to lie and say the plumbing had been repaired and not leaking. I thought back to my own job, and how I had been taught to never, ever lie. I thought back to how I have always practiced telling the truth and how it serves as a guidepost. Knowing I would be honest probably kept me from exhibiting behavior that could lead to terrible consequences—even more lies to cover up.

CHAPTER 115

His new job in entertainment brought a change to Jemal's outward appearance, as well as to his disposition. Perhaps it was the strenuous effort he put into the diving and dancing. Learning the choreography and performing three times a day was quite a physical workout. His body was tall, slim, and taunt. It reminded me of mine when I was in the Corps. Boy, did he look good! He let his hair go natural, wearing it in long dreadlocks. The hint of browns, copper, and gold in it and in his newly grown beard came from the chlorine in the pool. Although I've never wanted to live an adventurous life through my children, I was awfully proud watching my son performing as a handsome pirate on the Strip.

As I spent time with him, Jemal seemed to be more content, happier—like he had found himself. He told me he was planning to work his pirate job for only one year. Then he would move to an ashram in Cal-Nevada to study Buddhism or Hinduism, yoga, or something—one of the Eastern religions.

CHAPTER 116

After Gavin's run-in with the law, like I had predicted, he lost his truck-driving job. Learning to make due, he took a job as a professional cab driver.

Although I never told him, I was afraid. I didn't want to see him in this job. All I could do was to think back to a time in my life, when I was a senior in high school.

****

Stanley was probably the brightest in our group. Thinking himself to be intellectually above the rest of us might have been the cause of his trouble. Being White didn't help. Stanley was raised from birth in our Black ghetto. Although we never discussed it, I've often wondered when his confusion regarding his racial identity began. All his life he acted "Blacker" than I looked. His genuine use of Ebonics, his dress, and his hood-rat gestures placed him in a lifestyle that was going nowhere.

None of Stanley's childhood friends ever entered his house—including me. We'd laugh, joke, and talk about the times we could sneak a quick peek from the front yard, times when Stanley would enter or exit his house from the front door. Through the gap, we would capture brief glances at disassembled truck and car engines or transmission parts laid out on tables and sprawled out on the living room floor. (Stanley's father was a professional automobile mechanic. He did lots of side-jobs literally in his home.) I'd wonder if Stanley developed a neurosis, an attitude of less-than by his friends not being allowed to come inside his home.

During our childhood, Stanley had a loving heart. He was an only child. To fit in where he could, he would smile a sheepish grin and give away his candy or money whenever asked. I never took advantage of him. He was a follower, a people pleaser—mostly brawn, with a little brain.

He once came to visit and told me, "Ronnie, the Court mandated that I see a psychiatrist."

"What for," I asked.

"In and out of trouble with the law. Small things, misdemeanors, nothing big."

"And what did you learn from your visits?" I asked.

"Nothing. I educated the shrink. I said, 'Man, you and I don't have nothing in common. It's a waste of my time and yours—my being here. You'll never be able to feel where I'm coming from. And I certainly don't understand your world. Like I said, this is a total waste of time.'"

His first car, given to him by his father, was a 1960 VW Bug—an old fixer-upper. It didn't surprise me the day Stanley and I were riding in his Bug and he got a flat on the rear-right, passenger side. Stanley didn't have a jack. "Here," he said, "I'll pick up the car and hold it up until you change the tire."

I worked as fast as I could, and in no time, we were on our way.

At seventeen, he somehow outsmarted the employer of a taxi company in our neighborhood. Stanley often bragged that he was legitimately earning good money driving his cab. But his job didn't last long. And it wasn't because the company discovered his actual age.

One late night around 2 A.M., a customer outsmarted Stanley. His passenger used a sawed-off, double-barrel shotgun to blast both barrels into Stanley's back. Robbed and left for dead, the doctor later clarified, "Stanley's 275-pound frame, his fatness, is what saved Stanley's life."

I believe Stanley's continual overuse of painkillers significantly changed his life. His self-medicating sped his life totally out of control—causing him to bump sometimes and occasionally to crash.

Donnie called me one day and shared that he was feeling sad—sad because he did not want to invite Stanley to a party. "I'm having a dinner party for my bosses at Hughes Aircraft. I've also invited our closest childhood friends. I'm not inviting Stanley because he won't fit in. It's not me I'm concerned about. I don't want him to embarrass himself and make my guests uncomfortable. You know, he doesn't fit in."

"Donnie, you are right; don't invite Stanley."

I was surprised when Stanley unexpectedly showed up. Donnie and I deduced a friend had invited him. Nevertheless, the party was a success. Stanley kept his mouth shut and didn't give his lifestyle away.

****

Stanley often bragged of buying ladies of the night—that is until his father, Stanley Senior, had to bail him out of jail for solicitation of prostitution.

"Is that what you want? Do you want me to kill you?" Stanley's father yelled into the streets as he threw Stanley out of the house and yard. Neighbors watched the show. "I'm completely through with you, Son. I disown you. You can't stay here anymore. You've got to go." Gossip spread throughout the neighborhood that Stanley Junior had used his own I.D. to withdraw twenty thousand dollars from his father's bank account.

Our childhood friend, Archie, came to Stanley's rescue. As his father had recently died from cirrhosis of the liver, Archie allowed Stanley to take up shelter in the family's motor home. Weeks later, and to Archie's dismay, Stanley stripped the motor home of everything—light-fixtures, seats, the compact mini refrigerator, and stove—everything. His insatiable need for drugs was driving him off the road of life.

Archie threw him out. None of our group saw Stanley for years. And when I ran into him on the streets, Stanley was ragged, toothless, and pockmarked. He weighed about one hundred pounds. I didn't know him anymore.

Going nowhere, Stanley eventually died from a drug overdose.

Saddened when I heard of his death, my mind replayed a quick overview of Stanley's life. *I can't trust skin color to determine someone's character, internal struggles, morals—anything about them,* was the life-lesson I learned from that relationship.

****

While Jemal was steadily improving his life, Gavin, on the other hand, was slowly plotting self-destruction. He worked regularly, but he was drunk all the time. He dressed like a bum, and often didn't comb his hair. I considered seeking mental treatment but knew his strong denial. So I never followed through.

After taking a riding class from the community college and saving enough money to make a small down payment on a brand new Harley motorcycle, Gavin rode to my house to show it off. It was a beautiful candy apple red, with lots of shiny chrome.

But Gavin was never satisfied with the way things were. He always had to modify them, twisting them to his own personal liking. He used the inside of my garage to strip and repaint his bike three or four different times. He constantly used my tools, never cleaning them or replacing them in their assigned place. And all I could think was how my daddy would yell and shout to Donnie and me when we were young, "Leave my tools alone!"

Gavin's "spray booth"—my garage—angered and frustrated me to no end. I spent a complete Saturday afternoon using mineral oil, wiping the residue of old paint, which he had taken off with a wire brush and drill, and new paint overspray from the white walls of my garage. I had to repaint, which totally aggravated me. But I enjoyed listening to the smooth, distant, beautiful roar of the motorcycle—vroom, vroom—as Gavin approached or left my home.

One day, Gavin asked me to follow him to Jemal's and his apartment. We took the Summerlin Parkway to Interstate 95. I intelligently drove my car. Gavin raced down the freeway. All of a sudden, he threw both of his hands high in the air.

Damn it. Damn it. What is it he's trying to do? Does the boy not have any sense? What is it that he's trying to do?

Arriving at the apartment, I didn't say a single word. Nor did I present any disapproving gestures. *I'm not about to give you what you want, Gavin. No way will I display any behavior you're expecting. I'm going to annoy the hell out of you, and I hope my unpredicted behavior hurts to the bone.* I decided to use the methodology of IGNORING, one I used to get the goat of students whenever they would do something negative to get my attention.

Some weeks later, Gavin told me the reason he lifted his hands from the handlebars of the motorcycle was to show me how much he was hurting from the loss of his mother, how much he was out of control, and how much that he, too, wanted to die.

I told him I would pay for him to see a doctor or therapist, that I loved him, and that I wanted to get him help. But he refused my offer.

Sometimes, when Gavin left his soiled clothes at my house, I'd take them to the cleaners, right along with mine. Believing that whenever I was dressed nicely, in starched, creased pants and shirt, my attire helped to lift my spirit. I wanted the same for Gavin. But I never saw him in his laundered clothes.

CHAPTER 117

O ver the next three years we took teachers and some of their Class of
'07 students to the national GEAR UP conferences held each summer.
Charlotte followed through on getting Clark to present a session at each
of these conferences. The conventions were held every other year in two different
locations—San Francisco or Washington D.C.

Bloom's Taxonomy is a matrix which ranks the different types or ways of learning.
The lowest, least effective method of teaching is by getting students to use rote memory.
The highest is application—applying what is learned to real-life situations. Knowing
this, we wanted both our teachers and students to soar while planning, developing,
and executing their presentation at the GEAR UP conferences.

They never let us down. Their presentations were the talk of the week's events—so
much so, after their first performance, other schools started presenting. *Oh, how the
program had changed since my first attendance.* I was glad to see the improvements.

On our first trip to San Francisco, my magnet theme coordinator prearranged for our group to have a personalized tour of both Stanford and Berkeley. We wanted our underprivileged students to see the type of postsecondary education they could get—paid for by GEAR UP. All they needed to do was take challenging classes, study hard in high school, and earn good grades. Part of the two-million dollar grant included four years of college for these children of poverty. How we wanted their lives to change. We wanted to do everything humanly possible to break them away from a family tradition of educational unawareness—a lack of interest for pursuing academic excellence.

Traveling by tour bus, a few students marveled at the palatial estates we passed along the way to both universities. "Wow, did you see that mansion?" one child chimed.

"I wonder who owns it, and how did they ever get rich enough to buy it?" another student questioned.

"You can have it, too," piped in one of our teachers. "Who told you you have to be at the bottom of the workforce? Put those notions, those self-fulfilled prophecies out of your head. Go to college. People will pay you a lot for what you know."

I don't think any of our students living within the community ever rode a trolley, and most likely, they probably didn't have family funds either to splurge on extremely fine dining. Therefore, based upon my belief, which I often used whenever I spoke to community partners, "If our children are to be, they have to first be given the opportunity to see," we made it a point to ride the trolley and have dinner in an expensive, fancy restaurant on Fisherman's Wharf. *Oh, what a wonderful waterfront tour, shared with Charlotte, our theme coordinator, teachers, and students.* We looked through powerful, big binoculars, viewing the Golden Gate Bridge and Alcatraz.

After returning home, one student stopped by the school, excited to share her photos of the trip. Upon her departure, my secretary and I both chuckled. Most of her "fabulous" pictures were of clouds in the sky. She shot these sky-scapes from her airplane window, during her first flight, what she called, "An hour's trip into heaven."

During the GEAR UP conference the following year, we toured Georgetown University and Howard University. We visited the Holocaust Museum, the National Cathedral, the Library of Congress, the Smithsonian, and lots of other museums. But I had been to Washington many times.

My first visit was when I was honored as principal of the year. I now wanted to share the sites I had seen with my students and staff. After the students gave their presentation, our group of forty-eight took a guided bus tour to all of the standard tourist sites. My favorites weren't the structures and statues on The Mall—not even

The White House. They were the bronze statues in the FDR Memorial—especially *The Depression Breadline*, people standing in a soup line. Each time I saw them, I thought of *The Grapes of Wrath*. I thought of how Eleanor Roosevelt was the great strength and backbone of our nation, the mother of our country. People can think and say what they want, but back then, in my mind, *We've already had our first women president—acting behind the scenes.* I thought of the Great Depression, and how she had to keep the faith and pull her "children" through hard and difficult times.

When we stood at the entrance to the Vietnam Memorial, looking at the three bronze statutes of the young, battle-dressed soldiers, one of my students asked, "Mr. Smith, you were a Marine and fought in Vietnam, didn't you?"

"Yes," I proudly responded. Looking at that statute always reminded me of the time in my life when I was physically at my best—a brick-house, young and strong. But I had to leave the group. I could not remain at the Vietnam Memorial wall for any length of time. When I first saw it, and every other time since, I wasn't able to stay. Too many memories of those comrades I fought with in 1967. I would never forget them, but standing next to the names of those who died brought them far too close to me. I teared-up and felt overwhelming anxiety—enough to make me sadly walk away.

When we got back on the bus, one student placed a gift she had bought in my hand. I hadn't said anything about my feelings to anyone—too professional to do something dumb like that.

When I looked, I saw she had given me a plastic replica of the three soldiers standing at the entrance of the memorial. I went to her seat and told her, "How sweet, how thoughtful; you could not have given me a more precious gift."

We even crossed the Potomac River, into Virginia to see the Iwo Jima statue and the Arlington National Cemetery. (In spite of my military background, I had nothing to do with adding these places to our agenda. I don't know who was responsible for doing that.)

One of our history teachers, Luanne, (the same one who had booked the Holocaust Museum tour) had made appointments, which got us into the Capital Building to see both Senator Harry Reid and Congresswomen Shelley Berkley.

I got to see the World War II Memorial during this trip with my group. I marveled and stood with great admiration for the monumental sacrifices these men gave for this country. I thought of my father, a Korean and WWII vet. *How sad. He gave so much of himself to a country—America, so steeped in blind, racial ignorance. When will this country ever change? Perhaps our children will change it.*

CHAPTER 118

In early spring, Gavin, Jemal, and I took turns driving my Trailblazer through Reno, Tahoe, and into Cal-Nevada. Jemal had quit his well-paying job on The Strip to embark upon his spiritual journey. I wanted to see for myself this monastery located high in the mountains above Cal-Nevada. I wasn't about to allow my son to live in a cult that would brainwash him and drain him of common sense. As we took turns driving, Jemal explained that the organization he was joining grew out of a love, peace, and harmony commune that started back in the sixties, on the same property where it is located today. I took what he was saying to mean free love transcended into Yoga and a dedicated search of each member of the community to follow a path leading to spiritual enlightenment. Jemal explained that each member financially contributed to the organization by working for the commune, performing the duties of their God-given, special talents for the good of the collective.

We arrived at the site about 11 A.M. The place looked like a four-star mountain resort. Mostly new cars and trucks were parked in the parking lot. All the buildings looked freshly painted and kept up. The shrubbery was manicured, and the grounds totally free of litter.

I paid careful attention to every word and gesture made by the man checking Jemal into the establishment. *Say one "red-flag" word, and Jemal, Gavin, and I will run to my car and speed away from here,* was in the back of my mind during the entire check-in process.

While carrying the few personal items from the car, we walked to Jemal's assigned dormitory. Four single beds rested, one in each corner of his room. One large window was at the opposite side of the door. There was no closet or restroom. Painted, wooden shelving ran above the beds along all the walls. A bright four-bulb light fixture attached to a ceiling fan hung in the center of the ceiling. A long, narrow hallway outside of the room led to a large toilet and shower area, which served the eight-room sleeping quarters.

We arrived just in time. Lunch was being served in the giant dining room. I noticed the sign saying, "Seating capacity 200." The food was displayed buffet style. So we got our silverware, entrée plate, and proceeded down the line. I piled on lots of fresh vegetables and baked bread, a bowl of lentils, and a glass of iced lemonade. I paid for three meals as I exited the line.

I saw to it that we didn't sit by ourselves. I scoped out a guy about Jemal's age. He was sitting by himself. "Mind if we join you?" I asked.

"Please," he replied. "Please have a seat."

"My name is Ronnie," I said. "These are my sons, Gavin and Jemal," while pointing at the two.

"My name is Steven."

"Glad to meet you, Steven. And how long have you lived here?" I asked.

"Two years."

"Sorry to bombard you with questions, but my son, Jemal will be living here starting today. Naturally, I want to find out as much as I can about this place."

Steven smiled and nodded. "Sure, I understand your concern. I didn't find this place. It found me—came along just when I needed it." He chuckled and smiled even more. "Life seems to work that way. I call it synchronicity." Steven looked at Jemal and said, "You are in the right place. This place will serve you well. Just open up your heart and your soul will follow."

I liked what I saw and even more what I heard. Steven was dressed in clean, regular civilian clothing. His head wasn't shaven. He wore a crew cut, with no beard or mustache. His fingernails were clean and trimmed. I was completely satisfied. He didn't need to say anymore.

We walked the grounds for a while and rested for a long time at the meditation pond. The water thrived with lotus flowers and leaves. *How tranquil, how serene*, I thought.

Then, Gavin cinched it for me. I knew Jemal would be all right staying here. Gavin bent over, leaned his head into my head, and whispered in my ear, "Dad, Jemal will be just fine. All he needs is a meditation pond, Lotus leaves, and flowers. He'll sit his butt down here and be just fine!"

That evening, after having an early vegetarian dinner with Jemal, Gavin and I left for home. We drove to Reno and stayed in a hotel for the night. By daylight, we were on the road again. Trading driving and passenger positions frequently, we raced down the highway until a highway patrolman pulled me over. I saw him pass me, on the other side of the four-lane highway. I saw him make an abrupt u-turn. Through my rear-view mirror, I saw him put his flashing red and blue lights on me. *I must have been going pretty fast, like exactly ninety-five for him to make that u-turn.*

I rolled down my window as the state trooper approached my car. I let him do all the talking.

"Do you know how fast you were traveling?" he asked.

"No, Sir," I humbly responded.

"Why the rush?"

"Sir, I just dropped my older son off at UNR. My younger son and I drove him there for his first year of college. I guess I'm eager to get home," I lied.

The officer's compassion for a poor Black man, wanting to "do right" for his elder son, worked. My con-job got me out of a ticket. Perhaps he had children, too, and knew how important it is for them to go to college.

"I'm going to let you off with only a warning. Drive the speed limit all the way home. Have a good day, Mr. Smith."

For a split-second I thought, *I wonder if he would have treated me the same if Elaine had been in the car with us? But then I would not have been driving that speed. She would not have let me. So the officer would not have stopped us in the first place.*

CHAPTER 119

I n May, of 2005, Donnie called me on my hotline at school. "Ronnie, come quickly. Mom's in the hospital, on a respirator. We all have to decide."

I knew exactly what he meant. *Where'd the time go? It seemed like only yesterday I called her to wish her a Happy Birthday when she turned eighty-seven.*

****

My sister, Betty, had summoned Mom inside the house, saying to me, "I've gotta get Momma and tell her you are on the phone. Hold on. She's in my backyard jumping on a giant trampoline with her grandchildren."

I waited for a minute for Mom to get on the phone.

Jumping on a trampoline? Is she trying to break an arm, a leg, her hip?

"Hello, Ronnie."

"Happy Birthday to you," I sang to the end of the song, and then immediately asked, "What are you doing jumping on a trampoline? You are way too old for that."

"It's out there. The kids are jumping and having fun. I wanted to have some fun, too. I wanted to try it out."

"Momma, come on, now. You're way too old for that."

****

My secretary, Linda, booked a flight for me. I drove home, packed a few items, and rushed to the airport.

Donnie picked me up at the Ontario Airport and drove to meet Betty at a hospital in Fontana. He explained that at age ninety-three, Mom had simply run out of life. We would have to decide to either leave or take her off life support.

"How do you feel about that?" I asked. "What do you think we should do?" After seeing so much loss of early life in Vietnam, I was grateful Mom had lived to age ninety-three. I had no problem letting her go, but I didn't want to share my feelings about taking her off of life support. I only wanted to support my siblings' decisions—whatever they wanted to do. I was actually feeling Donnie out, wanting to know where he stood before arriving at the hospital. I figured by knowing his decision, I'd have more time to think things through—especially if Betty disagreed with Donnie.

"Let's just wait and see what the doctor has to say. Maybe we won't have to make a choice," he replied.

It took us no time to get to the hospital and to join up with Betty.

Sitting in a lobby, waiting for the doctor, I thought it best not to question Betty regarding life support. My sister looked tired and weak, as if she had not been sleeping, only worrying herself over my mother's health. There were darkened bags under her eyes, and she seemed to be having trouble breathing. Empathizing with her anxiety, I watched her take long, labored breaths. Although she was only a year older than Donnie and I, she looked several years our elder. *Had the time she spent caring for our mother caused Betty to age so quickly?*

A lady looking to be in her thirties entered the lobby. She walked up to Betty and introduced herself to Donnie and me. We returned her salutation.

"Your mother, Mattie, is in no pain right now," she said. "Mattie has simply reached the end of her days. She's worn out her life. The only thing keeping her going is a life support system. If she were my mother, I would take her off and allow her to take her well-deserved rest." She paused to read our reactions.

Looking into the eyes of my sister and then my brother, I tried to show no emotion. But I felt terrible for Betty. Her eyes were red and sobbing. And Donnie wasn't much better. I was glad that I could be their strength. "Soooo, what I hear the doctor saying is Mom is dying from growing gray." I said this, trying to cheer them up. "Let's just take a moment for prayer," I said. "Mom and all of us are in His hands. God certainly knows what to do." I think all three of us prayed one after the other, with my starting and Betty finishing the prayer.

Next, the doctor chimed in saying, " I don't have the authority to take your mother off of support. The three of you will need to reach consensus. Take time to think it over, and then let me know." Being Asian, she bowed, and then quickly left the area. I did not know if her bowing was out of respect for us or for our mother.

The three of us looked at each other, and then I popped the question, "So what do we do?"

Donnie was hesitant to speak and waited for Betty.

I looked at Betty, waited, and finally asked, "What do you wanna do?"

"I don't know," she responded. "What do you guys want to do?"

I waited for Donnie, thinking, *Round one is over. Now, what do we do? I'm not going to be the first to suggest anything.*

We went through this process three or four times without getting anywhere. Then the doctor retuned announcing that Mother had regained consciousness and was breathing on her own.

"Hallelujah," exclaimed Betty. "Thank you, Jesus."

Later that evening we were told that if Mother's condition continued to improve, she'd be released back to the care of the assisted-living facility my sister placed her in a few months previously.

Betty rode in the ambulance the next day while Donnie and I drove to the assistant-living facility. I watched as the attendants placed my mother into her bed. Her limbs were skinny and brittle. She looked a little more rounded than a toothpick. With sunken cheeks, glazed-over eyes, and long, shinny, white hair, and with the exception of her frailty, she looked good for her age.

We were all relieved that we didn't have to decide to bring Mom's life to an end.

I stayed with my brother for another day and then took a plane back to Vegas.

On May 23, 2005, Betty called and told me that Mom had died.

I drove to L.A. and took Gavin with me for comfort. The funeral, although it was a Black traditional ceremony, with open-casket and all, was the easiest I had ever attended. *How long can a person expect to live?* Mother had lived a good, long life without any health complications along the way.

Looking at her resting in her coffin I thought about one of my previous visits with her—the time I told her how proud I was of her for the way she raised me, putting my needs before hers.

She died knowing we thought she was an excellent mother. I know this because when I told her how I felt, she smiled, looked at me, and said, "Betty and Donnie have told me this, on separate occasions. I have loved you with all my heart."

Taking my last, final look, I thought, *What more could a mother do?*

CHAPTER 120

Because of Mama's death, thoughtful Donnie wanted to ease the sadness for both Betty and me of not being able to continue our annual Thanksgiving and Christmas family gatherings at Mama's house. He invited and offered to pay for us to join him and his wife, Joyce, on a Thanksgiving cruise to some islands in the Western Caribbean. We accepted, of course, but only if he would allow us to pay our own way.

Getting my first passport and making all of the necessary preparations for the trip brought about great anticipation and excitement. *I'm going to Belize, the Cayman Islands, and Jamaica!* All of these places carried their own significance or special interest for me. I wanted to visit Jamaica because of the song, "Jamaica Farewell." That particular song and the banana song would easily evoke a peaceful, relaxing fantasy every time I heard Harry Belafonte sing them. Being a certified diver, who wouldn't want to dive the Cayman Islands? And Belize—my students and their teachers were participating in a special virtual tour of the marine studies conducted by the researcher,

Tom Ballard, in the very waters I would dive. *I would soon get a first-hand visit to the ocean we saw and heard him talk about so passionately.* How good it felt, knowing we would be going all out, splurging on this trip. We even booked separate, balcony accommodations.

During the actual trip, I got all that I expected—even more. One afternoon, Betty and I ate lunch by ourselves on the ship. As I chomped on my salad, she said, "Ronnie, remember that time at Mama's when you caught me in the kitchen alone? Remember when you said, 'Betty, I've got to talk to you, and you know what it's all about?' I knew for some reason what you wanted to talk about. I said to myself, *Dear Lord, please don't let him continue with this conversation. I'm not ready.* I held my breath and waited. Boy, was I relieved when you let it go."

I stopped eating and gave her my full attention.

"Ronnie," she continued, "When I was about twenty-five, Mother told me who my father is. It was difficult for me to process, learning that I had a sister, who attended my same church. I think she hated me, and I didn't care that much for her. But we eventually got through it, and we became good friends."

I took time to truly listen. I even tried to imagine how the two of them had to work through their initial pain.

"Ronnie, I can easily talk about this now. And it gives me great joy in knowing that our daddy, Robert Tee Smith, always loved me. He never once withheld his love from me. He always treated me the same as he treated you and Donnie."

By then, I was all choked up. Tears started to form in my eyes. *That's my daddy. His behavior took courage and love. That's my daddy. I'm part of him. In essence, that's who I am—I'm formed with some strength of solid steel.*

I appreciated her openness and thoughtfulness. Although Betty didn't discuss her business at the time I initially confronted her, I was overjoyed with the intimacy and honesty she finally disclosed to me on the ship. All I could say was, Thank you, Betty. Your sharing this means so much to me."

Sometime later, long after our trip ended, I thought about my daddy. I thought about me. Sometimes there was a clearing along the pathway of my journey when I could easily recognize pretense from simple truth. Back at the time when I thought about Elaine's first pregnancy, *Is the baby mine or somebody else's?* I knew exactly what the final outcome would be if the baby was not mine. Although I struggled with making a decision, deep in my heart I knew.

CHAPTER 121

" Defibrillator Crew, Defibrillator Crew, Room 321. Defibrillator Crew, Room 321," blared from my walkie-talkie. I jumped up out of my desk chair in my office and headed toward the room. I did not run. I had learned from experience that running causes others to panic. I walked at a brisk pace. Along the way I saw the nurse and her assistant. The nurse was carrying a defibrillator strapped over her shoulder like a purse. Her assistant pushed a wheelchair in front of her. Leaning forward, she looked like she was in a pushcart race. The three of us must have looked like we were in a walking competition. Heel-toe, heel-toe, we all swiftly swished down the hallway—pumping our elbows as fast as we could.

This must be another one of those defibrillator drills set up by a team from the district's health department, I thought, *as we raced down the hallway. What a waste of district money and personnel having them come to the school monthly to hold a drill. What a waste having them bring their rubber, high-tech mannequin. What a waste, timing us on our medical response and procedures—what a waste of time, personnel, and money.*

Someone needs to cut them from the budget.

I opened the door to the room and let the two of them enter first.

The room was utterly quiet, as if no one was in it. All I could hear was our dean of students' blowing air into the lungs of a male student lying on the carpeted floor, in the middle of an aisle created by two long rows of desks. Blank stares filled the room. Every face I saw looked as if it was in shock—even the teacher's. I looked again at our dean giving mouth-to-mouth-resuscitation to the student.

The entire defibrillator team was present. "Get my secretary, Linda, on your radio. Tell her to call 911," I instructed one of my assistant principals. I pointed to another and said, "Get the name and student I.D. number of the injured student from the teacher. Take that information to Linda." I knew Linda would contact the parents and make copies of the student's information, so we would have it available for the paramedics as soon as they arrived. I took my ring of keys from my waist and addressed the teacher. "Here, take these. Take your students to Room 315. That room is empty this period. Take your students there." I handed her the ring with my thumb and pointer finger holding onto my master key. "I'll send someone later for my keys."

The nurse switched places with the dean and continued performing CPR. I noticed the dean had already attached the two electronic nodes of the defibrillator onto the boy's chest.

"I'm losing him, I'm losing him. He's about to go!" the nurse hollered out.

No, you can't, I thought. *You better bring that boy back to full life. I ain't about to lose a kid on my watch. This can't be happening to him or me. Bring that boy back to full life.*

I envisioned yellow police crime-scene tape crisscrossing the front of the classroom door. In my mind, the signage on the tape transformed to, "Corner's Investigation Site."

I ain't having this. That boy ain't gonna die.

"He's gone. I've lost him," the nurse muttered. "Stand clear," she immediately screamed. "I'm going to keep on trying." Counting each pump, she pushed hard on his chest after using the electronic jolt from the defibrillator. A few seconds later she yelled, "I've got him back."

"Go to all the entrances of our school. Let me know when and where the paramedics arrive," I instructed to the crew remaining in the room.

Linda called me on my cell. "Mr. Smith," she said, "I've tried contacting Leroy's mom, but I've been unsuccessful in reaching her. She's the only one listed on his 704 student information form. I've tried the home phone, the work number, and the emergency contact numbers.

"I've gotten no answer, but as soon as I reach her, I'll let you know."

As soon as I hung up, a call came over the radio, "Clark Five to Clark One, Five to One."

"Go Five," I replied.

"One, the paramedics are approaching the main parking lot in the front of the school. Again, the paramedics are approaching the north parking lot."

"North parking lot. I copy. Out."

"I'm losing him again," the nurse shouted.

I left the room and ran down the hallway—I ran!

Meeting the paramedics as they were getting out of their ambulance, I quickly introduced myself. "I'm so glad you're here. Please hurry. I've got a child who is unconscious in a classroom. Please follow me." I started rushing back to the room. I looked behind me. They were nowhere near. They were taking their time.

"I need epinephrine if I'm to keep this child alive," came from my radio. It was the nurse. I recognized the voice.

I turned to the paramedics and tried to rush them along. "Did you hear that last radio transmission? My nurse said she needs epinephrine to keep the boy alive."

"It's probably a drug overdose," one of the paramedics casually commented to the other, but they didn't walk any faster.

"I must have epinephrine if I'm to keep him alive," came over the radio again.

Is the nurse saying this to me, hoping that I'm hearing it, or has she flipped out and lost her mind? I don't even know what epinephrine is. Is it some kind of strong stimulant like ammonia, some wake-me-up like smelling salts? Why is she repeating this over the radio?

Then as I looked back at the two men casually strolling alone, I became extremely angry. *Why are they being so slow? What caused one of them to assume the boy is a worthless, Black, druggie? That must be what they're thinking—walking so slowly.*

I felt powerless because I wanted to chew their asses out, but I knew that I couldn't. We finally reached the room. One of the paramedics relieved the nurse. They placed an oxygen mask on my student, put him on the gurney, and rolled him to their wagon. I had one of my assistant principals ride along in the ambulance as a surrogate parent of the child.

"When the parent arrives at the hospital, I'll have someone come to get you. I might come myself. I will have someone come to bring you back to school."

The incident concluded minutes prior to the passing bell sounding. Most people didn't know what had happened. I retrieved my keys, praised the teacher for her quick action in notifying the office of the emergency, and told her she could return to her own classroom. I returned to my office to read the student's cumulative folder while Linda continued trying to reach his mother.

Linda finally made contact with the mother at her work place. The parent had made it to the hospital, and my assistant principal had been transported back to school by noon.

While reading the child's folder, I discovered that he had been diagnosed with a heart condition. That he was not to exert a lot of physical energy while in P.E. I wished his counselor had taken him out of the class. But my wish was hindsight. I needed to find out if the boy exerted himself in P.E. that day.

Thank God, he hadn't.

I went to the hospital to visit with the mother after school dismissal. Being a single parent, I knew she needed support, all that I could give her.

She shared with me how the doctor explained to her that her son would have died had our nurse not been there to treat him. In confidence she told me she needed to miss

work in order to look after her son. She had no one to help her with her finances.

I've never told anyone other than my secretary; my heart went out to this parent. I wrote a personal check from my own checkbook because I believed she honestly needed the money. I didn't do it out of guilt or with the hope that she might want to try and sue. I did it out of compassion and my thankfulness to God for not letting the child die.

CHAPTER 122

" Mr. Smith, I don't know how to tell you this," Gavin's best friend, Paul, said as he spoke to me over the phone. It was a Sunday night, May 27, 2007, Memorial Day weekend, about 7 P.M.

"Just go ahead and say it, Paul. You know me. You can tell me anything."

"Mr. Smith," he said, and then paused. "Gavin is dead."

I jumped out of my chair. "What? Paul, what did you just say? What? Tell me what happened."

"Gavin called me at my apartment. Said he was sick. He asked me to come over. When I got there, I gave him water—lots of water. He passed out. I called 911. They arrived too late. They told me they couldn't tell me if he was dead or alive, but not to expect the best."

"Where is he now?" I asked. "Are you sure he's dead?"

God, where are you? It's Sunday night, I thought. Where is my son?

"From the way the paramedics sounded, I know that Gavin didn't make it. When you get to the hospital, UMC, call me. Tell me what the doctors said."

Was he shot? Motorcycle accident? Drug overdose? Alcohol poisoning—what? But I don't think I ever asked.

Something told me to grab a copy of Gavin's birth certificate on my way out of the house, so I did. I drove to University Medical Center. *This can't be happening. When I get to the hospital, the doctors will have pumped his stomach. He may be in critical condition, but he'll be alive.* Foul play never entered my mind.

I went to Admissions, showed the nurse the birth certificate and my driver's license. "May I see him? Please tell me he's all right," I begged.

The nurse sitting at her desk, behind a glass encasement handed me Gavin's wallet and keys. "These are the items Gavin had in his possession. I'm sorry." Then with no emotion, spoken completely flat, she continued, "He was dead upon arrival. The coroner will contact you. There has to be an autopsy. He died so young."

I thanked her and stood there in shock as I watched her leave her station. "He's gone. My baby is gone. All I have is his wallet and set of keys," I said out loud to no one.

Driving home, all I could think about was a poem by Robert Frost, entitled, "Out-Out." I learned in college Frost wrote this poem while reflecting upon Shakespeare's "Out, out brief candle." *There's nothing more for him to build upon: Gavin's dead, at age twenty-four.*

I spent the sleepless night rifling through Gavin's wallet, which contained his certified driver's license, a taxi-driver I.D., one credit card, a Blockbuster' card, and three one-dollar bills. I remember reading every word on the cab card. "Professional Driver," along with Gavin's picture, are the parts that stood out. Although he hadn't finished college, I was proud. Gavin had gotten a professional driver's card, his CDL, and a motorcycle license. So young; yet, he had all the traveling credentials he needed to go somewhere.

How I ached. I'd never again hear "vroom, vroom," the loud sound of Gavin's motorcycle coming and going to and from my home.

Tuesday morning, I got up and went to school. I needed my work for sanity. I could lose myself in running a school with 3,000 students. I figured if the job became too hectic, I could always cut work short.

Paul phoned me often. "Did you learn anything new?" he would ask." I never returned a call to Paul. I offered nothing. In fact he called so much, I began wondering if he played a part in Gavin's death.

Cleaning Gavin's apartment kept me busy at night. Dirty dishes, pots, and pans filled the kitchen counter and sink. I washed them all and placed them in boxes. I figured I'd donate everything to Goodwill—everything except his motorcycle. A friend with a truck helped me store it in my garage.

I cleaned the apartment alone. I needed my privacy as I frequently cried. Pills like Oxycodone, several rolled marijuana sticks, and a line of cocaine resting on a mirrored plate with a razor blade and card occupied the room. *Damn,* I thought. *Gavin's been into drugging far too much. Did Paul played a role in Gavin's death? Was he drugging with Gavin when Gavin died? Was Paul too far gone and waited until he had "come down" to seek help for Gavin?* I decided asking all these questions could drive me crazy. With all the illegal drugs about the place, I wondered why the paramedics didn't inform the police, why the cops didn't come and conduct an investigation? Perhaps both were simply too busy. I let the questions go, thinking, *There certainly was no way that an investigation would add to Gavin's life.* I concentrated on cleaning the room and neatly boxing up all the items.

I wept inside his closet while boxing up his shoes. Holding onto a familiar pair, I leaned against the doorjamb, dropped the shoes, and slid to the floor. I picked them up again. *These are more than shoes. They're Gavin's.* I could feel his presence in those shoes. I had to end it there.

After stepping out of the closet, I looked about the apartment. Most of my intended work was completed—the kitchen emptied, the counter and floor sparkled. The carpet in the living room had raked marks from the vacuum. Neatly stacked boxes stood against the wall. *I don't have to be strong.* Knowing what was best for me, I shook my head from side to side. *The unfinished bedroom and closet—I can't. I can't hold or box up any more of Gavin's possessions. I've got to let him go.*

I locked the apartment door, and headed to the manager's office. Handing her the keys, I probably babbled something like, "I'm sure that you are aware of my son dying in your apartment. I wanted to leave your place in excellent order, bringing polished decorum to the end of my son's life. But here are the keys to Apartment B-3. Please donate everything in the apartment to charity. I don't have the endurance to execute my first, well-meaning intentions."

While accepting the keys, I don't think she possessed any sympathy, feeling, or concern for what I had just said.

From what I could hear and see, there were no words or gestures expressing hints of, "I'm sorry" or, "be strong," or "my condolences," or anything.

Instead, not wanting to enter into my world of grief and mourning, she stood stoically, like a robot, showing no sign of compassion. "Thirty days, I'll have to keep everything for thirty days before I can legally donate them to charity."

"That's okay. I'm glad I was able to make it this far," I replied and then left.

Paul called me daily to know the findings.

"Gavin died from a heart attack induced by drugs," the coroner explained when he called me several days later.

I never told Paul.

CHAPTER 123

In keeping with Elaine's family tradition, I had the body cremated. Linda, my secretary helped me plan the memorial service. We scheduled the going-home celebration three weeks from Saturday, June 9, 2007, at 10 A.M. I needed time for Jemal to travel home from India. He had started living there after "graduating" from his monastery near Cal-Nevada, where he learned the renunciation of his western way of thinking. Linda put me in touch with a minister who officiated the service. I contacted all of my family. Linda notified Gavin's and my friends. I decided to have the service and repast at the funeral home. Linda planned the refreshments. My sister-in-law picked up Gavin's remains. I didn't have the emotional strength to do it. They were in a brown, cardboard box. I selected the urn and tortured myself viewing numerous family photos. I choose three pictures of Gavin and had them enlarged to twenty-by-twenty-four-inch posters to display in wooden frames, on easels borrowed from the art department at my school.

I arrived early at the mortuary the day of the service to make sure everything was in perfect order. I hugged and greeted family and guests as they came in. It felt good seeing most of the Gene Ward faculty, especially my former principal, Mr. Twitchell, and his wife. I thought about how quickly time flies, how I had known this group of educators since 1975, and how we were all still so very close. *I guess that says a lot about the principal—his ability to build lasting relationships.*

Gavin's Uncle Edley spoke, followed by my brother, Donnie. Then all three of Gavin's girlfriends spoke in succession. *What a mess,* I thought. *He dated all three at the same time and was very involved with each young lady. Worse yet, they all knew what he was doing.*

Next, my band teacher's wife (the one who sang a solo instead of a student when we went to Carnegie Hall) sang "Starry, Starry Night."

Paul, Gavin's best friend spoke, telling of how the two of them would camp out in caves in the mountains west of Las Vegas. Paul also told of the fun both he and Gavin had riding motorcycles together. Paul took the opportunity to hint that Gavin would want him to have Gavin's motorcycle.

Grandpa Ed didn't speak at all. I figured he must have felt a lot like me. I simply sat and listened. I didn't dare take the chance of breaking down and losing all of my composure. I knew I didn't have to put on a strong, steady, mendacious posture, and I was afraid if I got up to say a word, I would be running the risk of losing total social propriety. I simply sat a listened. Something inside me had changed. I didn't want to pretend to control anything anymore. It took all I had to barely control myself. I sat there thinking about all of the losses in my life—how I never really allowed myself to truly grieve. By not daring to even slightly open any of those doors holding excruciating pain, afraid of what I might find and equally afraid of how it would all come out—probably with an emotional breakdown—I overly guarded every emotion regarding all of my losses. My children were all I truly had. With one of them now gone, a new me emerged. I allowed others to be in charge.

One female colleague, Gavin's principal when he was in middle school, gave a short speech, which helped me considerably. She said, "Ronnie, if you could have chosen to have or not have Gavin in your life, I'm sure you would have decided to be his father the brief time you two had together. Better a little time together than none at all." Her wise words wished comfort to my heart.

Others talked about how smart Gavin was and how he spent his life helping others. One said, "He didn't talk down to me, but I always felt he was ten times smarter than I would ever be. Gavin had a talent for figuring out how things worked. He always helped me whenever something in my life went wrong."

Interesting how some people can always help others when they can't find a good path to travel themselves. But hearing their words helped me to smile. I thought of the lyrics in an old gospel song, "If I can help somebody, then I will not have lived my life in vain."

Jemal finished the ceremony. Dressed in his white Kasaya robes, he delivered his speech with eloquence and superb articulation. He ended playing an instrument, called a harmonium, flawlessly. It's a bellow-pumped instrument that slightly resembles an accordion. As the notes sounded Middle Eastern, he sang some kind of Buddhist chant. I was proud of his sincere courage and strength to not be pretentious, but to be himself.

****

As he played his instrument and sang, I closed my eyes and thought back to the time when an owner of a doughnut shop called out to his brother in a back room hollering out,

"Jamal, please come to the front counters. I need help with the customers."

Jemal was about seven. I wanted to introduce him to Jamal. My son and I approached the counter after we had finished our doughnuts, and I said to the clerk, "So which of you is Jamal?"

He looked to be both nervous and horrified. I think this was about the same time as our war in the Middle East—Desert Storm. The clerk looked Middle Eastern. Looking at his countenance, I knew immediately that he was troubled, that I could have used a better introduction.

I immediately changed my approach. "Oh, my son," I pointed at Jemal, "his name is Jemal. I wanted to introduce him to your coworker, Jamal."

The man broke out in hearty laughter. "Jamal, Jamal, come back to the front," he hollered. "Yes," he added, "Jamal is my brother. We are from Jerusalem, and the name, Jamal, in my native language means "beautiful."

****

Returning to his song, I thought, *Jemal, you are truly beautiful, and I thank God for giving me such a son—someone I will now need to lean on.*

My two band teachers, two orchestra teachers, and my guitar teacher played soft music as a quintet throughout the repast held at the mortuary. At the end of the event and after clean up, I said my goodbyes and went home, calling it a day.

Jemal stayed with me a few days before going back to India. I remember giving him the urn containing Gavin's remains. I told him I trusted his judgment and shared that I didn't have the emotional strength to keep the urn. Later, Jemal shared with me that he had scattered some of Gavin's ashes at Red Rock, some at the ski lodge at Mt. Charleston, and some at Brian Head. He released the urn and poured the remaining ashes into Panquich Lake, in Utah—all Gavin's favorite places.

CHAPTER 124

Not having any family in Las Vegas, I put most of my life force into my job to keep from going crazy. Having a faculty who shared my teaching philosophy and students who valued their education made it easy. We were all on a roll. With me as the principal, metaphorically driving our big school bus, we were all going somewhere. We did everything possible to not let any of our stakeholders crash.

From time to time, I looked at the various plaques on my wall—loads and loads of them. *I don't need anymore. I have earned enough for a lifetime. Let me get busy helping those who need the recognition most.* Based on that thought, I spent a lot of time writing grants and completing special teacher recognition award applications. *If we can get extra money for the school, why not?* Even though we didn't need it, receiving a grant added prestige to our school. On a sheet of letterhead, which included our fancy gold and black embossed logo, I wrote our school's bio—a promotional strategy I learned while attending the GEAR UP conference. My administrative assistants and theme coordinator, Shirley McLees, rallied with me. We listed the most recent and top awards, achievements, and facts about our school on the report. Whenever we received better school data, we'd delete less significant, less noteworthy items, replacing them with pieces that carried more weight. Knowing that philanthropic organizations went wild about evidenced learning, we were careful to include information like, "Clark continues to participate in professional training conferences and symposiums. By continuously using the information learned, along with trending school data, Clark is making significant gains toward becoming a national model school, one that any inner city school may opt to emulate." We also stated, "As a comprehensive and magnet school, Clark serves 2,729 students in grades nine through twelve. Approximately 25% are enrolled in one of three magnet programs: The Academy of Mathematics, Science, and Applied Technology (AMSAT), the Teacher Education Academy at Clark High (TEACH), and our Academy of Finance (AOF). The diverse ethnic and economic student body consists of 10% African American, 18% Asian or Pacific Islander, 21% Caucasian, and 51% Hispanic. Approximately 44% are on free or reduced lunch." We made it a point to state that our goal, our dream, was to have 100 percent of our graduating students pursue college. Our current data revealed that the majority indicated a strong interest in pursuing a postsecondary education. We talked about many of the colleges and universities our grads were attending, like Harvard, MIT, Stanford, and Yale. We wrote about the average $5,537,756 scholarship dollars annually awarded and that *U.S. News & World Report* repeatedly designated Clark as a Silver Medal High School. We shared some of the names of our teacher recipients who earned impressive recognition, like our calculus teacher who received the Siemens' Foundation Award for teacher of the year. We ended the document saying, "Clark is moving forward because we are capitalizing on formal and informal affiliations whereby every student has a genuine, authentic place of belonging within the school, with the beliefs that every student must experience a sense of connection and affiliation; and each teacher must constantly analyze methods in which his or her class can become a unique place of belonging for each child in our school. Clark truly is a place where students self-actualize our motto, 'Earning an Education Today for Tomorrow's World.'"

CHAPTER 125

Could it be my son's death was the catalyst that brought me back to life? I don't know, but it was then I started to change. With Helen gone, my dad gone, my mother, and Elaine—especially Elaine and the way that she went—Gavin's death ended my seeking to control feelings to the point of excluding anyone into my heart. Over a short period of time, I started opening up—not so much to my family since I had none living near me in town. But I allowed close friends, my staff, and my students to see a little more of me—not all of me—just a little. One student's parent wrote me a letter. "Mr. Smith," a part of it said, "I am a certified, clinical psychologist. If you find that you are having too difficult time with the loss of your child, I offer you my service, free of charge."

I called her and thanked her for her kind and generous invitation—not that I went around broadcasting, "Oh, look at me, oh, look at me. My world has fallen apart." I guess tragic news travels fast within a community that genuinely cares, and the outreach of stakeholders within my school was abundant. Their concern for me helped to increase my emotional awareness. When giving motivational or student recognition speeches, my eyes would tear up and my nose would begin to run. I blamed my condition on my allergies, but everyone in the audience knew the truth—I treated all of my students as if they were my biological children. I wanted all of them to succeed.

Children can do the most amazing things to make their parents proud. One evening, during our magnet school recruiting season, our theme coordinator invited several students to present most of the program. Interested eighth-graders and their parents from all over Clark County were in attendance since students had to apply for acceptance into the magnet program. Our students and staff were dressed in black blazers, which carried a gold embroidered crest saying, "AOF, TEACH, and AMSAT."

Steven, a senior, came to the microphone. "I'm an Academy of Finance student who has been attending Clark High School for the last three and a half years—going on four. I've been shown nothing but love and acceptance by staff and my peers the entire time I've been here. What most people don't know is that prior to attending Clark, way back since I was two, I didn't talk—not to my parents, not to anyone. I never said a word. Then one day, while at school, I started talking. I love this school."

Steven's presentation brought tears to my eyes. Prior to his part in the program, I had no knowledge of his condition.

Then tears swelled in my eyes at a district board meeting. It was when our student body president gave an annual report on the state of affairs at our school. She stood at the podium facing the board and said, "Dr. Martin Luther King is smiling down on our school. Students at Clark are living his dream. We're family, where Blacks, Whites, Asians, and Hispanics all treat each other as one." Immediately after her speech, our student council—a rainbow of color—all stood, clapped, and sang our fight song in support of their president. I stood and sang, too. Filled with emotion, I cried. *Our kids aren't learning from a teacher and textbook about multicultural education. They are living it everyday. They make me proud to be their leader.*

During home and away football games, our band would yell, "Good evening, Mr. Smith," as I walked onto the bleachers. They trained me to walk across them just so they could call my name. Waving back at them as I passed, I felt comfortable and cared for.

The start of our home basketball games opened with our announcer hollering into the microphone, "Go o o o o d evening, Everyone. Welcome to the house that Ronnie Tee built." Our band's drums would roll, and the brass instruments would sound. This acknowledgement made me bubble inside. I felt like a superstar, like I had just shot an exceptional three-pointer at the high-point of the game.

To spread icing on the proverbial cake, our orchestra teacher would send a quartet to my office to play "My Girl" on my birthdays. Although I couldn't drop one-hundred percent of my cynicism, thinking he did this as leverage for later, watching and listening to my students always put tears in my eyes and joy in my heart.

Our school hadn't evolved into a campus like one dropped from heaven—we had our troubled kids and their problems, too. Or is it possible there are problems in heaven, too—as God seems a prankster at times. We had a series of fires in both boys' and girls' student restrooms. One was so bad—set by nail polish, used as an accelerant—my assistant principal and I couldn't put it out. Girls had dumped all of the paper towels, toilet paper, and trash out of the two trashcans. They created a large pile next to a tiled wall. (Anytime a fire alarm sounded, there was a machine called an enunciator that showed the room number of the fire. It was located next to my office. My job was to race to the machine, locate the correct area, call out on my portable radio for the closest responder to go to that area, and let me know exactly what was going on. Most times, if I was close, I ran to the area.) This time the fire was close to my office. My assistant principal, who was also close to the area, and I were unable to extinguish the blaze. He wanted to remain and continue fighting the fire, but the smoke was doing us in. I insisted that we give up the battle and get out. Since our school's enunciator automatically notified the fire department of a possible fire, I knew firemen were on their way. As the enunciator was linked to the nearest fire station, it automatically alerted the firemen to rush to our school under siren, cherries and berries, if the school did not call them and explain that a pull-down alarm box was malfunctioning.

The fireman arrived immediately and put out the nail polish blaze. No damage was done since the room was all ceramic tile, but smoke was everywhere. This was only one of several fires intentionally set that week. I knew how important it was to catch the culprits. I personally got involved in hunting down the perpetrators.

To solve a crime, I had learned long ago—during my days as a dean—to work backwards. Find the puzzle pieces, and put them together. I sent a memorandum to all of the teachers in the nearby area, asking for names of girls who were out of their classrooms at the exact time of the fire. My deans and I also looked at surveillance cameras of the area to see who was in the hallways. Using these leads, I began my fact-finding—carefully examining the pieces. I never called two kids into my office at the same time. The name of the game was to divide and conquer. I started individually interviewing the girls caught on camera. "Tell me again what happened. Remember, honesty will get you everywhere. I'd hate to call in the fire inspector who is hungry for punishment. I'm not. I just want the truth. I'm here to help, not to prosecute." I paused and read the child's reactions. Sometimes, facial expressions or sheer nervousness gave it all away. I carefully ran with what little clues I got. "Come on now, when people are in a restroom just prior to a fire breaking out, they had to see what happened. Common sense tells me not to settle for anything less. All I want is the truth. The truth will set you free. Don't worry. Your information is confidential. I won't share it with anyone."

It didn't take me long to get the full story from the one who was least involved. And I always got it in writing so the story wouldn't change when parents got involved.

Why did they do it? Was it out of boredom and curiosity? Did they want to see if they could get away with it? This hurt me to have these two freshmen girls arrested and expelled for arson, but I couldn't put others lives into jeopardy. I did it for the safety and welfare of the entire school.

A few days later, my student council advisor—motivated, excellent, and talented—told me that to promote school spirit, he purchased a t-shirt for everyone on campus, all staff, and students. He proudly showed me a white t-shirt with our logo—a large charging horse, galloping into red and yellow flames. The caption read, "CLARK ON FIRE."

"Rodger," I said, "I wish you would get my pre-approval on these purchases before making them. I can't allow you to distribute any of those t-shirts at this time. Save them for later. Maybe you can hand them out during the next school year."

CHAPTER 126

I called the hospital immediately. This was after I had returned to school at 6:30 A.M. Tuesday, following a three-day weekend. While listening to my phone messages I heard, "Mr. Smith, I'm calling from Summerlin Hospital. Your father-in-law, Ed, is here. He could not remember his son's telephone number. All he could tell us was that you are the principal of Clark."

I called and learned that Pampaw was in a coma, dying from stage four melanoma and prostate cancer. My next call was to Edley. I shared the tragic news. "Edley, your father is in the hospital. They are ready to send him to Hospice." I gave Edley full details—as much as I knew.

That night after work I went to the hospital. I rubbed Ed's hands and feet. I talked and talked, repeatedly calling his name, trying to bring him back to consciousness. "Pampaw, it's Ronnie. I've gotten in touch with Edley. He is on his way. Pampaw, Pampaw, Ed, Ed, Edwin, Ed, Pampaw," I repeated and rubbed even harder, trying to awaken him. But it didn't work. I ended my visit saying, "Pampaw, I have loved you. I will always love you for being you. Watching your life I've seen Jesus inside. Thank you for sharing your family. Helen's strength and ability has taught me a lot. I'm sorry I did not do better in loving Elaine."

A couple of days later, Edley called to tell me his father had died. Worse, yet, Edley had to spend most of his time in Las Vegas countering Pampaw's young girlfriend's manipulations. She intended to get full benefits from Ed's social security. Had Edley not been able to end her conniving, sugar-daddy-chicanery, she would have robbed the government, taxpayers, and this dead man for the rest of her life. Edley ended our conversation by saying, "I'll get back to you regarding arrangements for a memorial service for my dad."

But he never did. Edley never had a service.

I had my talk with God during sunrise, while driving to school early one Monday morning. I thought about Ed. I thought about Gavin and Elaine. Next, came my mother, Mattie, and Elaine's mother, Helen. I thought about my dad. They were all gone—all gone, except for Jemal. *Jemal, you and I are the only two left. You're a monk, and I'm old—certainly too old for having more children. I always thought that you and Gavin would have kids. Elaine and I would enjoy our grandchildren during our golden years. So much for plans. They twist, they turn, and sometimes, they seem to double back.* Then I laughed although I wanted to cry. I shook my head, having been once more amazed, and outsmarted by the irony of life.

God, I know I'll never have a grandchild, someone I can help raise far better than I've raised my children. But it's okay; I can accept it. I'm going to have to live with that.

A few minutes after being in my office, Briana, one of Gavin's last three girlfriends called me. "Ronnie", she said, "I called to tell you you are a grandfather—the proud grandfather of my daughter, Krystana."

What? Oh, shit! Somebody's lying. Since Gavin was dead, I thought, *What has Jemal been doing?* "What, what did you just say?"

"Yes, I waited to tell you because I wanted to make sure. Krystana was born December 24th.

She's a most beautiful child who looks just like Gavin."

"When can I come and see her?"

"Why don't you come over tonight?"

"I will—just after work."

Immediately after hanging up the phone I smiled—a great big smile. *Isn't that something? God, You are truly amazing. You knew all the while I was praying. You truly are incredible.*

Then, anger set in. *Why'd she wait so long to tell me? Gavin died in May, and she waited until now, a year later to tell me this news? Why didn't her parents let me in on the pregnancy? One of them could have said something—waiting all this time. Family secrets never come to any good.*

Switching my thoughts to what I had learned about anger, I asked myself, *Ronnie, why are you so angry? Where's this anger coming from?* I took my eyes off of me and started thinking about others. *I guess I have to accept everyone's point of view; people have their own reasons for doing what they do. I can't control everything and have all life around me subjected solely to my wishes—my created world.*

All of my understanding was interrupted by the thought, *Oh, oh, here we go again—the sins of mothers and fathers . . . Is the child really Gavin's?*

Holding Krystana in my arms that evening brought tremendous joy. It was like having a living piece of Gavin pressed to my side. She looked just like him, too. I thought back to both Gavin and his grandfather, Ed. *One goes, another comes . . .* How I wished that Elaine was there to share this new life with me.

Elaine must have somehow heard my thoughts because she came to visit me that night in a dream. I was walking on an unpaved street in Mexico when she called out from what appeared to be an old, abandoned garage—a defunct auto shop. The rolled-up, metal door was halfway up. With no sunlight or electric light, I could barely see. But I recognized her voice. "Elaine, Elaine," I called out as I started to venture inside. The room was dark. Squinting, I made out fine dust and cobwebs. I smelled the stench of decay.

"Ronnie, you are here. I knew you would come."

I located her, following the sound of her voice. Dressed in dingy muslin, and a bit ethereal, she hovered one foot from the ground.

"Won't you stay with me? We can be together forever."

"No, I'm not staying here," I screamed—loud enough to wake me up.

I asked myself, *Did this dream have anything to do with the saying, "When someone departs, another one arrives?" Had Krystnna taken the place of Grandpa, Elaine or Gavin?*

Although I had no idea what that dream was about, I wondered for several days if I had chosen to remain with Elaine, would I have died in my sleep? Would Krystana have taken the place of all three of us?

CHAPTER 127

By having dedicated teachers on my faculty who knew what they wanted, and in most cases, exactly how to get desired student results, I was able to change my supervision strategies. I no longer spent valuable time trying to uselessly prep, plead, pry, and persuade teachers to do their jobs—to put planning and passion into their profession. Instead, I exchanged my focus on teacher behavior in the classroom, shifting to student performance and outcomes. Moreover, I taught my administrators to do the same. We looked to see if the kids were sitting in traditional long rows, or were they in a circle, or a circle within a circle, engaged in meaningful discussion? Who was at the marker-board—a student or the teacher? Who was doing all the talking?

Fourteen cushioned, wooden chairs, with arms, sat around a polished, oblong, walnut table in one of our Academy of Finance classrooms. The furniture was donated by one of the local casinos. I enjoyed taking community partners into this room to show how our students learned and discussed their business plans. They had a poster on one of the walls, which read, "Come learn with us now, or work for us later." I was extremely pleased that our students were completing tax forms for people in the immediate neighborhood, completely free of charge. This was sheer "Application"—

according to Bloom's Taxonomy; learning at it's best. Many of these students were employed after school by banks and casinos. In the casinos, they worked in accounting, not on the floors as dealers or serving cocktails. I swelled with joy watching these students, adorned in business suits and dresses, learning in their classroom. Sometimes, if I had V.I.P.s. visiting the school, I'd take them into this room and introduce them to the class. Students, without my prompting, presented them with one of their business cards. Our students had learned this essential while in the program—to be ready whenever opportunity knocks.

Seniors in our Teacher Education At Clark High magnet school program engaged themselves in a full semester of student teaching. They taught at nearby feeder elementary or middle schools, and they got college credit through UNLV for their services. "Learn by doing," was a mantra our school fully embraced. Freshmen in the program were required to give educational presentations whenever and wherever we could find a venue.

I, along with members of the TEACH advisory board, set up an affiliation with Clark County School District's Human Resources Department, especially with Personnel. HR sent personal letters to our new, in-coming freshmen, thanking them for showing an interest in teaching. Encouraging them to stay in the program, our students received a more detailed letter every year, enclosed with real, district-used advertisements, including salary schedules and other benefits.TEACH students not only mentored students within their academy who were having trouble passing State proficiency exams needed to acquire a high school diploma, they also reached beyond their school-within-a-school to other students in our Charger Family.

One TEACH student mentor, Vivian Washington, tutored a regular student who was not in the academy. Vivian worked with her in the discipline of mathematics, only to discover the mentee had failed the mathematics proficiency exam in the tenth, eleventh, and twelfth grades. As a senior, the mentee came to me devastated and crying. "Mr. Smith," she said, "Vivian said she's quitting. I'm too slow. She can't work with me anymore."

"What?" I replied.

"Yeah, she said I'm worthless. I'm never going to pass."

"What? No she didn't, " I retorted, but something completely different was going on in the back of my mind—*Vivian, Vivian, Vivian, I'm not going to let you get away with that.* Then I comforted the mentee by saying, "Don't worry. You are not worthless or slow. You are very bright. You just haven't been taught how to pass the test. There's still time. You'll have another time to retake the test before graduation."

I saw her to my office door and thought. *How sad for those not passing all of their proficiency exams by the end of their senior year. They will be able to participate in the graduation ceremony, but they won't get a diploma—only a certificate of attendance. How sad.*

I summoned Vivian to my office.

"Girl, I've known you all your life. I used to teach with your mother. I know she's proud of you following in her professional footsteps. What's this I'm hearing about your giving up on your mentee—that she's worthless and never going to learn?" I wanted to say, "Vivian, your mother would roll over in her grave." But I would never be that cruel an uncaring.

"Mr. Smith, she can't do the math. She's got the problem, no me. I don't know what more I can do."

"Vivian, good teachers never give up on their students. Talk with your colleagues. See if there are other teaching strategies or methodologies that you might use." I looked her straight in her eyes. "Vivian, don't you ever, ever, ever give up on a student. Don't take the common, acceptable excuses. Find a way to solve the problem."

After the next time to test, I checked to see if the student had passed, but it didn't take long for the student and Vivian to rush into my office, exclaiming the good news.

CHAPTER 128

“ These kids are smart, much smarter than I'll ever be," I heard all the time—especially from new teachers to our Academy of Mathematics, Science, and Applied Technology program.

The teacher disclosures, plus the presentation I had heard during a national conference about a senior inventing a device that would start a car from a mobile phone, sent my mind racing. *How wonderful it would be for our seniors to take a class creating, designing, or constructing a project? The students would do the work. Their teacher would merely facilitate.* One thought led to another. *Let's see, our students would have to utilize community partners as resources. This would be beneficial for our school, local colleges, and businesses, as well. Their projects could be either tangible or intellectual property.*

When I returned to school, I immediately discussed my idea with my administrative team, magnet school coordinator, and AMSAT teachers.

We shared our thoughts with sophomores and juniors. I introduced the concept to the AMSAT Board and to our Parent Advisory Council. As we all agreed, the next step was to seek approval from the Clark County Curriculum Commission, of which I was a long-standing member.

Having obtained state and district approval of the course, seniors took the class the following school year. I stayed in continuous contact with our magnet school theme coordinator and with the teachers to monitor the program.

Our AMSAT seniors worked well with their community mentors. We utilized this venue trying to find after school jobs dealing with math and science for our students, but companies were not interested because of our students' young ages. We even tried to convince local business to consider long-range planning and recruitment. "Why go after college seniors? Capitalize upon some of the best and the brightest while they're still in high school. Consider growing your own; you'll get first-dibs for your personnel." But it did no good. High school students, perhaps, were viewed as too young. Companies did not want to invest that far out.

At the end of the year, our magnet theme coordinator charged into my office. "Mr. Smith, Mr. Smith, one of our AMSAT seniors developed a device in conjunction with a college professor. I hear it's going to be a huge success."

"What is it? Who is it? Tell me more."

"Well, the student's not going to get any accolades. The professor talked the kid out of receiving any credit. 'You're young. You'll make a name for yourself. I need this invention for the college and for myself,' is what the mentor used to persuade our senior from taking any credit. Everything is secret at this point."

For some reason, I didn't pursue the theme coordinator's allegations any further. Perhaps something else of major importance was going on, taking up all my time. Maybe I had reached that point in my life where I was tired of trying to run and control everybody's lives. All I knew for certain is that I did not delve any further into the allegation. Knowing all too well that there's a price to be paid for causing change and standing up to injustice, I was tired of being ridiculed and emotionally beaten up. I settled for being happy in knowing something good came out of the course. I was pleased the students and our facilitating teachers had done their jobs well.

CHAPTER 129

D o I stay? Do I leave and take a job elsewhere? These were questions
recurring in my head. In 2005, I was in my twenty-ninth year of working
for the Clark County School District—eligible for retirement. I would
make about 90 percent of my annual salary if I walked at the end of the year. Still
young enough to start a second career in education in another state, coupled with my
retirement pension, I could make a lot of dough. But I hadn't finished what I started.
Maybe I'd "walk" with my GEAR UP class, my Class of 2007.

How pleased I was with this class. Their test scores were off the charts—the highest
in the district. Using rigor, and my staff pushing them, we did all we could to motivate
the Class of 2007 to excel. Concurrently, my spirit was pushing me. I had never lost
the deep desire to be like that character of Chaucer, The Good Clerk from Oxford. I
still carried my burning, inner banner—my passion to "Gladly learn and gladly teach."
Based on some information I had learned while attending a symposium, about being a
risk-taker, I decided to up our ante. The presenter talked about that kindergartner or
first-grader who was always the first to throw up his hand to answer the question—how
he would let his hand fly into the air, long before the teacher completed the question.
During the presentation, I thought of my second-graders, how they easily wanted
to be first at answering my questions. Then I'd sadly remembered my fifth through
twelfth-graders, way back when I taught. I could see those who had been discouraged,
publicly humiliated, and beaten down, those who would never raise their hands again.
*Oh, what had some so-called teachers and some parents done to these children—pulling
risk-taking out of their spirits and replacing it with fear and apathy toward learning?*
Coupled to that, I also thought about a fact that I had learned while teaching in the
prison long ago. Whenever a state wishes to build a new prison, research is conducted

to examine I.Q. and academic test scores of all current second-graders within the state. This data, along with other information, provides an accurate prediction of how many inmates will populate the prisons in the next fourteen years.

I decided during the presentation to become more of a risk-taker—to not allow fear of embarrassment to keep my hand from flying up first—especially whenever I thought I knew the correct answer.

I began practicing this new behavior wherever I went. Perhaps Charlotte, the local GEAR UP director, picked-up on my actions. She asked during one of our council meetings if I'd be the chairman-elect of our GEAR UP board the following year. Now, I didn't know anything about Robert's Rules of Order. For me, simply being on a board was stretching my comfort. Chairing the board would be completely out of my character. I wasn't the chairman of any of our Magnet School boards. And I wasn't uneasy attending the GEAR UP council meetings—since I wasn't the one in charge. I wanted to empower others, so why would I want to take this on?

I forced myself to accept Charlotte's invitation—of course the board had to vote on my taking the position. After the "All in favor, say aye . . ." I was voted in. My heart raced, but not to the point where major anxiety set in. I knew I would have a lot to learn, but I was up for the challenge.

I began to really pay attention to everything the chair said and did from then on. Seeing all of the educationally talented, degreed people on the board, I felt a little less-than qualified. After all, there were Ph.D.s., college presidents, university directors, and state educational department officials on the council. When my time came to take the position, I wanted to be ready to do the job—and do it well. I not only wanted to be proud for myself, I wanted to please Charlotte because she knew I didn't know what I was doing in this position; yet, she gave me the opportunity to stretch and grow. My ego wanted to elevate me to the level of a self-important blow-wind.

It was then I learned more about myself. I finally understood why I was so troubled with fear and anxiety during the administrative meetings way back when I first became a dean of students and a new assistant principal. It was now time to bring everything out into the open. Back then, being an administrator for the first time, I didn't know what I was doing. I felt like a phony, an imposter. Worse yet, I didn't want anyone to find me out. Now over the years, with aging, more maturity, and looking through a new pair of bifocals, I saw the real issue clearly. Growing up in the Black ghetto during that time in my life, I felt that I could not be sensitive, kind, and caring. I felt in order not to be taken advantage of, I had to isolate myself, pretend to be calloused, insensitive, and to act real tough and strong by pretending to be somebody I wasn't.

Tired of running from this perception, I wanted to be set free.

I sat in my high-back chair, dressed in a three-piece suit, but I was scared almost to death. Although I wanted to tuck and hide them under my butt, I rested my hands on top of the long, outstretched counter. With my fingers interlocked, I tried to look confident and poised. It was time for the vote. "All in favor for the motion to elect Ronnie Smith as Chairman of our GEAR UP Council for the 2006-2007 school year say aye." I felt good that no one abstained or opposed.

By the end of my term, with opening and closing each meeting, I had almost escaped from my position unscathed, without a single flaw. Then came my big testing moment. Discussion on the floor revolved around paying one hundred percent college tuition for all GEAR UP high school graduates. Some council members adamantly felt students should fund a small portion of their bill—totally free gifts aren't generally valued. If they don't pay at least a little, recipients won't do their best. Words of near anger flew around the room.

Opponents fervently voiced and sometimes furiously argued, "Forcing the students to work would decrease student study time, causing them to focus less on their educational goals and objectives."

I sat, looking like I was watching a serious ping-pong match. I was not thinking about each different point of view, or remembering my stipend and totally free college tuition funded by Teacher Corps. I was consumed in survival thinking. *How do I effectively chair this discussion?*

"Call for a vote. Call for a vote," someone yelled.

I was stuck. I didn't have the slightest idea of what to properly do.

"Call for a vote. Call for a vote," again came the cry.

What the hell does that mean? Stalling for time to think I asked, "Do I have a motion to call for a vote?" Then, I announced, "Will someone second?"

The ayes received two-thirds of the vote. I can't remember how I voted. I don't know if I followed the rules, but how glad I was that no one complained or called for point of order. *Hallelujah*, I was overjoyed when I adjourned the meeting and even more joy flooded my being when the new chairman of the board took over my position.

CHAPTER 130

W as it heightened sensitivity, or was I headed for emotional breakdown? I didn't know, but I cried all the time. I felt good allowing myself to just be me. Finally, I had matured to the point I didn't feel the need to always be on point, guarding my emotions and not letting anyone into my heart. I even started to occasionally wear a yellow dress shirt on Fridays since yellow and black were our school colors. I thought the sunshine-yellow shirt went well with the black and yellow smiley-face tie. The least little incident caused my eyes to tear-up— like when a special education student, designated by the system as learning impaired, was giving his presentation at our last GEAR UP national conference. He spoke on how one of his teachers changed his life. He told of how she taught a special class called "Clark Challenge." This was a heterogeneous class, with "regular" kids and academy students. "In this class," he said, "my teacher, Mrs. Cynthia McCoy, treated us all the same, as if we all were smart. Eventually, I believed her. Now I'm on my way to college."

My eyes swelled with tears. How proud I was of him and his teacher. She exemplified the adage, "All students can learn. It's teacher expectation and attitude that determine student achievement." Some teachers, like her, truly believed. They got great student results. Agreeing with her and even taking the concept farther, I believed expectation is somewhat metaphysical—spiritual—too difficult to explain in words. Others believed it was a crock. Their students, accordingly, seldom rose above expectation.

At the end of the student's presentation, while the audience applauded loudly, I looked at his teacher. She was crying as much as I. I went over and hugged her and thanked her for her belief and dedication.

I didn't bother to bring a handkerchief to the Class of 2007's graduation. How stupid of me. Watching the procession, all the students draped with honor chords and special medallions march down the aisles filled my heart with glee. How special it was seeing all of the GEAR UP students wearing their white stoles, which dangled from their shoulders and chests. (The last of GEAR UP money was spent to purchase these sashes to commemorate our students' achievement and success.) Not only did my eyes run with water; moreover, my nose flowed with snot as I stood at the podium. Fortunately, there sat a box of tissues resting on the podium's inside shelf. I blamed my eyes and nose on allergies, but everyone knew I was lying. For me, this was the best day of the school year—my time to tell all of our graduates not to ever forget Clark High School because this is where their greatness started—not at their college or university. This was also the time for me to give our students to the superintendent and school trustees, telling them our students had completed all required work and were now ready to receive their diplomas. What a joy it was to end by saying, "And now, on behalf of our entire school community, I present to you, the Clark High School Class of 2007."

As our symphony orchestra played the recession, we stood and watched about five hundred joyous students march down the aisles and out of the arena. About half of them would be going to college, some to the military, and the rest to work. *I have done all I could. I've given my best. I have no regrets. Some will have to learn the hard way. People aren't always going to do what I would like them to do. I can't make them. I'm not God. I don't know what is best for them.* I thought all of these things, convincing myself not to hurt for the kids who were not going to take advantage of the GEAR UP college tuition funding.

It's over, I thought *as I walked to my car. No more students, parents or teachers, I've got the school and the next three months basically to myself. Just the school banker, the registrar, my secretary, and me—I've got the best job in the world, and all through summer, I'm free.*

CHAPTER 131

With my GEAR UP kids gone, I felt I had accomplished my dreams as an educator. I could now leave the profession and glory at the zenith. I thought of a parent who worked in a warehouse. One day he said, "I don't work on Fridays. I go to the job, but I do as little as possible. Friday's my mental day off." I didn't want to be like him. At the beginning of the next school year, my thirty-third year in the district, I debated over the idea of retiring. *If I stay for thirty-six years, I would retire getting ninety-nine point nine percent of my pay. Right now, I would get about ninety-one percent.* I calculated the dollar amount. Staying, I would be earning about sixteen percent more than I would be getting from my pension. *School is easy. I'm not working. I do only what I want and delegate the rest.* I decided to stay the year.

At the end of my thirty-third year, I again weighed my options for staying another year. *If I left, I would get about ninety-four percent of my current pay. If I stayed, I would earn about twelve percent more than I could get retired. But I don't do anything—only what I choose. My subordinates do the work. I play. I can go into the guitar classes and play music with the children. I can go into the orchestra room or band room and conduct. I can attend field trips with the kids. I'd be a fool to give this up.*

I thought about a fellow high school principal, a longtime colleague of mine. He had worked as a counselor at Las Vegas High School with me. "Ronnie," he would say, during my thirty-third year, "you're the second most senior administrator in the district. Bob retires this year, and then you'll be number one. I'm number three. I came into the district three months after you. I can't wait to be senior administrator."

"If that's your goal, you'll get there one day. I don't think I'll do the full thirty-six. I'll decide year-to-year. But I'm not the one keeping watch on the administrator's longevity list. That's you. Good luck."

Once I had thoroughly convinced myself to stay, unpleasant news would appear, causing me to waver—like the time I had to tell one of my support staff she was being terminated for lying on her application. She was now in her silver sixties but was arrested for prostitution way back when she was a teen. I delivered the news with empathy and compassion, telling her, "I'm not here to judge. I'm simply the messenger, following directions from personnel."

I never did like going to hearings to have teachers terminated for sexual abuse with a minor, one of our students. I didn't, however, delegate this task to one of my subordinates whenever it occurred.

What about the time I escorted a student to my office, dripping in blood? He had been engaged in a physical altercation in the main office area. I sat him in my office to separate him from his opponent. I later learned he was HIV positive when the dean of students sent custodians in to disinfect my office. Worse, yet, I had to inform the parents of the other fighter in writing that they needed to have their son tested, as blood had been exchanged during the scuffle. My secretary, highly displeased with my approach, argued with me, telling me I needed to be totally upfront with the parents.

"I can't, Linda. The Health Insurance Probability and Accountability Act (HIPAA) stipulates that I cannot disclose to others any information pertaining to a child being HIV positive. The school has eyes—people gossip, telling everything.

As principal, I'm not even privileged to know this information regarding students on our campus."

The one problem I had in providing testing information to the parent was when the parent asked, "Why are you so insistent in my child getting tested?"

"In this day and age, anytime body fluids are exchanged, it is wise to be tested," is all I said—as straight-faced as possible. I didn't want to become too pushy or possibly insult the parent, so I didn't add, "If money is an issue, I'll gladly check with Risk Management to ascertain if there is District insurance to cover the cost."

My decision to either stay another year or retire came down to this. *Am I willing to accept the responsibility for everything happening on my campus or not—even though I can't control the actions of anyone other than myself?* In keeping with the thought, *Quality schools don't just happen; they're made. Do I want to let things happen, or do I wish to continue working with others making them happen?* I also thought about time actually spent at school.

There was the two-week Winter Break, one week Spring Break, staff-development training four times a year with no students on campus, and tons of three-day holidays throughout the school year. Out of a nine-month period, taking out all of the non-school days, I hardly worked at all. But I didn't want to behave as though I was retired before I actually retired. My character would never allow me to perform like that. I decided to give it another year.

CHAPTER 132

The school year came. It went. As growth requires change, it wasn't the same old routine. We continued allowing our students to give presentations at conferences sponsored by the Nevada State Department of Education. My boss and boss' boss would ask, "Ronnie how do you consistently get your high student achievement results?"

"I don't know. We just try," I'd respond—not wanting to get uppity or pedantic.

"I sure wish the other principals would try. You know, we spend thousands of dollars each year sending principals to special, out of state training. We could save our district lots of money by having you present the training."

I didn't let any of her politeness go to my head. I merely responded, "Thank you." Her comment reminded me of a time when the television news media came to my school, interviewed me, begging the question, "Why is Clark so different than the other local high schools?" *No, you aren't going to get me to make of fool of myself, talking about any other school.* I thought back to the time I had said far too much to the interviewer, way back when I was a new middle school principal. *No, I won't be pulled into your web. No one will mistake my comments as arrogance. I'll continue repeating one short sound byte.* "I can't speak for any other school. All communities are different. I can only speak for Clark."

"Yes, yes, but tell us why is your school so different from the other high schools?"

"As I've said before, I don't compare my school to any other school; I can only speak for Clark. We continue analyzing our school data, using the trend data in planning new goals and objectives for school improvement."

"Yes, yes, but why is Clark so different from other schools?

Why are they continuing their tactic? Repeatedly asking the same question isn't going to yield a different answer. Calmly and politely I said, "I can only speak for Clark. I put all of my time and energy into keeping my eyes on Clark. This is my school, the only one I'm responsible for leading."

"Thank you, Mr. Smith, Thank you for the interview."

I confidently walked away thinking, *I didn't give them too much information they could twist and take completely out of context.*

I continued attending conferences, looking for effective strategies we could incorporate into our school. I focused on the topic of technology in the classroom. Gone were the days of the black, green, or brown chalkboards. Smartboards now ruled the day. These modern, interactive display boards enhanced student learning. Talking about student engagement, any information in the world could easily be loaded onto the screen. Handwritten notes could be typed, organized, printed and filed, all emanating from the board.

While attending conferences I learned that to get the most bang for my buck, to only provide Smartboards to young, new teachers. Generally speaking, compared to veteran teachers, Smartboards in young teachers' classrooms would be used, not sit gathering dust. Conference presenters suggested younger teachers could mentor the wise, experienced teachers on how to utilize the boards. This could be a stipulation before doling out the limited boards.

I applied for and received a grant for getting twenty Smartboards into our school. We followed the suggested prescription of young teaching old.

The more technology sessions I attended, the sadder I became. I started feeling old, a bit outdated. So much had changed since my first days of teaching. Teachers no longer used a typewriter. CDs. replaced the phonograph. Teacher fingertips were no longer purple from running class worksheets on the hand-cranked mimeograph machine.

Worse yet, as I conducted observations in the oldest teacher's classrooms, I had to admit many of these veteran teachers were trying to teach concepts that applied to a country—a world—that no longer existed.

I knew at the end of my thirty-fourth year it was time for me to go.

CHAPTER 133

Late in the night, June 29, 2009, I lay in bed peacefully drifting off and thinking of tomorrow, my last day of work. *Thirty-four years in the making, retirement had finally arrived.*

I thought I was still awake when craziness entered my world. I was at a wedding chapel—getting married. Inside the right breast pocket of my tuxedo, I carried a polished, wide, men's gold band ring, inlaid with 18-karat diamonds completely circling the outer circumference.

Although all my friends and relatives attended the ceremony— including everybody I had ever met—only the minister and I participated in the wedding. At my request, Donnie did not stand beside me to serve as my best man. Nor was there a bride.

I had gone all-out, spending a fortune to marry the best person I knew—myself. Incased in a room filled with an abundance of broad, silk ribbons, an ostentatious display of flowers; and splendidly dressed, I wanted all attention focused on me.

At the last minute the minister tried to convince me that he could not perform the marriage because I did not have a marriage license.

I immediately pulled a written copy of my wedding vows from the inside breast pocket of my tux.

He took it, looked it over, and started to explain. "From my professional point of view, what you are doing portrays the pinnacle of narcissism. I can't marry you. Your wanting this declaration is simply unconscionable. It's straight-out anti- social. If I followed through with your request, what would people think?"

He could have at least had the courage to read my vows aloud. A few in the audience would have understood my transformation when they heard, "I, Ronnie Tee Smith, do hereby promise to love myself unconditionally, without any reservation. Not allowing others to influence who I am, I'll be faithful to myself, in facing all situations and circumstances for the rest of my life."

Shaking his head from side to side and looking downward he replied, "I don't know what to do with this. Storming out of the room he hollered, "But I'm certainly not going to officiate this disgraceful debacle you're making of yourself."

"It doesn't matter," I clarified. "It's not about you and what you are going to do. This is my symbolic ceremony, and I know exactly what to do."

I took the ring from my pocket; slipped it onto my finger, and then thought back to the time I would not wear a ring, when I wedded Elaine. "It makes me all jittery, Elaine. A ring on my finger gives me the heebe geebies."

The next morning, time I awoke, I first thought back to that time in my twenties, when I had that dream about Archie getting married. I thought about how we, his best men, carried his bride down the aisle, in a coffin. I remembered my interpretation of that dream—Archie was far too young, not the least bit mature enough to marry. Moreover, I remembered my dream interpretation professor saying, "Everybody in your dreams is really you. Often, your unconscious state will provide a character in your dream that your conscious mind is not ready to accept."

Comparing that old dream to last night's, my new dream was refreshingly easy to interpret. Placing that gold band on my finger symbolized how bright I had become, just how far I had journeyed. I was no longer afraid of crippling fear—no longer afraid of what other people thought. Wearing that ring told me I was mature and ready. I realized that like an unassembled puzzle, completeness—healing—comes by finding, acknowledging, and then connecting all the separated pieces. I finally found myself. Transformed through my journey—reborn—I discovered that like a diamond-studded, gold, wedding band, I am complete. I am enough. I am whole.

CHAPTER 134

Looking back over my life, I have learned a lot—especially about feelings. I started out discovering them. I embraced them. And then I learned to repress them. Although I practiced self-control most of my life, what I truly longed for was emotional effacement. This simply deadened my capacity to feel. While gladly teaching and learning, I discovered almost everyone around me goes through life in a similar manner. We think each of our individual journeys—living broken—is normal.

Thinking back to the time when I first attended a twelve-step program reminded me of when I got it—when I first felt like chains imprisoning my feeling and my life had finally been unlocked. What a conundrum! Talking about mind-blowing, elegiac— once I discovered that since I started seriously drinking at age thirteen, I hadn't grown emotionally until I stopped at age thirty-four. Realizing this, I wanted to cry—all those wasted years of drinking. What self-induced craziness, not adding one bit of quality to my life.

Today, I'm kicking butt; I'm freer—much freer. I seek the ability to explore my feelings. Yet, there is control. I've learned, and have placed in the back of my mind, this governing thought, *Just because I think it, doesn't mean I have to say it or do it.* I seek to be able to feel life most sensitively. As I look back from where I came, I am comforted and confident in knowing that evolution comes from learning. The good news is that today, even though I sold my Bug a long time ago, I'm still going somewhere. Although I wasn't an Olympic gold, silver, or bronze medalist, how pleased I was to receive the Citizen-for-the-Day proclamation from our city council a few days before retiring.

I'm no longer seeking degrees, titles, accolades, or extra finances to define my status or self-worth. I'm traveling, discovering, vacationing in present feelings, wanting to explore them to their depths. Today, I am able to genuinely care about how others and I are feeling. I can talk to them about their feelings and communicate mine. I can rejoice while wearing a genuine smile, no longer ignoring feelings—hiding behind pretense or a mask. I'm no longer playing a real-life game of charade. There's no laboring under mendacity, or simply saying, "I feel fine." It feels incredible, making the journey from stoicism to self-expression. Today, I'm going somewhere within my heart.

Epilogue

Today, whenever I run into one of my former students, my first thought is about Gavin—his saying, "I bet we're going to see one of your students, and they are going to say, 'Mr. Smith . . .'"

After the student and I greet each other—and it's great when I can call him or her by name without their reminder or prompt—a sudden delight, yet uncomfortable feeling, overcomes me. It happens immediately when they say, "Mr. Smith, you were the best teacher I ever had."

Sometimes, they go on, telling me about the family problems they were enduring during school, and how being in my class added hope to their frustrated situation. Hearing them explain more of their past circumstances, I felt like life was a sharp spear being stabbed into my heart.

I wanted to do more—so much more to help. But patiently listening to their story coming to an end, how good it finally felt to hear them say, "You helped me, Mr. Smith."

Bittersweet is what I felt for their lives and mine, too. To relieve the painful part, I'd jokingly conclude our conversation by saying, "At least I did something right in my life." Then I'd leave their presence thinking, *I guess the pain comes from all the horrible decisions and executions I haven't yet totally forgiven myself for putting my family through.*

I've reconnected with Donnie and talk with him almost daily, but what I'd seriously like to do is to wake up from writing this book in a dream. I'd settle for it being 1969, the day when I was honorably discharged from the Marine Corps. Knowing what I know now, I'd make two major corrections. I would keep that aborted child and work harder on saving my marriage. Otherwise, most of my life's experiences—like teaching, having two sons, and a granddaughter—I would gladly do all over again.

STUDY QUESTIONS

Being an educator most of my life, I would be remiss in not offering an end-of-the-book test. Accordingly, I invite you to reflect upon the following questions:

What was Ronnie's greatest fear? Did the story bring a fear that you've been carrying for a long time to mind? (Optional—mind sharing?)

What exactly is Ronnie predominately struggling with throughout his journey?

What is resolved and what is still left unanswered for him?

As many young children of poverty live in a dreamworld, they don't take getting an education seriously. Many fantasize that one-day they will become a professional athlete. Incorporate this concept into a discussion regarding Ronnie's athletic sub-theme/motif.

What social statement is Ronnie making by having Stanley in the story?

Ronnie often utilizes the convention of the dream to move his story along. Choose one of his dreams and analyze it.